MUSIC: MOTION AND EMOTION

The Developmental-Integrative Model in Music Therapy

D1568182

Chava Sekeles

MMB MUSIC, INC.

MUSIC: MOTION AND EMOTION
The Developmental-Integrative Model
in Music Therapy
Chava Sekeles
English translation by Reuven Morgan

Cover design: Chava Sekeles
Typesetter: Gary K. Lee
Printer: Walsworth Publishing, Marceline/Brookfield, MO
1st printing: May, 1996
Printed in USA
ISBN: 0-918812-88-7

For further information and catalogs, contact:

MMB Music, Inc.
Contemporary Arts Building
3526 Washington Avenue
Saint Louis, MO 63103-1019

Phone: 314 531-9635, 800 543-3771 (USA/Canada)
Fax: 314 531-8384
E-mail: mmbmusic@mmbmusic.com
Web site: http://www.mmbmusic.com

To my husband, Eliezer, and my sons, Barak, Raz, and Sharon.
C.S.

CONTENTS

FOREWORD

This work has a special character, based on professional experience rather than on simple academic research. The range of subjects discussed is most impressive: the writer displays a firm grasp of all aspects of a complex multidisciplinary field.

Her musical skills added to the knowledge acquired in both developmental and clinical psychology, neurophysiology, medicine, and anthropology give the work a sweeping breadth of understanding and clarity. The Developmental-Integrative Model presented here in such a concise and systematic manner, is a wide-ranging integration of all these varying disciplines. In this it surpasses all others which are not so "multilayered" and even lack the "developmental" aspect.

Her rationale regarding the therapeutic effects of musical elements serves as a firm theoretical basis for the model she describes, a model which is a significant breakthrough and contribution to the sphere of music therapy.

The case histories are eye-openers: live illustrations of the way in which music therapy works, and of its hidden possibilities. The variety of the patients, of their ages, social backgrounds and physical or mental disturbances, lead us into a number of therapeutic approaches.

I was most impressed by the descriptions of the work on both physical handicaps and emotional stresses, and the combination of musical, vocal and other creative means of expression. Musical activity emerges as only one element within the entire reservoir of psychotherapy, which can include the use of other means of creativity such as poetry, play, and painting. The last two case histories (Rita and Alon) are among the most compelling I have ever encountered in clinical literature. The very fact that in all of these cases there was significant improvement points to the hidden potential of this therapeutic approach, even in cases of extreme physical and/or emotional disability.

Prof. Yoram Bilu
Hebrew University, Jerusalem
Department of Psychology and Anthropology

PREFACE

Over the last forty years music therapy has developed as an established profession in the Western world. It is a profession which utilizes the inherent therapeutic potential to be found in the basic components of music (*frequency, duration, intensity, timbre*), and in music as a complex art form, in order to preserve the patient's healthy capabilities, to promote beneficial change and development, and to enable the achievement of a better quality of life.

Music therapy consists of a patient-therapist interaction in which the latter employs skills derived from specific interdisciplinary training combining a thorough knowledge of both music and of therapeutic theories and methods.

Music serves as an essential intermediary agent in the therapeutic process, in order to express and elaborate threatening subject matter, and to form a link for human interaction. The role of the therapist is to guide the patient through auditory experiences—both as a receptive and/or active participant—and thus develop those qualities essential for health and growth.

The adoption of music as an agent which can influence and activate both body and soul is universally accepted in East and West, in primitive and sophisticated societies. More than this, it may elicit positive or negative qualities, may assist or hinder.

Despite the fact we cannot begin to discuss any unity of musical style within differing societies (or within certain societies themselves), it has nevertheless been established that basic components do in fact influence different human beings in an identical—or supercultural—manner (Alvin 1975, 60–70).

This enables the establishment of a fundamental theoretical model, using the basic elements of music in therapy, regardless of the differences between age groups, educational achievement, culture or religion. In the same way the therapist is enabled, to a certain degree, to confront the culture gap which can often occur between patient and therapist, to adapt himself to the specific needs of the patient, and to be able to contain the patient's habitual musical culture.

Quite apart from the auditory components, studying the literature of past civilizations and listening to recordings of the healing rituals of traditional societies reveal that certain musical principles do in fact repeat themselves in quite surprising ways in differing cultures.

These principles, which might at first glance appear to be quite similar in practice, reveal themselves as very different once we examine the concepts underlying therapeutic considerations and their application.

For example a change of the organism's equilibrium by means of auditory overstimulation has always been a characteristic of traditional societies which indulge in ecstatic ceremonies. This has been documented by past civilizations, and even today can be employed in music therapy.

The technique is similar, the dominant element being a strong rhythmic stimulus by means of percussion instruments. The spontaneous reactions to such rhythms are manifested by turning, whirling, leaps and somersaults, all of which are dictated by the music.

According to modern researchers such auditory stimuli and the resultant physical activity can lead to physiological changes in pulse rate, breathing, blood circulation, digestion, muscle tone, brain activity, and so on (Critchley & Henson 1977, 202–233)

Emotionally, the patient undergoes catharsis and is able to release physical and emotional blockages. All this in a nonverbal manner and without the elaboration used in psychotherapy. When this ecstatic activity takes place within a group framework, the individual gets a temporary legitimacy to shake off social taboos and to express his urges in a protected environment.

Traditional healers, however, would describe this differently: in the Moroccan Atlas Mountains, for example, they would tell you that the drums, cymbals and hand clapping were aimed at driving out the evil spirit from the body and soul of the sufferer. Similar descriptions of ecstatic activity are voiced by young children who still possess magical thinking and make use of noises to banish their fears; as well as by psychotic patients who create noises (either organized or at random) in order to rid themselves of delusions and hallucinations (Sekeles 1979).

Even in rituals or musical activity in which the music serves as a soothing element, we can perceive the effect of supercultural principles. The auditory stimuli are characterized by repetitive hypnotic components which lead to a reduction of physical and physiological activity. Here too, despite the obvious similarities, the music therapist's explanation will be quite different, for example, from that of the North American Indian tribal healer.

Both these examples, of excitation and relaxation, are to be found within the broad axis of music therapy dynamics. Both are made possible by the natural ability of music to transmit emotional messages to the patient without the use of words or cognitive participation. Such messages serve to lay the way for further elaboration both in music and in speech.

The tribal healer, on the other hand, will be satisfied with the act itself which serves both as process and end result. Should he employ words as metaphors or magic amulets, this will be only to explain away the exorcism of evil spirits according to tribal custom. The concept of elaboration or working through has no place in his thinking, even though he too attaches symbolic meaning to problems, according to the traditional thinking within his own culture.

This book divides into three main parts. The first two parts are theoretical and deal with two major subjects: the ancient origins of music therapy which still exist within certain ethnic groups in today's world, and the *Developmental-Integrative Model in Music Therapy (D.I.M.T.)*, which was formed during my years of clinical experience (1963–1990) in psychiatry and neuropsychiatry with chronic and acute patients.

The third part of the book attempts to illustrate the practical application of *D.I.M.T.*: five long-term cases are discussed (ranging from two and a half to four and a half years) which represent a variety of patient problems, all of them from differing cultural backgrounds, with a wide range of age groups and a variety of developmental and therapeutic intervention.

Ron's case presents music therapy with a child suffering from multihandicaps from birth, both neurological and psychological. Anat shows us music therapy with a Down's Syndrome child, Jacob's case represents music therapy in order to rehabilitate an adult whose musical skills were damaged due to C.V.A. Rita is an example of music therapy as applied during an adolescent crisis rooted in a traumatic childhood, and Alon serves as an example of the combined problems of neurological disorders from birth and problems of emotional development.

It should like to stress that in this book I am not dealing with the principles of group music therapy, but rather with individual treatment. In analyzing the case histories I have tried to offer a glimpse of the therapeutic space, its atmosphere and the equipment used, and to enable the reader to follow both the therapeutic considerations and the meaning of the patient's progress.

Careful record keeping by means of sound and video tapes, transcriptions and reports enables the therapist to maintain an accurate follow-up of specific processes and at the same time permits an overview of therapeutic thinking, practical approaches, musical techniques and the application of interdisciplinary knowledge to the music therapy process. It should be stressed, however, that the written word cannot fully describe the music therapy experience, and there is a vast difference between reading about it and actually hearing it. This is not a gap which can be bridged even by musical notation, particularly when dealing with improvisations, transitions from instrument to instrument, from instrument to voice, etc. A partial solution may be found in the recording archives which can be of help in actually hearing the various aspects of music therapy in both theory and practice.

The major aspects stressed in this work are as follows:

1. Physiological and psychological descriptions of research into the processes of excitation and relaxation as practiced in traditional healing rituals.
2. The differences in therapeutic aims, the use of music and the therapeutic rationale, between traditional healing methods and modern music therapy practice.
3. The differences between the use of music in special education and in music therapy as such. These find their expression in the concept of music as an element to be exploited in various ways, the aims of musical activity, and the attitudes towards the creative process and its results.
4. The opportunities for using music in a variety of creative modalities which emerge both spontaneously and deliberately on the part of the patient, rather than being dictated by the expertise and creativity of the therapist.
5. The sense of continuity which music affords to various activities: vocal, instrumental, movement, etc.
6. The concept of music as a supportive, communicative link (both inter- and intrapersonal), in cases where impaired development, either mental, physical, or a combination of both, hampers normal communication.
7. The links between primary and secondary communication and the assumption that treatment through music can contribute to the self-expression of various parts of the personality and hence to a greater sense of completeness.
8. The concept of the human being as a complete entity (psychophysiological) which demands an integrated therapeutic approach.

In conclusion I should like to express my warmest thanks to Professors Amnon Shiloah and Yoram Bilu of the Hebrew University, as well as to Doctor Jacob Avni of Hadassah Hospital, for their constructive criticism of my manuscript; to my son Barak for his photographic skills, and to Reuven Morgan for his efficient cooperation.

I also owe a great debt to my colleagues and my former students in the field of music therapy, as well as to the patients and their families who so willingly gave so much of their time and assistance to this project.

Chava Sekeles
Nataf, Israel, 1993.

I

THE ROOTS OF MUSIC THERAPY IN TRADITIONAL RITUALS

Introduction
Hypnotic Healing Rituals
Ecstatic Healing Rituals
Physiological Aspects
Psychological Aspects

INTRODUCTION

Traditional healing rituals serve as the most ancient origins of music therapy. Archeological and anthropological evidence has revealed that such rituals existed as far back as the Paleolithic culture of Ur of the Chaldese (La Barre 1970). La Barre refers to shamanic[1] rituals in which to the best of our knowledge music was a major and permanent element.

I have chosen to discuss this subject with examples from those societies which even today do not possess a written culture (such as certain groups to be found in remote regions of Africa, South America and Asia), as well as societies which exist on the fringes of a literate world (such as certain groups of Moroccan Berbers). In these societies it is the oral tradition which dominates and it is music as a therapeutic agent which precedes the written word (amulets, inscribed blessings, etc.).

Traditional medicine is known by a number of names such as primitive, ethnic, rural, folk, shamanic and so on. There are also various subclassifications: Jane Achtenberg (1985) speaks of two main types, technological and shamanic. In her view the first consists of the use of herbs, piercing the skull, the removal of tumors and so on, whereas the second is concerned with the spirit. If technological medicine strives for the elimination of symptoms and a relief from pain, shamanic medicine is devoted to the overall health of the whole being by means of suggestion and fantasy.

Foster (1976, 1978), phrases it differently, his two chosen categories are naturalistic and personalistic. The first takes into account the objective factors such as natural forces, or obvious symptoms of imbalance such as fever or chill, whereas in the second there is a deliberate intervention of various agents which he further subdivides into human (witches and sorcerers), extrahuman (demons, evil spirits, ancestors), and superhuman (the gods and their emissaries). Whereas naturalistic healing perceives only the disease and its symptoms and treats them as best it can, personalistic healing is rooted in the overall perception of the human being and therefore also touches on religion and magic.

The healer or shaman engaged in personalistic healing is first and foremost concerned with such questions as "Who caused this affliction, and to what purpose?" For many the diagnosis is of graver importance than the actual treatment. In this connection Foster presents an example from Sudan: the shaman goes into an ecstatic trance in which he discovers the cause of the ailment and how it came about. He then hands over the actual healing process to someone else (ibid., 778).

It is held that disease attacks man because he has infringed certain taboos and thus exposed himself to the invasion of evil spirits which are capable of stealing his soul (as Eskimos believe), to rule over it (the North African belief in being "possessed by the devil"), or to torment it by means of visions and dreams (North American Salish Indians), and so on.

According to Foster's definitions it would seem that the main role of music is in personalistic healing. However there is evidence that music is not the only art form utilized in healing rituals. There is an integration of movement, costume, headdress, dramatic action, the ritual decoration of musical instruments (in Asia and

Africa for example), painted bodies and faces (North American Indian tribes) as well as more unique phenomena (such as the sand drawings of the Navajo Indians in the southwest of the United States). Indeed, in traditional societies, art forms have a mainly magical significance; unlike in Western civilization they are not solely devoted to aesthetics.

At this point I should like to comment that the integration to be found in such traditional healing rituals could serve us well as a model for music therapy, and a means of exploiting the basics of intercommunication and primal expression. An example is included among the case histories to be discussed in later chapters which touch on the natural and spontaneous links between music and other art forms.[2]

As opposed to art music which might be employed in music therapy, the music in healing ritual makes it easier for us to explore the degree to which both the physiological organism and the emotional mood of the patient can be influenced. This is due to the comparative simplicity of a musical texture based only on a few components. Even in the Voodoo rites in Haiti, in which the drummers make use of highly complex rhythms, a basic beat is maintained to serve as a framework ("holder") for both music and participants. It should also be noted that apart from drumming and stick beating there are almost no additional musical elements.*

It is possible nowadays (as will be described later on) to assess under clinical conditions the influence of drumming on the human brain and thus, to a certain degree, the effect it has in healing ritual.

On the other hand, the music therapist wishing to evaluate the effect on his patient of a complex musical work (such as a Beethoven Quartet, or Berlioz' *Symphonie Fantastique*) must be prepared to break these down into their components, to analyze, to raise questions both about the musical and nonmusical aspects. What, for example, is the dominant element which influences gross or fine locomotion? What influences breathing, and how? When were there head movements, hip movements, or movements of the hands and feet? Which sections or elements aroused personal associations in the patient, and just what were they? What angered, what stimulated, what saddened, what gladdened?

The more complex the music, the heavier the task for the therapist (even after the most detailed analysis) to truly assess its influence on the patient. Apart from analyzing the music, the patient's own personality must be taken into consideration, his education and cultural background, his past and present experience of music, the effect of his accumulated memories (and their content) on his flow of free association, and so on. It is these questions which dictate a fresh approach and prolonged observation as far as each and every individual patient is concerned. This is, in my view, a crossword puzzle whose solution is to be found in a combination of various and varied disciplines.

As has already been stated, the music of healing rituals contains very few components: often it is only the rhythm, expressed by drums, hand clapping, foot stomp-

---

*Sekeles Recording Archive: "Exorcism of Kita" Voodoo ritual in Haiti, 1974.

ing, stick beating, and occasionally by jangling bracelets. Should there be any semblance of melody, it is minimal and repetitive.

In ecstatic rituals in Asia, Africa and Australia for example, drumming is the major component.* In certain rites, such as those of the Hamadsha in the Moroccan Atlas Mountains, oboes are added; on the other hand in the hypnotic rituals of the North American Indians it is singing which is dominant, accompanied by rattles and now and then by a monotonous, repetitive drum rhythm.**

In a comparative study of the components and typical developments of such ecstatic rituals as opposed to the hypnotic, I found a remarkable similarity of basic processes, despite vast geographical, cultural and other differences between the groups examined (Sekeles 1981).

In all such ecstatic rituals (whether they last a few hours, a full day, or even several days), the rhythmic and dynamic development is extremely similar. The ritual begins with a drum (or other rhythmic means such as foot stomping, hand clapping or stick beating) in a repetitive metronomic tempo of 60 to 80 MM (between largo and andante), a tempo which matches the normal human heartbeat. Gradually there is an acceleration which can advance to more than 200 MM; thus from a moderate tempo the music and the locomotion of the participants reach the equivalent of presto–prestissimo.

Along with this acceleration comes an increase in volume, and at the climax of the ritual we can hear a multirhythmic texture in which the melody (if there was one) shatters apart as do the words (if there were any). An excellent example of this is the Ahouache ritual from the Moroccan Atlas Mountains which moves from 76 to 200 MM, resulting in an inability to either reproduce or understand the words, particularly if we take into consideration that the participants are in continual motion, which increases in tempo all the time.*** (Later on we shall examine the symptoms induced by intensive rhythmic stimulation combined with movement from both a psychological and emotional point of view).

As far as hypnotic healing rituals are concerned, the musical aspects are different. The beat begins in a moderate tempo suited to a relaxed heartbeat, and maintains this throughout. Now and then stimuli may be inserted, by means of a single drum, and often by rattles whose sound is more ambiguous.

Frances Densmore (1954), found that in North American Indian rituals of such nature the rattles and drums maintain a steady rhythm while the melodic line is irregular, characterized by a shift of both accent and duration. Densmore stresses that this is an unusual phenomenon for a Western musician and concludes that it is the maintenance of a steady beat which permits melodic freedom.[3]

I would like to present here a few comparative examples:[4] At this stage we are not taking into consideration the actual duration of each ritual—only its degree of acceleration.

---

*Sekeles Recording Archive: Music from Ecstatic Healing Rituals
**Sekeles Recording Archive: American-Indian Healing Rituals
***Sekeles Recording Archive: Berber Healing Rituals, 1972–1975

Ecstatic Healing Rituals

No.	Location	Musical Activity	Start Tempo/MM	Peak Tempo/MM
1.	Manchuria (Tungus)	Drums, some singing	78	206
2.	Siberia	Drums, some singing	72	200
3.	Borneo (Kita)	Drums, cymbals, some singing	76	152
4.	Haiti	Drums, sticks, cymbals	80	208
5.	Malagasy (Atandory)	Hand clapping, Foot stomping, singing and hyperventilation	70	200
6.	Guinea	Drums, cymbals	72	205
7.	Kenya (Gerengany)	Drums, singing, Natural horn	72	184
8.	Ethiopia (Zar)	Drums, clapping, Stomping, singing	72	192
9.	Morocco (Hamadsha)	Drums, oboes	70	198
10.	Morocco Atlas Mountains (Ahouache)	Drums, singing	76	200

Hypnotic Healing Rituals

No.	Location	Musical Activity	Start Tempo/MM	Peak Tempo/MM
1.	Dakota (Sioux)	Singing, drumming	72	72
2.	Colorado (California) (Yuman)	Singing	88	88
3.	Nebraska (Pawnee)	Singing, rattles	74	74
4.	U.S.A. N.W. Coast (Kwakiutl)	Singing	82	82
5.	Canada South Coast (Chippewa)	Singing, rattles	88	88
6.	Ecuador (Napo)	Singing, leaf rustling violin and whistle	84	84

Before going on to discuss the specific musical elements of healing rituals and to analyze their effect from a psychophysiological point of view I should like to furnish brief descriptions of four examples for purposes of clarification.

HYPNOTIC HEALING RITUALS

The Navajo Indians

The Navajo tribe has inhabited parts of the southwest of what is now the United States ever since the year 1500. The Navajo adopted the agricultural methods and well-known weaving skills of their neighbors the Pueblo. From the Spanish they learned animal husbandry, and from the Mexicans (in the 19th century) the art of the silversmith. The Navajo are the richest of all American Indian tribes and live on a sixteen-million acre reservation which stretches over parts of Arizona, New Mexico and the Utah desert. It is an area rich in oil, coal and uranium. Despite having adopted the English language, the tribal chieftains nevertheless endeavor to teach their offspring their original tongue, folk legend and tradition, and this within the regular school system.

Modern Western-style medicine and the medical practitioner are the lowest on the list of their priorities, together with the traditional herbalists. On the other hand the tribal healer is still considered to be the best diagnostic, his advice and medicines are considered to be extremely powerful, while his extranatural and supernatural powers go totally unchallenged. Among the Navajo, both naturalistic and personalistic medicine (Foster 1976), are accompanied by chants and song. These are conducted over a nine-day period either by the healer himself or by a specially-trained singer. The Navajo believe that singing and incantation are the central means by which harmony can be restored both to the patient's body and soul and to his surroundings[5] (Deloria 1974, 374).

It is interesting to note that the American establishment, including the National Institute for Mental Health, recognizes the value of traditional healing methods, and even provides partial financing for the training of traditional healers.

As mentioned, among the Navajo the use of herbal cures is considered to be the simplest of all healing practices, and is much less widespread than in other tribes. Far more esteemed are symbolic methods which employ singing and sand drawings. These are executed on a bed of dry sand in colors produced from plants, soils and minerals. Such drawings are composed by some fifteen people during the course of a full day and comprise dozens of complex symbols. These symbols together with the singing and chanting are designed to banish the disease, or the misfortune which has befallen the tribe, the witchcraft or whatever. The following example of such a hypnotic ritual describes the case of a sick infant: The group of healers arrives at the home of the sick infant bearing sheets of cloth on which the clean sand is to be spread. Once the area to be drawn has been smoothed out, pinches of sand are grasped between finger and thumb, and the design begins. The symbols are chosen according to the patient's complaint, and in this case they create a figure with arrows and lightning flashes radiating from its outstretched arms. During the ritual, mother and child are seated in the centre of this picture, and the figure portrayed in the sand transmits its healing powers to both. The medicine man plays a rattle, prays and sings, laying hands on both mother and infant with elaborate, stylized gestures. Both prayer and song have a quiet and soothing dynamic. The vocal range is limited, the rhythm slow, and the rattle provides a constant beat, leading to a sense of security and relaxation which, combined with the magic thinking and faith of the participants, becomes a formidable therapeutic force (Maxwell 1978, 239–241).

Frances Densmore (1927) stresses the soothing atmosphere of all the healing rituals she witnessed in Indian tribes from British Columbia to Florida.[6]

The healer has been given the songs he employs in a dream or in a hypnotic trance (experiences the Indians believe to be supernatural). The healer sings and his patient listens, motionless. This example of receptive therapy can be seen as a primeval example of Guided Imagery in Music as experimented with and formulated by Helen Bonny (Bonny & Savary 1990).

Once the ritual is over, each one of the participants is permitted to take a handful of sand from the drawing. From now on such sand is believed to possess special healing powers. The remainder of the drawing must be swept away in a northerly direction. The Navajo also use masks in those rituals which last a number of days, and healing drugs in the most severe cases.

One of the most interesting phenomena of Navajo song and incantation is the existence of the nonsense syllables (which seem to have no logic in speech). The sequence of these must be painstakingly rehearsed otherwise the healing process will not succeed. The tribespeople believe that these syllables comprise a magical structure, or charm, and must not be altered in any way lest they lose their power (Herzog 1933). According to Ida Halpern (1967),[7] who researched the songs of Indian tribes on the Northwest Pacific Coast, such sounds (which are also characteristic of this region) are actually derived from genuine words and from the cries of animals, which may explain their magical powers.

Whatever the case it appears that despite the uniqueness of the Navajo sand drawings, the atmosphere created by the music in their healing rituals is typical of many other Indian tribes. It is prominent at every stage of the ritual and serves as a basis for relaxation and soothing.

The Napo: Upper Amazon—Equador

In 1967 Neelon Crawford and Dan Weaks photographed and recorded a shamanic healing ritual in the Napo River region of Eastern Equador. Since this ritual involves the use of hallucinogenic drugs (as do other rituals in this region), I have chosen it as an additional example of hypnotic ritual.

At the outset the shaman is seated on an ornate wooden stool in the shape of a sea turtle which symbolizes the feminine force of water, and drinks a potion made from Banisteriopsis Caapi (of the Malpighiaceous family).[8] People in the region refer to this in the feminine gender as "Beautiful Spirit" or "Mamma." With the aid of this drug the shaman is assumed to be able to enter a different world of experience, to gain strength and clarity of thought, acquire knowledge and thus be able to trade with the spirits.

The sick woman who has been brought before the shaman lies on a straw pallet at his feet. The ritual begins with a prelude played on three-stringed musical instruments, this is known as the "Visionary Song." The two upper strings play both the rhythmic and melodic pattern, while the lower string serves as a drone to attract the spirits. The sick woman is also given a dose of the drugged potion, and once it begins to take effect on her the shaman begins to play a bone flute whose function is to summon up the Spirit of the Jungle and the Spirit of the Sea.

Later on the shaman speaks rapidly with the sick woman and the husband who has brought her, reassuring them that he has the power to heal her, that the spirit he has summoned appears in his visions and that the healing can proceed.

The shaman then takes a bundle of leaves, purifies them with water and uses them to produce a soft, rhythmic rustling; he calls upon the spirits to emerge from his stomach, sprinkles water and banishes the unwanted spirits by blowing his breath at them. All this time the sick woman lies silent; all speech and music are restrained and repetitive. The woman and the shaman experience visions which are described by him in song. During this he swings his body from right to left and back again in a steady rhythm, performing magical journeys from this world to the world of spirits and returning.

From a musical point of view the melody consists of a single major chord, alternating occasionally with a minor. The range of voice is confined to a fifth, while the melody moves down from high to low (as in any typical lullaby). When reaching the central tone the shaman plays a soft tremolo. It should be noted that the style of playing, the singing accompanied by the rustling leaves, and the melodic structure, are all typical of traditional societies in the indigenous cultures of the South American Lowlands. The rattling, or rustling, which accompanies the singing are, however, typical of all Indian tribes in both North and South America.

At a certain stage in the ritual the shaman snatches out harmful objects from within the woman's stomach, chews on them and spits them away.

Then the woman, for the first time since she has been brought before him, suddenly informs him of what actually happened to her:

"I went to the garden to get Maniok" she says, "a stick of Maniok broke and hit me in the side and I fell. The wound kept hurting and now I'm almost dead."

The shaman reassures her that he knows the identity of the evil spirit who did this, and will repay him in kind.

The ritual is conducted at night, and after some eight hours the shaman remains alone with the woman, speaking to her gently and comfortingly with no musical accompaniment (Whitten 1976).

During the entire ten hours of the ritual the soothing melody and andante tempo is consistently maintained, even in the hallucinatory and terrifying passages.

It should be stressed that despite the vast differences between the Navajo Indian healing ritual described earlier, and this one from the Jungle Quichua of the Napo River Region, the hypnotic components of the music are common to both and are integrated into all stages, with their purpose clearly understood by both healer and participants alike.

The melodic range is limited, as are the dynamics. The rattles or the rustling leaves which accompany the singing in both rituals, contribute to continuity and a gentle flow. The Napo stringed instrument contains the same components as those of the singing and can thus be included in the same melodic category. In both rituals the patient remains passive, prone or seated, allowing the music to be absorbed and to arouse visions. Some of these visions may be dictated by the healer or the shaman, as is occasionally done in guided imagery. It may well be that part of this imaging is personal, but we have no way of knowing this.

Whatever the case the ritual leads to soothing and relaxation, to a maximum concentration on the patient, and to the summoning up of mental powers and resources. Later, we shall be discussing the rationale of such therapy from a psycho-physiological point of view.

ECSTATIC HEALING RITUALS

The Vezo tribe—Madagascar

The Vezo live in the southwest of Madagascar and are a minority group within the Sakalava. They are a seminomadic people who inhabit the forests along the shores of the Mozambique Straits and subsist, in the main, from fishing. According to their beliefs, disease and other disasters originate in a supernatural world peopled variously by the kingly spirits, the spirits of important persons drowned at sea, and the spirits of their ancestors who constantly look down upon them and observe them. It is the first two categories of spirits who are most likely to take possession of a personality and cause illness. The reasons for such domination are a punishment for the transgression of social norms or family unity. The penalty is an interference with the smooth progress of a normal existence.

In order to pacify the punitive spirit, it has to be identified, contacted as soon as possible, and negotiated with in order to ensure its exorcism.

The ritual itself resembles total theatre with a huge cast of characters, each of whom is playing a well-rehearsed role. Each group of spirits has its own specific musical repertoire.[9]

The roles played by the music are many and varied: to prepare the healer for his task, to soothe the patient, to assist in diagnosis, to appeal to the spirits and the gods, to act as emissary to and fro, to serve as a basis for the dancing, and so on and so forth.

It should be noted that all other styles of music employed by the Vezo tribe, which concern hunting, farming and similar matters, are limited to the singing of poetry. It is only the tribal healing rituals which are characterized by a collective musical endeavor within such an impressive theatrical format.

As in other parts of the world, here too the healer draws his strength, either in a dream or in a vision, from a godly spirit or from the spirit of his ancestors, which is henceforward acknowledged to be his own.

This particular ritual was recorded in the years 1967–9 by Koechlin from the Ethnomusicological Department of the Musee de L'Homme in Paris. Like many other ecstatic healing rituals, it takes place in the open air. In the area reserved for the rites stands a kind of altar on which are laid out all the ritual paraphernalia.

The ritual is divided into four stages:

1. The patient is brought before the altar and faces east as he listens to the instructions of the healer's assistant. The women play and sing under the guidance of a tribal music master; the melody is simple and repetitive, thus permitting improvisation and the moulding of verbal phrases while seeking out the spirits or demons; the singing itself is backed by the repetitive beating of two drums and by hand clapping. By degrees this combination is joined by the maruvaani (the local version of the lyre) and by the rattle. These are played by the men. The role of the lyre is to attract the spirits. The participants react with movement, which at this stage remains slow and relaxed in accordance with the stimulus of the sounds. Once the evil spirit has been identified the overall tempo advances to allegro, cries of encouragement are heard and incense is scattered.

2. At this stage the evil spirit brutally invades the body of the medium (usually a member of the patient's immediate family), causing him or her to lose consciousness. The music ceases abruptly, signalling the beginning of the process which the tribe defines as resurrection. Even after the medium has been "restored to life," he or she remains in an ecstatic trance. From here on the dancing steadily accelerates to include spins and leaps and so on.

3. This is the stage in which the healer/shaman transmits his signals to both spirits and patient. The music accelerates to presto and dancing is based on twirlings and gyrations. Mothers dance their way up to the altar and absorb the benevolent spirits which it houses. Occasionally the tempo is relaxed, only to return to its former frenzy.

4. At this stage the spirits are banished by fast-paced music and dancing. The spirit departs from the body as it entered it, aggressively and violently. The more evil the spirit is considered to be, the more frenziedly dramatic the ritual becomes, with the musical tempo reaching prestissimo.[10] The music breaks off entirely when the Medium emerges from his or her trance and returns to normal.

The Moroccan Berbers

In Morocco there are several Berber groups who conduct festivals, circumcision rites and healing rituals. One of these, the Hamadsha, has been vividly described by Crapanzano (1973). They are divided into two subgroups named after Moroccan Saints whose tombs lie a few kilometers northwest of the town of Mekness (Sidi Ali Ben Hamdush and Sidi Ahmed Dghughi). They see themselves mainly as exorcists of the devil, thanks to the powers and special blessings they have been granted by God, his servant Mohammed, and his Holy Brethren.

According to Crapanzano the achievements of the Hamadsha are remarkable even by the standards of conventional Western medicine. They successfully treat a variety of syndromes including hysterical paralysis, mutism, sudden blindness due to psychological causes, severe depression, anxiety, and more. Their aim is not necessarily to restore the patient to his former ability as a member of society. They frequently adopt him into their own, or a similar, group framework, giving him new functions and new aims.[11] In this way his life takes on a new meaning, possibly more suited to his needs, and even altering his social status.[12] The Hamadsha impart to the patient their own interpretation of his affliction, and a description of the proposed cure, by means of the accepted symbols of the patient's own society. Since the ecstatic rituals are conducted within an extremely organized pattern, the participant has the constant opportunity of a release from tension and pressure, while still feeling secure.

Music for the Hamadsha rites is provided by three guwwalla (an hourglass shaped pottery drum), one tabbal (snare drum), and two oboes known as the ghyyata. A major role is assigned to the leader of the ceremony and master of the dancing (known as the Muqaddim), as well as to the two men who collect cash contributions from the participants.

The group assembles in a semicircle with the musicians at one extreme, facing them is a troupe of about twenty males ranged shoulder-to-shoulder. The dancing (a reaction to the music of the oboes and drums), develops stage-by-stage (according to the rules of ecstatic ritual we have already encountered), the Muqaddim, serving as a kind of role model, directing the actions of the other participants. His movements, as in other ecstatic rituals, include leaping (similar to that of the Asian shaman), spinning and twirling (similar to that of the Ahouache or the Vezo) and heavy landings on the heels which may sometimes be accompanied by breast beating with his fists. When the women join in, their movements are typified by bold gyrations of the hips and bowing backwards and forwards with their loose hair flying in all directions.

The number of participants steadily grows, the drumming increases both in dynamic and in tempo, and on this basis the ghyyata play the "Rih" (a tune symbolizing the evil spirits) specifically aimed at the demon which has been identified as the inflictor of the disease. It is here that the significant role of the wind instruments comes into play. On occasions the identity of the evil spirit is known in advance, but if this is not the case it must be sought by means of a series of melodies (the "Ariah"). This might take hours until the patient displays what the Hamadsha perceive as a positive response to the music.[13]

The more the ecstatic trance takes hold, social taboos (such as both sexes dancing together, or the use of sexually suggestive movement and gesture) diminish. At the climax of the ritual the Muqaddim and his followers are quite likely to group together and slash their heads with knives in an act of self-mutilation. The blood is believed to be sacred and strength giving, and so the other participants daub themselves with the blood streaming from the Hamadsha and beseech their blessing. At the climax of the ritual, the evil spirit is exorcised.

Like many other ecstatic healing rituals, all this takes place in the open air, often in the market square—a venue for a variety of other rousing events. In addition to the already described means of exorcism (the rhythmic stimuli, the Ariah on the oboes, the ecstatic dancing, etc.) the Hamadsha prepare themselves beforehand by drinking highly-sweetened tea, by snake charming, and at climactic moments of the ritual by drinking boiling water and eating cactus fruit, spines and all. Such phenomena and their possible explanations will be discussed later.

At the end of the ritual, which can last anything from hours to days, the participants fall into a lengthy and well-earned slumber.

Despite the fact that the Moroccan intelligentsia and the Moslem authorities openly disapprove of such events, and attribute them to marginal illiterate groups, they turn a blind eye to their existence, and in so doing, it would seem, display a discreet understanding of the psychological and social value of such functions.

We have noted identical characteristics in two examples of hypnotic rituals, as well as in ecstatic rituals, conducted a continent apart, or at a distance of some six thousand kilometers one from the other.

For the purposes of this study, the essential similarities between the musical components in ecstatic ritual consist of the rhythmic stimuli created by drumming, hand clapping, stick beating, and rattles or cymbals (depending on any given culture). Such rhythmic stimuli provoke and influence a motor response which is systematically developed to a degree which allows the participant to enter into an ecstatic trance without which the healing process would be impossible. At the climax of this trance the evil spirit is exorcised.

On the basis of this rhythmic stimulus, as already mentioned, can be added the playing or singing of melodies which have a therapeutic significance. In the fastest-moving moments of the ritual the rendering of these melodies is often taken over by nondancers, whereas sometimes it is the only role played by the musicians and the singers. When the singing is integrated with frenzied movement it becomes impossible to perform, hence in a ritual such as that of the Ahouache Berbers, in which all participants both sing and dance, at the ecstatic climax words and syllables become completely incoherent.

Following is a table of comparison between ecstatic and hypnotic rituals from the point of view of their musical components, the characteristics of movement and physiological phenomena, the psychological gain, and their spiritual significance.

Comparison	Ecstatic Ritual	Hypnotic Ritual
a. Components of sound, rhythm and dynamics	1. Stressed beat units, increasing in tempo from largetto to presto prestissimo	1. Fixed beat units at a normal or low heart rate
	2. Dynamic at peak reaching *fff*	2. Same tempo until end of ritual
	3. At climax: multirhythms and a disorganization of components	3. Moderate, repetitive dynamic
		(continued)

Comparison	Ecstatic Ritual	Hypnotic Ritual
b. Musical instruments	1. Drum, or drums solo drum (occasionally) 2. Other percussion: stick beating, rattles, hand clapping, hand/body cymbals, foot stomping, body slapping 3. Wind instruments: flutes, conch shells, natural horns	1. Rattle or leaf-rustle 2. Occasional string instrument
c. Vocality	1. Not always used: breaks out at climactic moments and may well be transferred to a substitute 2. Yelling, yodelling, hyperventilation	1. A key element 2. Brief repetitive melody 3. Occasional transfer of melody from Voice to Instrument
d. Vocabulary	1. If words are used they are generally in hypnotic ritual.	1. Words are usually given to the healer in a dream. 2. The origins of these words are to be found in the animal world, in mythology and tribal history. Words, syllables and phrases are endowed with magic meanings. Some of these chants may be composed of nonsense syllables.
e. Movements of healer and movement-reaction of participants.	1. Participants form a circle 2. Circular movements 3. Jumping upwards and sideways 4. Heavy descent onto heels 5. Pronounced hip movement 6. Pronounced shaking of shoulders 7. Running 8. Strong head movement 9. Healer drums, sings and dances	1. Permanent seated or prone position facing healer 2. Patient remains motionless 3. Healer moves with caution, plays gently, touches patient in silent, ritual gesture.

Comparison	Ecstatic Ritual	Hypnotic Ritual
f. Physiological phenomena among participants	1. Increased muscle tone up to spasm 2. Trembling, hands and feet in particular 3. Sweating, blushing 4. Accelerated heart-beat and respiration 5. Fatigue and pain (which diminish during ritual 6. Lowering of blood-sugar level to point of hypoglycemia 7. Reduced sensitivity to pain (self-mutilation, fire, freezing, etc.) 8. Sleep at ritual's end	1. Decreased muscle tone up to trance and sleep 2. Pallor and sense of chill 3. Slowing of pulse rate and breathing tempo 4. Sleep at ritual's end
g. Spiritual factors of greatest influence	1. Total faith in healer and his powers 2. Magical meanings of song given to healer in his dream, of dance, of the structure and iconography of the musical instrument 3. Sense of security bestowed by structured ritual	As in ecstatic ritual
h. Psychological benefits	1. Psychophysiological relief from oppression, aggression, sexuality, anxiety 2. Sublimation 3. Catharsis 4. Group support for, and legitimization of, vocal and physical behavior which is often socially unacceptable 5. Maximal attention during the ritual process 6. Possibly altered social status	1. Experience of meditation, relaxation, physical and mental tranquillity 2. Experience of passive acceptance 3. Satisfaction of primary needs in object-relation 4. Maximal attention during the ritual process 5. Possibly altered social status

To this should be added the observation that in both ecstatic and hypnotic healing rituals, the patient enters into an altered state of consciousness (due either to an ecstatic or hypnotic trance), and by way of this undergoes the experience of beyond reality situations (according to traditional perceptions) and intrapersonal experience (in terms of accepted therapeutic dogma in the Western World).

We shall now discuss in further detail the physiological and psychological aspects of healing rituals, as indicated briefly in these charts.

PHYSIOLOGICAL ASPECTS

In our examination of traditional healing rituals, we encounter two opposing rhythmical processes: one of which steadily intensifies by means of a systematic acceleration of tempo and an increase in dynamics, with the participants responding with energetic movements as dictated by the musical development; and the second, which preserves a constant rhythmic beat, generally with no change of tempo or dynamics, and in which the participant remains in a state of quiet receptiveness. In both cases, stimulus and reaction can lead to a state of trance, typified by an altered state of consciousness.

This has been defined as a situation in which "The person experiences a clear sensation of qualitative shift in the structure of his mental processes" (Tart 1969, 2).

This phenomenon, well known to music therapists as a result of Guided Imagery in Music has been described in detail by Ludwig (1968) who observed it in various, sometimes contradictory situations:

1. A decrease in exteroceptive stimulation.
2. A increase in exteroceptive stimulation (Crapanzano 1973; Sekeles 1996).
3. A decrease in the alertness of critical human faculties.
4. Selective and focussed alertness.
5. Various psychophysiological conditions connected with hyperventilation,[14] hypoxemia, hypoglycemia, dehydration, sleeplessness, and exposure to extreme temperatures.

This last is a phenomenon to be found in many healing rituals. The drinking of boiling-hot tea and water among the Moroccan Hamadsha, and the performance of the ritual in the open market square under the blazing sun (Crapanzano 1973); massaging the body with glowing coals as is done by the Kung in the Kalahari Desert (Katz 1982); the inducement of fever by means of powerful metaphors describing the sun in various parts of the body and a sun-kissed world, which is a part of the technique of the Tibetan shaman (Evan S-Wentz 1967); the extensive and continuous dancing which can continue for hours, and even days on end, resulting in the symptoms detailed in #5 above—all these are characteristic of ecstatic healing ritual.

On the other hand the experiencing of states of extreme cold is also a part of many healing rituals. The dance of the spirits of the Salish Indians on the northwest coast of the United States, opens with the patient situated in a darkened tent watched over by "Nursemaids." Here he undergoes a womb-like experience[15] while the shaman and his assistant seek the most suitable *Demon Song*.

The song represents the healing process, and the dance of the spirit its intensity and power. At a certain point the patient enters into a trance and experiences dreams and visions which symbolize reincarnation and a new birth. After four days of fasting and total isolation, the "Newborn" chants his new song, accompanied by the drums and voices of his companions. He then rushes into the forest to undergo the agonies of bathing in an icy stream. The shaman breathes upon him the "breath of life" which symbolizes rebirth (Jilek 1982). All participants in this rite are called upon to repeat it each winter.

This ritual decreases sensory stimulation and enables a return to the womb simulation, as well as a symbolic purification in the icy waters—a parallel to purification by fire.

Percussion possesses a tremendous ritual significance, due to the magic thinking associated with it. The instruments are constructed from special materials, they have specific shapes and forms, bear special and symbolic decorations (iconography), and there are strict taboos regarding their use and how they must be played (Sekeles 1995). According to Drury (1982), the drum is the central ritual element since the sound of the drum acts as a focusing device for the shaman. It creates an atmosphere of concentration and resolve, enabling him to sink deep into trance, as he shifts his attention to the inner journey of the spirit.

Apart from occasional Eskimo rites, the drum figures in all ecstatic rituals as an essential instrument for the inducement of trance.[16] The magic properties with which it has been endowed (as already described) make of it a multipurpose tool. Its shape enables it to be employed as a vehicle, and as a receptacle, as well as serving its purpose as a musical instrument. The Asian shaman can use it as a boat in order to reach the spirits under the sea, as a bird in order to reach the heavenly spirits, or as a stag, a gazelle or a horse if he seeks spirits on earth (in which case he makes use of the drumstick as a whip). Once the spirits are captured, they can be trapped within the drum and brought back to earth.

Because of its special qualities the drum is often made from rare species of timber. For example the "tree of the universe" which the Ostiak-Samoyed tribe believe to sprout from the centre of the world with its trunk linking humanity to the upper spheres. Other examples of the sanctity of this instrument can be seen as the result of dreams and visions. Crapanzano and Garrison (1977), describe a Moroccan healer who was commanded in a dream to find a tree struck by lightning, and construct his drum from such wood.[17]

The shaman believes that the drum has a soul, which must be awakened before the instrument is played. The Altai shaman anoints his drum with beer (Rutherford 1986), whereas the Moroccan healer will expose his drum to fire, thus both stretching the skin and at the same time breathing into it a spirit of life.

In addition to these spiritual attitudes, there are however various physiological aspects connected with drumming and its influence on the participants in such rites which also merit discussion.

In a pioneering work, Neher (1961) researched one of these when he exposed a group of normally healthy people to low-frequency, high-amplitude drumming under controlled laboratory conditions and recorded their EEG readings, in an attempt to discover whether such percussion can lead to the reaction known as auditory driving (an expanding reaction firing frequencies to surrounding systems). Neher found that such a firing reaction did in fact occur with a stimulus of 3, 4, 6 and 8 drumbeats per second, and that under these conditions the subjects reported both visual and auditory imagery.

Furthermore it emerged that response to rhythmic stimuli increased according to the degree to which the subjects were in a stress situation, or suffered from metabolic imbalance (such as hypoglycemia or fatigue), symptoms typical of ecstatic healing rituals.

Auditory stimulation which ranges between 4–6 cycles per second has been found to be the most effective in healing rituals since these frequencies enhance the Theta rhythms in the temporal-auditory regions of the cortex. Theta rhythms can be registered under conditions of light sleep (particularly among adults) and are apparently characteristic of the shift from full alertness to an altered state of consciousness. Theta rhythms are also connected with states of creativity, and imagery (Green & Green 1977). Despite the fact that in the actual rituals (such as the Salish tribe's "Spirit Dance Ceremonial") more drums were employed and more intensively than in the Neher experiments, the recorded frequencies were nevertheless extremely close to the range of theta rhythms.[18]

In a further article (1962), Neher comments that in the majority of controlled laboratory experiments conducted into the influence of rhythmic stimuli on healing ritual participants, use was also made of visual rhythmic stimuli, whereas in the actual rituals stimulus is confined to the drums.

Neher's research led him to a number of conclusions:

1. One single drumbeat contains many frequencies. When transmitted to the brain it activates a larger area of the auditory cortex.

2. A drumbeat contains mainly low frequencies (particularly the oversized drums usually employed in healing rituals), and the low-frequency receptors within the human ear are more resilient than those designed to receive high frequencies. Hence the drum is capable of transmitting more energy to the brain than high-frequency stimuli (such as that provided by flutes). In ecstatic ceremonies we find a combination of low frequencies, intense volume, and an acceleration in the tempo of the drumming.*

3. Reinforcement of the basic rhythm by additional rhythms increases participatory response. (We have already seen how in ecstatic rituals use is made of additional rhythmic structures such as hand clapping, idiophones and various percussion instruments).

4. When the rhythmic stimuli are variegated in terms of sensory modalities (sound, sight, touch, proprioception, kinesthesia) response becomes even stronger. In ecstatic rituals we find such visual stimuli as the flickering of candlelight

---

*Sekeles Recording Archive: "Comparative Acceleration in Healing Rituals Utilizing Music" 46: Ecstatic Rituals & 52: Hypnotic Rituals.

(Zar, Ethiopia) and of course the kinesthetic stimuli of frenzied rhythmic movement to be found in all societies which practice ecstatic healing ritual.

Since it is this insistent stimulus which leads to a steadily growing physical reaction, which in itself leads to the physiological symptoms already described, one can
say that in this chain of events music can be defined as the initial link whose task it
is to ignite and activate all the others.

Field researches by Jilek (1982) serve to authenticate Neher's conclusions, since
they were conducted in the natural settings of such rituals. Nevertheless
Achterberg (1985) claims that Neher's pioneering work suffers from a lack of
follow-up, and that his conclusions have never been verified by additional research
into the physiological effects of the drum. Achterberg supports the views held
by Drury (1982) concerning the role of percussion in concentrating the
shaman's mind during his ventures into the Lands of the Spirits, and adds her
own hypothesis.

The auditory tracts enter the reticular system of the brain stem. This massive
nerve net acts as the coordinator between sensory input and muscle tone, alerting
the brain to incoming information. Sounds transmitted through the auditory system are capable of activating the entire brain. Strong and repetitive neuronal firing,
as would be experienced from the drums, can theoretically create a state of cognitive awareness. This is an hypothesis which contradicts the Western belief which
perceives trance as an illusory state similar to that of the dreamer, and reinforces the
theory that at least the shaman who conducts the ritual is in fact capable of clear
control of his thoughts and actions.

A significant contribution to the understanding of the shamanic phenomenon
comes from the ongoing and developing research into endorphins.[19]

Endorphins are endogenous healing mechanisms similar to morphine and other
opiates which act upon the brain as analgesics to relieve pain, to create euphoria, as
well as leading to alter consciousness. Their greatest concentration is to be found
in the extra pyramidal system of the brain which controls muscle and the integration of movement. Other concentrations are to be found in the limbic system
(connected with conditions of amnesia, euphoria and altered states of consciousness, as well in those areas responsible for transmitting pain impulses and the
perception of pain. Pain has always been a major research subject for all those
concerned with opiates. Prince (1982) differentiates between the "hypnotic analgesia" of shamanic ritual[20] (the lessening of stress, anxiety or pain), and what he
terms "endorphin suggestion" or "endorphin-related phenomena."

In the first case (the hypnotic), there exists a psychological mechanism based
on belief (faith analgesia), unblocked by naloxone which neutralizes morphine.
The second case is a natural result of the interaction between various endorphins (opiates) and their receptors. It is this which allows of changes in the
sensation of pain, of movement, of mood, and of the reactions of the autonomic nervous system.

Interaction between an opiate and its receptor depends on pressures, or on deep-
tactile stimulation (such as acupuncture). Such stimulation can also be originated
by intensive rhythm and movement (as in ecstatic ritual).

Prince (ibid., 413) quotes the example of marathon runners who suffer from pains and exhaustion during the first twenty minutes of the race and then enter into a state of euphoria in which all pain is dispersed.

Appenzeller and others (1980) pointed out that during a marathon race the endorphin level increases considerably.

According to Prince this ties in with the earlier works of Cannon (1957) and his hypothesis regarding "FFF" (fright, flight, fight). Both man and beast share the same system which regulates both pain and fear and finds its expression in situations of danger and self-defense in which the choices are either to run away or to do battle. An injured animal or man, even in a serious condition, is nevertheless capable of self-defensive action. Today this is explainable by an understanding of endorphin activity.

"The pain threshold rises slowly, reaching a maximum after approximately forty minutes. It remains at a plateau while stimulation continues, and when it is discontinued, the pain threshold falls gradually over a period of fifteen to twenty minutes" (Prince 1982, 412).

We should bear in mind that ecstatic rituals involve extreme states of fatigue, and certainly muscular pain, as well as other agonizing situations involving extremes of temperature, self-mutilation with knives and needles, in addition to the state of extreme anxiety experienced by the patient which is reinforced (consciously or unconsciously) by the healer and the entire process of the ritual. This is an anxiety which can be fed by actual causes and events but also by inner fears and imaginings.

The organism experiences anxiety without any reference to its origins, and activates a hormonal reaction (and according to recent researches, an endorphin reaction as well). Incidentally, the realization of nightmares and horrific fantasies triggers an intensive hormonal reaction to stress situations. This is something practiced by various tribes as part of their maintenance of mental health (e.g., the Iroquois Indians in Canada's St. Lawrence River region) and serves as an integral part of music therapy in which the patient is encouraged to express by way of music, song, or any other artistic means, his own fearful fantasies (see Case Histories: Rita and Alon).

Prince stresses that endorphin is especially active under extreme stress situations. This is also true of hormonal activity, such as an increase of the adrenaline level in the bloodstream.

In conclusion it can be stated that the above mentioned studies propose an added dimension (widely researched over the last ten years) to the possible function of the endorphins in the ecstatic rituals we have already described in detail.

We shall now examine the physiological effects of the hypnotic ritual on its participants.

We have already noted that the singing, accompanied by rattling or rhythmic drumming, is characterized by repetition, by a very limited dynamic, by a steady and moderate tempo, and by a general atmosphere of soothing and limited movement. From the point of view of a music therapist such musical characteristics, movement and surroundings, provide the ideal setting for the total relaxation of the patient and his or her descent into slumber.

Both in the ecstatic ritual, as in the hypnotic, the rhythmic opening is characterized by repetition and monotony, thus focussing the personal consciousness inwards.

This is not simply a mental process. It is also affected by one's physical posture and the effort needed to counteract the force of gravity. During a hypnotic ritual, the healer (mostly seated), and the patient (mostly seated or lying down) invest no physical energy in movement or posturing. As a result (and also due to the repetitive melo-rhythmic stimulation) they can restrain and slowdown their breathing process, blood pressure is reduced, as is muscular tone and other physiological parameters already described. Stage by stage the healer brings both himself and the patient to a state of relaxation from which it is possible to reach a hypnotic trance and an altered state of consciousness.

While it is true that some of the rituals include the use of hallucinogenic substances, it would seem that pure relaxation without their use can also lead to a state of hypnotic trance and to the emergence from it with no harmful aftereffects (Bonny & Savary 1990).

The patient is exposed to music and suggestive words when in a totally passive state, reacts with an inner ideo-sensory and ideo-motor activity. According to Maurice Kleinhause and Pazit Sela:

> *Suggestion* is an unqualified acceptance of an idea, an idea accepted by the patient without any intellectual persuasion but rather due to a bypassing of all intellectual-analytical processes. Any *ideo-reaction* can be transformed into *suggestion* by means of neutralizing the normal physiological stimulus and turning it into a reaction aroused by the therapist's instruction. The suggestive reaction of the patient is dependent to a large degree in his faith in his therapist and his expectations that his therapist can help him (Kleinhause & Sela 1986, 7).

The more suggestion suits the psychophysiological structure and social characteristics of the patient, the easier it will be for the therapist to make use of such suggestion. This is a feature of hypnotic ritual, in which both healer and patient share an identical social and ideological background.

Kleinhouse and Sela further claim that:

> The therapist must make suitable use of every aspect of communicative behavior: tone of speech, musicality, mannerisms, the implied meanings of words, movement and so on (ibid.).

All of these are to be found in hypnotic healing rituals.

Since traditional societies regard the majority of illnesses (even if they display physical symptoms) as spiritual maladies, it is hard to differentiate between the processes of physical and psychological relaxation. This is equally true of music therapy as I perceive it in our day and age.

Above and beyond the psychophysiological relaxation and the imagery of hypnotic rituals which employ music and other elements, there remains the question (as in ecstatic ritual) of the influences which create the ability to overcome pain and stress.

One explanation is provided by Prince (see above) who differentiates between the easing of pain due to endorphin activity, and that due to hypnotic suggestion. Another explanation can be found in one of Achterberg's researches (1982) concerning severely-burned infants.

Instead of anesthesia she used recordings of fetal heartbeats, very similar to drumbeats. These rhythms (which probably match delta brain waves of 4–5 cycles per second) created an effective sensory block against pain, which facilitated even extremely painful treatments. Once the infants got used to the presence of the tape recorder in their cots, they would fall asleep within a minute or two after hearing the sound.

Achterberg bases this clinical research on the Gate Theory of Melzack and Wall (1965) in which they claim that since pain sensations are transmitted by very sluggish fibres, the perception of pain can be blocked, or limited, by rapid and powerful counterstimuli. This could be acupuncture, mild transcutaneous electrical stimulation, massage, and even repetitive percussion.[21]

The anesthetizing of infants, children and even adults, by means of monotonous and repetitive pulses is recognized and accepted as effective in a variety of schools of relaxation therapy. This is generally attributed to psychological causes (see later), or to physiological causes associated with a loss of alertness due to the continuous and monotonous stimulus which holds no changes and no surprises.

Achterberg (as we have seen) presents another viewpoint in which she claims that rhythmic stimulation can be employed not only as an anesthetic but also in order to block, or delay, the sensation of pain (see Case History: Ron).

An additional theory regarding relaxation concerns that structure of brain matter known as the reticular formation, which serves as a modulator between sensory input and motor output. When stimulus (such as sound) is extensive, it can excite, and when limited, can relax. In particular it is the ascending reticular formation which influences the state of alertness; reduced activity of this portion leads to a state of hypnosis, trance or sleep.

PSYCHOLOGICAL AND SPIRITUAL ASPECTS

Traditional healing is aimed at those individuals who sprang from the selfsame cultural and societal roots as did the healer/shaman, and who share his own philosophy and beliefs. It is these shared faiths and the confidence of the patient in the abilities and powers of the healer which serve as the rock-solid basis of traditional healing. Alongside these there exists a clear social code of the forbidden and the permissible, any transgression of which can lead to imbalance and hence to illness.

The healer is acknowledged by his patient as being possessed of an expert knowledge of traditional law and an ability to restore equilibrium due to his inherent powers and his ability to make contact with the forces of affliction. These (at least as far as the personalistic category of illness is concerned) are part and parcel of the magic thinking of traditional societies (see Foster).

It should be stressed that while such magic thinking which embraces the concept of supernatural powers may be regarded by Western psychology as a form of pathological regression, within traditional societies the supernatural remains a concrete part of reality. Spirits, demons, ancestors, gods and demigods all inhabit their surroundings and watch over them all the time.

Within this web of beliefs music is also considered to possess magical powers due to the merits perceived in it over the centuries and the manner in which it influences mankind. Accordingly, music makes its own special contribution in a variety of functions:

1. As a means of return to primal object relationship during hypnotic healing rituals. Vague, soothing and sleep inducing. In this context the patient returns to infancy, the healer takes on the role of the mother, and the music serves as a lullaby. In other words a regression to the oral stage of life.

2. As a release of sexual and aggressive energy during ecstatic healing rituals, by means of strong rhythms which develop in an orgastic manner and elicit energetic, cathartic movement. If we compare the hypnotic ritual to the symbiotic-oral stage, then the ecstatic ritual can serve as a metaphor for adolescence in which sublimation serves as the most effective defense mechanism (sport, music, rock and so on). Statistics reveal that in most ecstatic rituals the healer is generally a man (father figure), whereas in hypnotic rituals we can often find a woman as healer (mother figure).

3. In all the rituals so far discussed, the group is an essential support for the individual through spontaneous action, the acceptance of transgressing accepted taboos (sexually explicit movement, shrieking and yelling, and so forth), and by a tolerant and absorbent participation.

4. The first, or active, category, resembles the dynamics of doing in music therapy. Here the patient initiates activity and takes part in creating the music. The second category is similar to that of being, in which the patient is passive and receptive. Both of these dynamics will be discussed within the case histories yet to be presented. Both can be traced back to ancient times as part of the history of healing and music as a meeting point.

5. In all the rituals so far described the major therapeutical factor was imagination (generally guided by the healer). Imaging, visions, dreams, transport the patient through experiences which differ from his day-to-day existence and release him, momentarily, from routine struggles, awarding him the chance of experiencing something out-of-the-ordinary. In some cases this could be described as re-birth (the Salish tribe), or a journey of spiritual purification and catharsis. Very similar phenomena can be observed when employing the technique of Guided Imagery in Music which in some ways resembles that of the hypnotic ritual. Guided imagery also involves collective symbolism (such as animals, structures, water, etc.), as well as the possibility of eliciting threateningly-laden personal matters.

Collective symbols appear both in hypnotic ritual and in guided imagery; however the music therapist encourages the awakening of personal issues, whereas the traditional healer stresses the collective material.

6. Traditional healing deals with the body, mind and soul as if they were one single entity. This is in fact a comprehensive therapy: suggestive stimuli provided by music, song and the word, affect body and mind together. Energetic movements exert their influence on both internal and external systems.

According to the Developmental-Integrative Model in Music Therapy, a patient suffering from what are diagnosed as mental problems will be subject to therapy aimed at strengthening the links between mind and body, whereas a patient suffering from distinct organic problems will undergo treatment aimed at linking body to mind.

A person is seen as a whole being, while affliction breaks this apart, causing difficulties of constant communication between motion and emotion, or in musical terms between the singing voice (which expresses emotion and movement) and the speaking voice (which expresses logic and thought).

As already stated, traditional healing rituals serve as the historic roots of music therapy. Despite the differences of concept, and in the therapeutic rationale which exist between the shaman (healer or medicine man) and the music therapist, part of their basic therapeutic activity appears to be remarkably similar. Not only that, all possible explanations of those physical and psychological phenomena which typify patients under treatment, and which are based on neurophysiological researches and on a psychodynamic concept, hold good in the main both for traditional healing ritual and for music therapy as we know it today.

II

THE DEVELOPMENTAL INTEGRATIVE MODEL IN MUSIC THERAPY (D.I.M.T.)

Introduction

Definitions

Musical Activity as It Affects Vital Human Functions
   1. Senses and sensations
   2. Movement
   3. Vocality
   4. Emotion
   5. Cognition

Psychoacoustic Qualities of Musical Elements and Their Therapeutic Relevance
   1. Rhythm
   2. Pitch
   3. Timbre
   4. Intensity

The Dynamics of Therapy
   1. The therapeutic triad (patient, music, therapist)
   2. Structure and significance of the therapeutic space
   3. Training of the music therapist
   4. Essential skills
   5. The patient-community
   6. Intake procedures (referral, initial interview, observation, therapeutic contract)
   7. Therapeutic considerations
   8. The therapeutic encounter (framework, developmental therapy, representation of stress situations in sound and music)
   9. The roles of the therapist
   10. Procedures for documentation, transcription, interpretation and evaluation

Conclusion

INTRODUCTION

I n 1962 I went abroad for supplementary studies in music therapy, and was employed in a major psychiatric hospital. The majority of the residents were chronic patients who had been there for literally scores of years, mostly diagnosed as schizophrenic. The hospital also housed an alcoholic ward, a day clinic, and an open ward for patients of various ages with a variety of psychiatric ailments. This encounter with severe chronic patients, almost totally cut off from reality and virtually incapable of verbal communication, forced me to reassess the well-known saying that music is an "international language," nonverbal and bypassing the need for speech. In fact this reassessment continues to this day, since the majority of my patients suffer from difficulties in verbal communication due to either physical and/or psychological causes.

The most severe schizophrenics had been hospitalized for periods as long as forty years and bore the characteristic symptoms of the illness. Linguistically, most of them possessed some kind of a personal language which emerged as incommunicative, with echolalic characteristics and neologism, incoherent mumblings and even a total abandonment of speech.

Behaviorally, the majority displayed a rigidity of movement, a compulsive sense of ceremony, a lack of physical coordination, and tended to catatonic states (stupor, rigid or excited). Many suffered from tactile, visual, somatic, olfactory and auditory hallucinations. Some of those undergoing music therapy displayed a paranoid anxiety when confronted with the recording equipment and its wiring, fearing that these might "transmit their thoughts," and thus endanger them.

My previous therapeutic experience either with handicapped patients in rehabilitation, or with nonhospitalized neurotics, was of no avail in treating these chronic cases—normal communicative speech was limited, even faulty, and so there was an urgent need to find ways of establishing confidence and trust between patient and therapist. As already mentioned, therapy can make significant progress only within a personal rapport between the two, hence the supreme importance of the links and interactions which can be expressed through music.

Music therapists tend to make free use of such expressions as creativity, creative freedom and creative joy. In my experience with a variety of patients, I have learned to regard such definitions with a certain wariness. The schizophrenic suffers from confusion, from sensory and mental flooding, from organizational difficulties and from flat effect. He is in need of an extremely clear and comprehensible supportive environment within which he may be able to function, to improvise, and to adapt to gradual change. Over-creativity on the part of the therapist can inadvertently sabotage such a process. The concept of beautiful and expressive, refined music as a predetermined positive influence is inexact, to say the least.

The patient's acceptance of music is not automatic. It demands emotional investment and patience on the part of both patient and therapist alike. Indeed, as opposed to traditionally accepted beliefs, D.I.M.T. does not see music as a magic formula for performing miracles.

In most cases, as in any therapy based on change and development, music therapy consists of a lengthy and exhausting exploration of advance and retreat, often of pain and sadness, sometimes of joy and relief. The more the patient reveals a greater interest in music, finds within it a means of self-expression and subconsciously senses its significance, the more it becomes effective for him as a means to be exploited on a level of consciousness and awareness.

By studying chronic cases I learned to observe both the integration and lack of integration of the personality and its various systems; to analyze developmental gaps; and to comprehend the psychological influences of the malady on the physiological being. I also learned that the patient's internal condition could not always be defined purely by means of psychological symptoms. Physiological blocking had also to be taken into consideration, such as surrender to the force of gravity, vocal pathologies, and more. It also became clear that the very nature of music, which enables it to affect vital human functions, is what gives it its genuine therapeutic power.

The influence of music on the senses, sensations, vocality, motion, emotion, and cognition, enables it to be used in Integrative Therapy when applied to such functions either in whole or in part. D.I.M.T. perceives this as one of the unique advantages of this profession. On the other hand, care must also be taken to avoid superficiality in these spheres, of which the music therapist has only limited experience.

However, I would like to stress that even with the most nonverbal patients (psychotic, retarded, autistic, mute, etc.) D.I.M.T. still advocates the use of speech. Thus the link with emotion is the role of music as a primary language, while the link with consciousness is the role played by words as a secondary means of communication. Just as the music therapist cannot analyze and understand the therapeutic process purely on the basis of music and body language, the patient also needs verbal expression in order to organize his thoughts and to link emotion with awareness, however primitive and limited his use of language may be.

If the aim of such therapy is to expand the consciousness and awareness of the patient, the therapist needs training in psychology and psychodynamic supervision, just as the treatment of physiological problems demands from him adequate medical training and supervision.

By treating chronic psychiatric patients (and later autistic children, psychotic children and neuropsychiatric cases), I became keenly aware of the power of music to penetrate the veils of the incommunicative and the inarticulate. The variegated influences of music therapy, and the results of detailed observation and other processes over a period of some twenty-five years, persuade me that there are clear conclusions to be drawn regarding the development of the patient and his ability to express himself during music therapy, as well as his psychological progress in his daily life outside of the clinic. This in no way resembles the accepted norms of a musical education aimed at an improved hearing technique, cognition and so forth, but rather a development within a human relationship. There are, after all, two major agents in music therapy, the first is the music itself which serves as a link between patient and therapist (interrelationship), as well as between the patient and himself (intrarelationship), the second agent is the therapist whose task it is to assist the patient to undergo musical experiences both actively and receptively in order that he may acquire those skills essential to his health and well-being.

DEFINITIONS

The term "Developmental-Integrative" demands a certain clarification. Developmental implies a basic concept of Man as a being who passes through various stages of development during his lifetime, including certain vital functions (senses and sensations, vocality, motion, emotion, cognition). Developmental psychology and physiology maintain that growth is characterized by supracultural or universal processes. Science seeks to describe, investigate and measure these, as well as to study deviations from their norms. Such research into deviationary patterns has indeed advanced our potential understanding and treatment of future pathologies.

Despite the apparent differences between various present-day psychological approaches[1] it would seem that rather than contradicting each other, their different accentuations tend to support the overall accepted view of infant development.

As a result of long-term observation (making use of music) of infants, children, adolescents, adults and the elderly, D.I.M.T. arrived at the following conclusions regarding its definitions:

DEVELOPMENTAL

1. Part of human health is determined by the degree of maturity and integration which exists within and between the vital systems which contribute to development. Observation by means of music can pinpoint deficits, gaps, regression and fixation. This is because music itself influences these very same life systems.

2. Should there be any health malfunction this must be examined according to its developmental significance. Identifying the developmental stage is an essential part of the intake and observation phase of music therapy. Without such data the therapist is unable to evaluate and consider any form of treatment.

3. There exists a certain parallel between the development of the persona in general and its development in music therapy. By observing musical activity we can identify stages of physical, psychological, cognitive and societal development.

4. D.I.M.T. sees each hour of therapy as a developmental microcosm and follows the patient's development as if it were a parallel of the life continuum.

5. D.I.M.T. stresses the need to stimulate and develop the surviving and healthy functions of the patient, without ignoring deficits and gaps, in order to bring about positive changes and to improve the quality of life.

INTEGRATIVE

1. The integrative treatment of deficits and gaps.

2. A holistic treatment of the complete individual (sensory-motor integration, motion-emotion integration, etc.).

3. The integration of the physiological and psychological persona, and the treatment of the whole person as far as music permits, whether or not the handicaps are defined as either physical or emotional.

4. Integration between the problems as diagnosed and the therapeutic approach, techniques, and the musical and verbal means at the disposal of the therapist.

5. Integration of methods and techniques in music therapy with knowledge acquired from relevant fields (musicology, psychology, medicine, etc.), in order to render as effective a treatment as possible.

This model can be either active or receptive, depending upon the needs of the individual patient, however the most desirable aim is to achieve a balance between receptive (being) and active (doing). Since development is perceived in terms of human relationships, even a receptive approach finds its fullest expression in the contact established between therapist and patient.

MUSICAL ACTIVITY AS IT AFFECTS VITAL HUMAN FUNCTIONS

Listening to and creating music may indeed affect specific vital human functions, but in fact all of these functions interact naturally. For purposes of clarification we shall discuss them separately.

1. Senses and sensations[2] play different roles in so far as the receptive or active music experience is concerned.

A 4–5-month-old embryo can already hear and move in reaction to auditory stimulation (Olds 1984; Pannenton 1985; Shetler 1985). In fact it responds to internal body sounds such as the mother's heart beat, as well as to external sounds.

Verny and Kelly (1981) assume that the infant has auditory prenatal memories which explain why it relaxes when embraced close to the breast, or when exposed to a steady rhythm. They also give numerous, often far reaching, examples in order to justify their claims regarding early memories of rhythmical beats within the womb as an influence on later tendencies in the musical development of the human being.[3] Among others they base their ideas on Michael Clements' research into embryo reactions to soothing or stimulating music, as well as his conclusions regarding the effect of prenatal memories on musical preferences and prejudices in later life.

Verny and Kelly further claim that apart from a physical reaction by the embryo to both internal and external sounds, it is particularly sensitive to the human voice. It would seem that the pitch and timing are what most attract the attention of the newborn and together with the sense of touch serve as an important element in primary object relation.

Music therapy, similar to the approach developed by Alfred Thomatis,[4] continues to take into account the in utero auditory experience, particularly as regards relaxation and soothing, and the recollection of previous experiences which may have led to neurological and psychological injuries in childhood.

Today there can be no doubt about the significance of in utero sound and rhythm. Verny and Kelly found that infants exposed to music gained weight and grew well, and Murooka's research (1976), emphasizes the relaxing and soothing effects.

The sense of hearing improves when it is integrated with other senses, sensations, movement and the process of learning. For example, in his earliest months the infant learns to respond to certain auditory stimuli (his mother's voice, his father's voice, a doorbell) by turning his head. He thus visualizes the world from a new viewpoint and so discovers the source of the sound. In one simple action he integrates sight, sound, movement, proprioception and the vestibular system. This is one of the first stages of learning, without which normal development will be impossible.

Playing a musical instrument also demands an integration between the sense of hearing and other senses; one needs sight before touch and spatial awareness will be sufficiently developed. Only then can one scan the notes and be able to play like the blind man who relies only on his sense of touch and of space. A variety of coordinations are required while playing an instrument—eyes-hands, hands-hands, ears-hands, etc.[5]

In other words, optimal musical activity involves a number of senses and sensations and demands a certain degree of maturity and integration between them. However, if we encounter deficits, or a lack of senses, we are still able to create alternatives. The degree of maturity and of integration plays a central role in considering and planning therapy.[6]

2. Movement is linked with musical expression in two ways:

a) By spontaneous or by directed reaction to musical stimuli which has a prenatal origin. The more the human being develops, so does his ability to react smoothly to musical stimuli. This is also true of the repertoire of movement, both in quality and in complexity.

b) By movement while playing, which is dictated by the actual production of sounds, and the aims, abilities and skills of the performer.

Whereas the first form of activity consists of perceiving and consequently physically reacting to musical stimuli, the second involves the active creation of music. Both of these undergo a process of development and improvement according to the degree of maturity and sensory-motor integration.

During both intake and therapy it is essential to be aware of the fact that spontaneous locomotor reaction is mainly composed of gross motor function, whereas movement in playing depends on fine motor ability.[7]

3. Vocality is the key factor in human communication, despite the fact that other means of expression can be utilized, such as body language, mimicry, graphic symbols, and so on. Voice is a movement with sensory feedback (in the main auditory and proprioceptive). When a baby is born it screams and simultaneously makes movements. Motor potential is inborn, as is vocal potential.

Quite apart from the very practical reasons which have made the human voice the central element of communication (due for example to its nondependence on visual contact, and its ability to be heard despite physical obstacles or by means of long distance transmission equipment), there is also a psychological reason—the human voice is endowed with a flexibility which allows it to express emotion, even without the use of specific words. The musical parameters which influence emotion can be expressed vocally by means of changes in tempo and continuity, accentuation, pitch and range, timbre and dynamics. All of these are characteristics of primary vocal communication and continue to perform their emotional role even after the acquisition of the powers of speech, the secondary means of communication.*

Careful listening to vocality helps in diagnosing various physiological problems (stammering, faulty diction, respiratory difficulties, etc.), as well as in the diagnosis of psychological complaints (limitations of vocal range, dynamics, tempo, etc.).

Within the therapeutic process the act of singing permits a wide range of expression which in normal speech would be considered either unacceptable or even ridiculous, but is nevertheless totally legitimate in song.[8]

4. Emotion. The art of music is endowed by its very nature with the ability to give expression to human feelings. Such expressiveness characterizes both physical and psychological situations and can therefore be exploited in order to evoke both kinds of reaction.

Emotional elements in music are basically expressed by changes of tempo, pitch, range, dynamics and timbre. Unblocked emotional excitation affects the tempo,[9] expands the vocal range and increases the volume and intensity. Should the patient improvise music containing these characteristics it would be logical to assume that he is expressing rage, joy, ecstatic trance, or so forth. In other words, this combination of fast tempo, increased volume and extended range, can be diagnosed as an expression of emotional excitation, but its exact nature should still be examined by additional means, such as analyzing the form and character of the melody, its harmonious development, its rhythmic structure, in addition to taking into consideration extra-musical information before risking a direct translation of music into emotion.

Susanne Langer (1979), who is critical of what she sees as the baseless assumption that music serves as a medium of emotional expression, quotes for example the differing emotional interpretations which performers and audiences can apply to the very same work, and it is certainly true to say that emotional interpretation of music is a many-faceted process. Even the most up-to-date research into this subject has been unable to provide an unequivocal answer to the question of why a low pitch, a moderate melodic range, a moderate tempo and a soothing dynamic, arouse feelings of sadness in one listener, of longing in another and of tranquility in a third. In this connection music therapy demands both an empiric and pragmatic approach which must examine each and every patient in an individual light. What are the personal motifs which best express his or her personality? What kind of music can arouse repressed emotions? In what tonal and rhythmic framework can the patient best find an associative expression for his or her feelings? What kind of music arouses metaphorical associations and can elicit subconscious content? And so on.

There are no specific scientific explanations for music's emotional power, but the model presented here sees in the subjective attitude of each individual patient toward music more of an advantage than a disadvantage. On the other hand, at the basic level of musical parameters we do have certain fairly clear answers concerning

---

*See also Note 16: Prosody.

their physical and emotional functions, this from observation and analysis of similar musical parameters in traditional healing rituals (see Chapter 1), and the concept of their being basically a product of the human organism (Appendix 2).

Susanne Langer, like many others, is concerned with the emotional impact of art music, whereas the music therapist who employs an active approach is concerned with the emotional impact of the music created by the patient himself, and with his emotional ability to create inter- and intrapersonal reactions by means of that music.

For example, when Alon (see Chapter 7) first started to react emotionally during music therapy, he gave vent to his passive aggressiveness by massive drum beating, thus initiating a new self-dialogue by means of which he was able to acknowledge his aggression and to dare give vent to it without feeling endangered. From a purely musical point of view his rhythmic creativity was of little value at this stage, but from a therapeutic aspect the drum provided him with a way of confronting his existential anxiety, expressing it, releasing it, and eventually coming to terms with it.

Anat (see Chapter 4) was a very erratic singer due to the vocal defects which characterize her syndrome. Her playing was also extremely irregular and she had difficulty in maintaining a simple drum rhythm due to muscular hypotonia. Nevertheless it was music which brought her into close contact with such emotions as anger and sadness, after which she was eventually able to phrase in words and even comprehend, despite her being classified as mentally retarded.

Concerning the emotional impact of art music Susanne Langer makes a salient point. "Music is not self-expression, but formulation and representation of emotions, moods, mental tensions and realizations—a 'logical picture' of sentient, responsive life, a source of insight…. A composer not only indicates but articulates subtle complexes of feelings that language cannot even name…he knows the forms of emotion and can handle them, 'compose' them" (1982, 222).

Such emotional forms succeed in arousing within the listener/patient an emotional identification which might stimulate self-searching. According to Helen Bonny (1990) it is quite possible that the very alienation of a certain musical piece from the here-and-now experiences of the listener is just what enables such individualistic identification with it. Pieces based on concrete metaphors (such as bird song, train whistles, thunder) merely arouse predictable visions in the mind of the listener rather that those uniquely personal reactions which we seek in therapy

With the mentally retarded, however, it may be preferable to employ such obvious stimuli in order to provoke any kind of reaction, as unabstracted it may be.

5. Cognition. The Cognitive System is more relevant to musical education than to music therapy. It is important, however, to note that there are often side effects to music therapy in the form of indirect learning such as acquiring the language of music, using music to symbolize an event or an emotion: conceptualization (short-long, fast-slow, duration, etc.), as well as analysis, memory and abstraction.

In treating the mentally retarded the cognitive system can be developed by the use of music in play situations (depending upon the degree of retardation) since the perception of music is not necessarily an analytical process and can exist on various levels of intelligence. One of the most amazing examples is that of Lesley (the boy described in "May's Miracle" 1980), who despite blindness and severe mental retardation from birth developed such an ability for absorbing musical structures that he could, by ear and with no musical training, repeat whole passages from piano concertos and play them quite well.

Whatever the case, in treatment D.I.M.T. accentuates the senses, vocality, motion and emotions. The fundamental assumption of the developmental concept is that a mature basis of these functions facilitates the development of the cognitive faculties. We must, however, insist that this is not a therapeutic model concerned with only one single aspect of the patient's health: it is an overall approach which takes into account all the various levels of development and maturity.

PSYCHOACOUSTIC QUALITIES OF MUSICAL PARAMETERS AND THEIR THERAPEUTIC RELEVANCE

1. Rhythm. Time expresses the duration of notes and pauses as well as including various other aspects such as beat-unit, rhythmical patterns, meter, tempo, etc. As in other musical parameters, the manifestation of time plays a cardinal role in music therapy due to its inherent linkage with the human organism. Here we shall concentrate on three basic rhythms—the biological, the movemental and the cyclical.

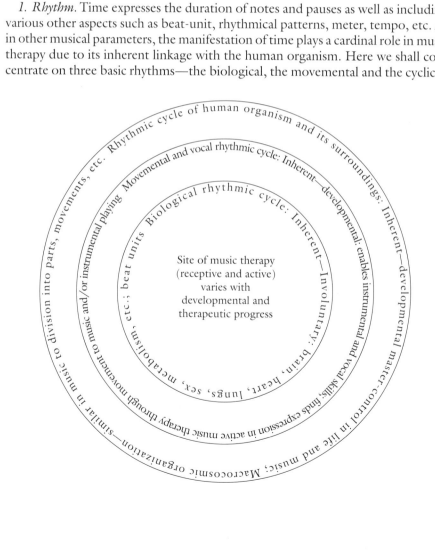

The innermost circle, the biological rhythm (beat-units), originates from the activity of such vital organs as the brain, heart, lungs, bowels, sexual organs, and so on. It is characterized by repetitive beat-units which are controlled by the brain stem. These beat-units serve as a primitive basis for both the organism and in the art of music (or at least did so up until the beginning of the 20th century when new concepts of composition changed the traditional role of rhythm). Within the human organism this inner rhythm is the first to exist and the last to be destroyed, even in vegetative conditions in which the patient is in coma.

In music, the beat is the cornerstone, whose degree of audibility varies from composition to composition. We have already noted that in traditional healing rituals, both ecstatic and hypnotic, it plays the major psychophysiological role; we have also noted various research which explains this phenomenon. The biological beat-unit can be altered by internal causes (such as illness, changing states of consciousness, etc.) as well as by external causes (such as excessive physical activity, time lag, climate, etc.). In other words, such change can be caused within the inner rhythmic circle in the same way it can occur within the middle or outer spheres.

Research has shown that the inner rhythmic circle can be reinforced by means of continuous action after birth (Murooka 1976). This can be both vocal and movemental, and bears a varied degree of significance which depends on the development and individual needs of the infant. For example, a mother who cradles her offspring in her arms and rocks it back and forth while crooning a lullaby does so in order to soothe it to sleep. Sleep is an important activity for a newborn infant and during the cradling ceremony and the lullaby it experiences the integration of several functions which are essential to its development: touch, movement, vestibular stimulation, hearing, and the exercising of its future means of communication.[10]

The use of a steady rhythmic beat at this stage in life fulfills the need for a soothing vestibular stimulation. On the other hand, when we consider the way beat is employed in rock music, which typifies adolescent culture, we perceive that energetic movement stimulated by strong beat-units serves a totally different purpose. Here too we find repetition (which therapy accepts as a holder) but its orgastic character and the movements it invokes are aimed at releasing sexual and/or aggressive energies. In this case the integration is between the biological beat-rates, the movemental, and the cyclical spheres (the adolescent phase and its special demands). In addition the adolescent is also capable of identifying with the lyrics which are generally composed by his societal contemporaries and deal with subjects which answer his urgent needs.

In both cases, that of the infant and that of the adolescent, we are witness to a combination of auditory stimuli and spontaneous physical reaction. In the first example, both actions are carried out by the mother, while the infant plays a receptive role. In the second example both music and movement can be performed by the same individual, or there can be a player and a dancer who reacts. These can be seen as equivalent to the events described in traditional healing rituals (Chapter 1), with the mother-infant dynamic likened to the hypnotic and the rock dance to the ecstatic.

Isaac Sadai, the Israeli composer and musicologist, regards the infant's discovery of sound and its repetitive realization as an essential stage in the development of musical epistemology. According to Piaget's theories (1958) the discovery of sound occurs during the sensory-motor phase which extends over the first eighteen months of life. The infant pounds with his hands and feet either on his own body or on some other object, and if he enjoys the sound or the rhythm he will repeat them again and again. This process of repetition by way of the sensory-motor feedback cycle "represents a key factor in the creation of rhythm and the structuring of form in every existing sort of music" (Sadai. 1988). By so saying, Sadai transports us from the sphere of inner or biological rhythm, to that of the rhythm of motion, beginning with the embryo's reactions in the seventh or eighth week of pregnancy (Hooker, in Payton, et al. 1977).

Generally speaking the infant's physical development follows two basic directions:

a) Head to tail (cephalo-caudal), which means it first moves its head, and by degrees the shoulders, the trunk, the hips, the knees and then the ankles.

b) From the inside out (proximo-distal), which means that the differentiation of movement begins in the center of the body and is transmitted in stages to the arms and legs. As progress is made toward the extremities and the more refined movements develop (the ability to separate and spread the fingers and to tap with one finger at a time), there emerges a more complex ability suited to the playing of musical instruments. It is the maturity of the physical-motor rhythm which dictates the degree of sophistication which can be employed to produce musical rhythm.

The motor development of voluntary movement achieved by professional musicians is so amazing that it defies comparison with almost any other day-to-day functioning. Furthermore, when these motor skills are developed to such a degree that each limb is capable of creating a different rhythm (such as playing a church organ), and the independence of the fingers has matured, complex polyphonic music can be performed. In other words the ability to perform music which is rhythmically complex is a natural outcome of motor skills and efficient praxis (motor planning). On the other hand, when there are defects in the motor system resulting in apraxis, these can in fact be improved by the use of various instruments (according to specific needs) and motor response to music.

Both movement response to music and movement while playing share an identical pattern of development: reflex reaction, repetition and improvement, complex voluntary movement, skilled movement which becomes automatic. The more the rhythmic motion becomes automatic, the more the mental and listening processes are free to acquire a greater awareness.

In the same way as the biological rhythms which are controlled by the brain stem can be compared to the basic rhythms (beat-units) of music, so can the rhythms of motion, which are controlled by the cortex, be compared to the variegated rhythmic events which occur in musical compositions. They exert a mutual influence one upon the other and both are influenced by the cyclical rhythm. This is a sphere which could well be compared with parts or whole movements of musical compositions—both embrace the extremities and the transformations within a given continuity. Both are perceived as an "overall timing" within which different rhythmic events occur, sometimes strict, sometimes flexible, and subject to influence.

Time (rhythm) is a parameter both of extreme exactitude and of dynamic flexibility.

Pathological symptoms as far as rhythm is concerned find their expression either in extreme pedantry or in extreme flexibility. In the first case this means compulsive repetition and perseverance, whereas in the second case this results in disorder, disorganization and incoherence. Examples of extreme pedantry can be found among neurotics who make use of rhythm as a defense mechanism, as well as with psychotics who tend to enter into movemental and rhythmic perseverance.

Eric[11] provided us with an extreme example of rhythmic obsession during music therapy when he would annotate his compositions with such exaggerated directions as:

This means repeat twenty times.

During therapy it was possible to observe a direct correlation between his improved psychic condition and the reduction of these repetition signs to the normal two.

For an example of organizational problems we can refer to the case history of Alon. Due to muscular hypotonia and passive-aggression he had difficulty playing in a steady rhythmical continuity. When his hypotonia was treated by ecstatic music thus enabling him to express his aggressions, his rhythmic control improved to a remarkable degree. This was not the result of rehearsal and practice, but rather a direct consequence of treating his basic problems.

Another example is that of Jacob, who participated in music therapy for rehabilitation. Jacob was a cantor who, as the result of a stroke, suffered from left hemiplegia. He underwent a lengthy and agonizing process of restoring his sense and performance of rhythm, especially the basic beat-unit in order to rebuild his melo-rhythmic abilities which had been almost completely destroyed.

Indeed, the various rhythmic spheres are perceived by D.I.M.T. as emerging from the human being himself. They facilitate both observation and diagnosis during music therapy, as well as treatment and reassessment during all stages of the process.

As a basic parameter, it is rhythm in its simplest form which serves as the central musical component of traditional healing ritual, just as it does in present day music therapy. The case histories which follow will illustrate, among other things, the various roles played by rhythm in music therapy, and also their links with the origins of the profession as described in Chapter 1.

In music therapy, as in complex musical works, the rhythmic elements (in all their various forms) serve as a unifying force (beat, rhythmic structure, meter), and as a linkage between excitation and relaxation (tempo, acceleration, deceleration). Organization, unification, excitation and relaxation, are viewed by D.I.M.T. as essential psychophysiological elements.

2. Pitch mainly depends for its psychoacoustic effect on a basic frequency, the number of vibrations per second. (Pitch is currently used to designate the psychological experience, whereas frequency designates the physical vibration). In purely musical terms a single sound generally has very little significance, whatever its psychoacoustic qualities (volume, pitch, timbre), may be due to the fact that significance in the art of music emerges from the relationships of such qualities within the composition itself. In music therapy, however, the individual sound can sometimes be endowed with specific content and meaning. Whatever the case, the human organism's source for the creation of pitch lies in the throat, from the very moment of birth the vocal system utilizes changes of pitch as both a primary and secondary means of communication.

Changes in pitch modulation which ultimately create melody, originate with the infant's first attempts at self-expression, and from the intervals which his vocal chords produce spontaneously. The development of voluntary movement within the vocal apparatus leads to stabilization in the production of sounds and intervals. Thus, along with the development of speech (which is not so dependent on the control of precise pitch), the ability to sing develops.

D.I.M.T. defines speech as verbal vocality and singing as musical vocality. The ability to translate pitch from the human voice to that of a musical instrument in accordance with accepted musical standards is an essential part of music development. In therapy this provides for an externalization of inherent internal elements in the same way that percussion provides an outlet for the internal psychobiological rhythms.

To sum up, music contains the ability to link internal and external processes, and as we shall see when we discuss the meaning of the Therapeutic Space, great importance is attached to this linkage in the process of development and growth.

3. Timbre "is determined primarily by the number, the order and the relative intensity of the fundamental, and its overtones as expressed in the Wave-Forms" (Seashore 1967, 20). It allows us to distinguish, for example, between A on a piano and A on a flute.

So far we have been discussing only two of the psychoacoustic qualities of music, duration and pitch, both of which are essential to the organization of musical composition. As we have seen, they both originate within the human organism and in therapy serve the need for order, continuation, stability, and emotionality.

From a therapeutic point of view it is important to note the patient's reactions to the timbre of certain musical instruments, as well as to that of the voice as this can prove to be a severe disadvantage if the therapist's singing and speech (strident, nasal, etc.) repels the patient. This critical question of matching the therapist's voice to the sensitivities of the patient deserves a more thorough investigation.

I have observed specific emotional reactions, due to neurological over-sensitivity among autistic patients, schizophrenics, and occasionally among minimal brain-damaged children to timbre, pitch and volume. In only two cases did I discern anxiety as a result of increased tempo, apparently due to traumatic associations (Sekeles 1989).

4. *Intensity.* Volume is expressed in terms of decibels. The decibel is a psychological unit representing the degree of loudness. Its physical counterpart, intensity, is expressed in terms of units of electrical energy.

The variety of intensities which can be employed in music is called dynamics. The expressive source of volume within the human organism is again the voice, and its emotional effectiveness is determined (apart from by the factors already mentioned) by dynamic change, which in everyday life consists of the whole range of volume between a whisper and a scream. Different degrees of volume can also be achieved by means of body-sounds, as we have seen in the case of other parameters; such expression begins at birth and remains active both in the art of music and in everyday life.

We have already noted how ecstatic healing rituals are characterized in part by steady increases in volume in a manner which serves to release aggressive and/or sexual energy, whereas in hypnotic ritual a moderate, unchanging dynamic is preserved throughout. The entire ritual remains relatively quiet from beginning to end, creating relaxation and a sleep-inducing effect, since the dynamics resemble those of the lullaby.

In therapy we must pay great attention to the gaps which may exist between emotional content and its vocal expression, with volume (or intensity) being one of our major guidelines. For example, Alon or Rita (see Chapters 6 and 7). While both of them suffered from an inability to express anger, their body language revealed obvious symptoms of passive aggression. They hardly ever made use of vocal expression, and even when they did the volume or dynamic they employed was a mere *p/ppp* (piano/pianissimo). One of the ways in which their therapeutic progress could be measured was by their ability to play musical instruments at extreme volume with a matching vocal energy.

D.I.M.T. observes and takes into account the free flow and balance between the dynamics of voice and body movement. For example Ron, (see Chapter 3), when suffering from a state of great anxiety would turn rigid, increasing the spasticity of the paralyzed part of his body, and scream. One of the first signs of improvement was his ability to master to a certain degree the dynamics of both voice and movement.

D.I.M.T. also attaches great importance to the fact that music is endowed with vast change and flexibility. It ranges from disciplined continuity to lack of continuity and order; from fast to slow tempo; from sudden, surprising changes and innovations to predictability and repetition; from broad to narrow vocal range; and from unexpected variations in volume to unity and a minimum of change.

The following chart attempts to show the relationships between the above-mentioned musical elements according to their vertical and horizontal flow.

Characteristic	Elements	Characteristic
Irregularity, inconsistency	BEAT	Regularity, Consistency
Irregularity, asymmetry	METER	Regularity symmetry
Variegated, nonrepetitive, unpredictable	RHYTHMIC STRUCTURES	Fixed, repetitive, predictable
Unpredictable	ACCENTS	Predictable
Accelerated, changeable	TEMPO	Slow, repetitive and predictable
High, with sharp variations	PITCH	Low, repetitive and predictable
Extremely variable, unpredictable	MELODIC RANGE	Limited, repetitive and predictable
Extreme variation within a brief time-frame	VOLUME— DYNAMICS	Unity, minimal variation

In this partial list (to which one could add further combinations such as musical texture) we can perceive certain principles. In the left column we find irregularity, asymmetry, acceleration, sharp variation and high pitch, all of these being qualities which arouse interest and identification in some, irritation and psychomotor unease in another, incomprehension in a third, and so on.

In the right column we find regularity, consistency, repetition, unity, and a moderation of tempo, pitch and volume, each of which can arouse boredom in some, and in some tranquillity, somnolence, etc.

As has already been noted, ecstatic healing ritual commences with some of the elements defined in the right column, and by a steady increase of both tempo and volume reaches the extremes of the left column, whereas hypnotic ritual remains rooted in the right column.

The Developmental-Integrative Model in Music Therapy makes deliberate use of these principles in order to create mood, excitation, relaxation, an altered state of consciousness, etc. As already emphasized, this is no simple task and it demands a profound understanding of the patient and of his individual needs.

Despite certain disagreement between researchers (Sekeles 1990, Chapter 2) regarding the exact psychophysiological influence of complex musical works, I should like to make my own contribution to this ongoing argument. This is based on numerous observations and reports which I have accumulated over the years.

A balanced combination of elements within any given musical composition can often induce a psychophysiological equilibrium within the listener and/or performer. Such equilibrium consists of a flexibility of movement in both vertical and horizontal axes and a balance between tension and relaxation, expressed in changes of rhythm, melody, harmony, dynamics, etc.

In music, just as in physical and emotional existence, we can observe the pressures and releases of tension, of conflict and its resolution.

Existing in a state of constant relaxation and a consistent limitation of tension has been proved to be antidevelopmental. Erik Erikson (1950) emphasizes the necessity for a certain degree of anxiety in order to progress from one developmental stage to another.

Pinhas Noy discusses art from a psychoanalytical point of view using the approach of Ego-Psychology which claims that artistic activity is by its very nature an act of mastery. "Just as in children's games, the ego in such activity, recreates those agonizing situations in which it used to be helpless, and by overcoming them, the painful experience becomes one of pleasure.... Impressive art makes its effect due to its ability to sweep the audience off its feet into emotional states of tension and anxiety, while at the same time ensuring the conditions under which they will finally be able to organize their experiences and get them under control" (Noy 1983, 351).

Such experience which induces tension and anxiety is recognized in music therapy as a result of musical structures which can lead to a certain identification in a certain patient at a certain time and in certain surroundings, but not necessarily in anyone else. A balanced musical composition can help the patient to identify with the musical solutions it offers, and might also afford the listener or the performer a sense of power and control.

It is this aspect which leads us directly from music per se and the definition of its therapeutic elements, to the Dynamics of D.I.M.T.

THE DYNAMICS OF THERAPY

THE THERAPEUTIC TRIAD (Patient, Music, Therapist)

The reality of therapy reveals that almost all the usually accepted generalizations regarding the influence of music on the human being do not necessarily apply in specific cases. Bonny (1969), and Eagle & Gaston (1972), arrived at totally contradictory conclusions regarding the exact same patient community. Indeed, the more complex the music, the greater the need for wider information regarding the patient in order to understand the possible influences it may have on him.

Despite this, however, the realities of therapy show that a number of overall characteristics are relevant for many patients, provided of course that these are anchored in a style which suits the patient's personality and cultural background. Music of a soothing nature, for example, exists in a wide and contrasting variety of cultures, styles, categories and even periods. We have observed the influence of such basic characteristics of music in the hypnotic healing rituals, and they have been examined by music therapists in a variety of clinical situations (Borling 1981; Scartelli 1982). Obviously in order to relax an Arab-Moslem patient we should employ a musical style with which he is familiar and which he is accustomed to hear, just as we should with a patient of Polish, or Anglo-Saxon origin. D.I.M.T. denies on principle the existence of an "International Language of Music" and instead puts a major stress on the cultural and personal background of the patient in the selection of appropriate music for therapy. There exists a parallel in verbal psycho-therapy, regarding the use of a language and lexicon which match the cultural experience of the patient.

So far our remarks have concerned receptive music therapy. In active music therapy great attention must be paid to listening to the nuances of the patient's musical expression, and to cooperating with him and identifying with his own particular musical culture (Sekeles 1983). Such identification can demand a famil-iarization with a style which might well be outside the therapist's usual repertoire and knowledge. For example, the world of music for Jacob (see Chapter 5) was rooted in his religious background and his education as a cantor. Most of his cantillation and prayers were foreign to me and forced me into a new field of study, and identification with a new kind of experience.

Similarly Rita (see Chapter 6), whose Netherlands background comprising the songs she learned in school within a certain age group and the music she knew at home, were also not a part of my own musical education. In order to help her I had to become acquainted with what was familiar and meaningful to her, to internalize it and then be able to make free use of it. This is more than simply understanding manuscripts and scores. It means fully comprehending the musical origins and the patient's cultural roots. This is especially true since D.I.M.T. lays stress on the fact that after the initial confrontation with the medium most of the musical material to be employed in therapy is produced by the patient himself and consists of rhythmic and melodic motifs, organization of the material, extra-musical connotations, the associations of music with emotions and events, the choice of instruments and their symbolism, etc.

According to D.I.M.T., the music is inspired by and emerges from the patient's personal world, both in receptive and in active therapy. It is up to the therapist to understand and contain this world, to analyze it and to make use of it in an ongoing therapeutic dialogue. During this dialogue the musical material will often undergo a metamorphosis and occasionally (as in the case of Eric) be transformed from mere improvisation into a comprehensible composition. In other words, alongside emo-tional and physical development there may well be a purely musical development. Despite the fact that this is not the declared aim of music therapy, the acquisition of skill and control in music can contribute to an overall sense of confidence.

Because it is so difficult to research and define the exact extent to which music can influence man, the music therapist often finds him or herself facing a profes-sional existential dilemma—can a therapeutic process exist even when someone sits at home alone, listening to or creating music by himself? If so, why apply for professional advice?

Similarly, can the musical dialogue which takes place between the players in a chamber or symphony orchestra be defined as therapeutic? And if so, can such players who conduct such a continuous musical dialogue be defined as a symbol of health in body and soul?

Another point to be clarified is the day-to-day dynamics which may characterize individual or group activity in music as opposed to the dynamics of the music therapy space. Music to which someone listens at home, or plays at home, can be excellent and extremely moving for the listener, or for the performer. This does not mean, however, that it necessarily opens up a window for self-awareness, or for a strengthening of personality. The potential is there, but in reality people tend either to cling to a professional analytical frame of mind (especially musicians) or to float on clouds of emotional experience, and no more than that. In the first case there exists a certain educational experience and intellectual approach to music, while in the second it is a purely sensuous experience. There remains no evidence of a therapeutic process, or the essential linkage which therapy seeks between emotion and intellect.

There also exists the phenomenon of professional players, in both large and small orchestras, who display a marvellous capacity for interaction and mutuality of sound in performance as a unified whole, and yet are extremely disharmonious in human relations when not on stage.[12] It is for these very reasons that D.I.M.T. perceives music therapy as a stage upon which the main purpose is to achieve a balance between the various personality needs of the patient. It is the therapist's task to assist in such linkage by means of mirroring, holding, elaborating the process of transference, and so forth.

Such techniques, adopted from psychodynamic therapy, are exploited in D.I.M.T. by way of music, words, and a combination of both. It would appear that without the mediation of the therapist such aspects would be hard to accomplish. It would also be difficult for any person, or his companion, to comprehend during musical activity the messages emanating from his body (fixation, distortion, pain), or the psychological expressions of repression, aggression, inability, and to exploit these by use of music in order to achieve efficient and satisfactory change.

Therapy demands an intimate framework within which one can work both physically and/or psychologically and focus on any possible change. Despite the fact that this model emphasizes an overall approach, it is not my intention to enter into the complex arguments regarding the links between body and mind, nor to prove their scientific existence.

From a philosophical point of view Prof. Isaiah Leibowitz, in an article concerning the apparently obvious and accepted links between body and mind claims that "Our mental powers are incapable of grasping the inevitable fact that the psychophysical link, which every one of us reveals in his own personality, is a logical impossibility" (Leibowitz 1982, 75–76). Logic, from a scientific point of view maintains that physical realities are measurable, while realities of the mind are not. Neither will we discuss here the viewpoints adopted by countless researches into psychoneuroimmunology (Lloyd et al. 1987, Pelettier et al. 1988). Possibly in the future such research will be able to provide us with a new approach regarding the powers of music as part of the body's struggles against illness.

At this stage we are not concerned with mind or body, nor with the immune systems, but with patients: Ron, Anat, Jacob, Rita, Alon (see Case Histories), paying attention to the special needs of each individual, in an attempt to enable them to achieve musical expression which includes not only words but also the experiences of music and that primal communication which preceded speech.

The psychodynamic process of music, according to D.I.M.T., shows us that from out of the musical chaos which often typifies the start of therapy, there emerges a dual conversation which the patient begins to conduct both with himself and with the therapist, and it is from this that order can develop. It is my contention, based on many years of experience, that the basic elements (such as rhythmic cycles) contain within themselves a basic urge for organization and balance, due to their parallels with the equilibrium achieved by the vital functions of the organism. Likewise, such organization has a reciprocatory effect on those vital functions and vice versa. When there exist blockages or regressions in natural development, be these due to cerebral palsy, blindness and retardation (Ron), muscular hypotonia and the Down's Syndrome (Anat), emotional blockage of speech (Alon), regression and a state of confusion (Rita), or the loss of vocal-musical skills (Jacob), it is our task as therapists to locate the problem by a diagnosis of the visible symptoms as well as the invisible causes. We must treat it with the means at our disposal, which are mainly the art of music and its components.

Should use be made of elements from other art forms, or from the fields of psychology or medicine, it should be done according to the special needs of the individual patient and a strict adherence to the professional responsibilities of the music therapist. The use of words does not make us psychologists; the use of movement does not turn us into dance- or physiotherapists, or indeed into any thing else. Music therapy is a discipline within itself, and D.I.M.T. takes a grave view of the employment of elements from other disciplines without sufficient professional knowledge and experience. Even so, the demands for interdisciplinary knowledge as outlined in the Preface are difficult enough to implement.

THE STRUCTURE AND SIGNIFICANCE OF THE THERAPEUTIC SPACE

D.I.M.T. sees the therapeutic space first and foremost as a "potential area for free choice," rather like Winnicott's "Potential Space," an area for activities whose roots lie in children's play activities, and whose nature depends on the ability of the child, or adult, to undergo experience. Winnicott sees the religious experience, the artistic experience, and the therapy room as an extension of the space between mother and infant: when in a state of satisfaction and a sense of safety the infant can allow himself to draw away from the mother and play by himself. "In the Potential Space between baby and mother there appears the creative playing that arises naturally out of a relaxed state. It is here that the child develops a use of symbols which stand at one and the same time for external world phenomena and for the phenomena of the individual person who is being looked at." (Winnicott 1971, 128)

" The symbolic use of music creates a place which allows emo'l exper to link the inner & outer world, & devel. a dialogue beta.

Winnicott defines this potential space as an intermediate area of experiencing, *then* " and a resting place for the individual in the perpetual human task of keeping inner and outer realities separate yet interrelated (ibid., 3). The therapeutic space embodies these characteristics since it serves as a place in which playing is possible. As artistic activities are on a personal level, the symbolic use of music creates a place which allows emotional experience to link the inner and outer world and develop a dialogue between them.

In practice the Therapeutic Space should be large enough to allow freedom of movement for at least six people. The floor should be close-carpeted and the musical instruments be moved to the side or be hung on the walls in such a way as not to inhibit movement, and at the same time attract attention and encourage the will to try using them. This allows the patient to choose his own area of activity, the instruments which interest him, what pieces he would like to hear, the physical posture he prefers (sitting, lying down, moving about), and so forth. This element of free choice is essential for learning the patient's problems and his latent strengths (initiative, self-control, responsibility, independence, etc.), and is especially important in gaining his cooperation and in strengthening his motivation for therapy.

The musical instruments themselves are of especial significance not only in terms of practical use, but also because of their symbolic significance (see Appendix 1). Because of this there should be the widest possible range of choice, including the usual selection (piano, guitar, a full set of Orff instruments, wind instruments, etc.), as well as folk drums and rattles, flutes and so on.

Special attention should also be paid to the patient's own self-made instruments which he decorates with his own personal symbols (see Chapter 1, Note 17), electronic instruments, and a vast and varied collection of discs and tapes. High-standard recording equipment is essential, and the space itself should be totally sound proof, thus ensuring the intimacy so important in therapy.

Summing up, the therapeutic space should be totally isolated from any outside disturbance, furnished spaciously without undue fuss, with a variety of high-tech equipment. It should offer a free choice of activity and serve as an intimate potential space for emotional and movement experiences through music.

THE TRAINING OF THE MUSIC THERAPIST

At the very outset formal training must include the professional study of music A physician or psychologist who is also a music lover and makes use of music in his treatments is not yet a music therapist, just as a music therapist who is familiar with and makes use of the basics of psychology is not yet a psychologist. It is the language of therapy which must serve as the initial basis for training. The demands made on the therapist to employ music in a flexible manner make it essential that music be a Calling, studied from an early age and springing from a natural desire.

The second stage of training should consist of studies in the fields of medicine and psychology of all aspects which concern the normal and abnormal development of vital functions.

Stage three should concern the development of self-awareness and an understanding of the therapeutic aspects of music and their relevance to the trainee himself.

Stage four should be devoted to the integration of these subjects into the specific field of music therapy. It should be stressed that stages two, three and four should not be taught one after the other but simultaneously, with a balance and integration between theoretical studies, workshops, and supervised apprenticeship in clinical settings.

After concluding these stages, the way is open for additional training which can optimally embrace music therapy for music therapists, psychodynamic therapy, other forms of artistic therapy, as well as intensive supervision of clinical procedures.[13]

ESSENTIAL SKILLS

The patient and his therapist are each burdened with his own set of values, cultural background, life-experience, musical preferences and prejudices. Indeed, the music therapist will be capable of authentic expression only insofar as he employs a musical language which is most familiar to him and permits him the greatest degree of flexibility. He must, however, be capable of transforming music into words and vice versa; and he must have the ability to select and improvise the kind of music which will influence the patient as and when required. He must also, at the same time, be able to objectively comprehend the therapeutic process.

Just as one of the aims of therapy is to expand the patient's scope of expression and range of experience, so must the therapist be open to an understanding of musical cultures which may be totally foreign to his or her own education. The therapist must be ready, willing and able to invest vast amounts of energy in improving and expanding his musical knowledge of styles, categories, unfamiliar instruments and vocal expressions in order to absorb and contain the patient's mode of expression and thus establish a dialogue.

The music therapist must learn to listen with patience and tolerance. The vast majority of patients arrive for treatment as nonmusicians who must undergo a process of chaotic trial and error which the therapist must accept at face value. Even though the therapist may have acquired vocal and instrumental techniques which could assist a patient who lacks any formal training, he must avoid any invasive intervention at this stage as it may well overwhelm the patient and sabotage the continuity of the therapeutic process. From a therapeutic point of view even the most primitive, limited and confused attempts at self-expression bear a physical and emotional significance. The therapist must be capable of a dichotomic analysis not only of the musical events, but also of additional phenomena (body-language, mimicry, physical and emotional blockages, verbal expressions, etc.), and recognizing the relationship between them. Listening must also be a dichotomic process, analytical (purely musical), and emotional (identifying with the messages the music attempts to convey). Listening not endowed with both of these abilities cannot be effective in therapy.

The music therapist must develop a dual sensitivity to the patient, both to his musical efforts and at the same time to his extra-musical activities. It is by no means an easy task to arrive at a swift answer to a patient's musical expression as it demands a developed ear,[14] the ability to transfer from ear to instrument, as well as the dangers of overloading due to excessive creativity on the part of the therapist, or the opposite—superficiality due a lack of sufficient creative input.

To sum up, the characteristics and development demanded of the music therapist are flexibility and broadening of interest in all fields of music and personality, which will enable him or her to listen with both patience and tolerance; to absorb, contain and understand the dynamics of transference and counter-transference: to be aware of and sensitive to the patient's musical and extra-musical forms of expression, and to be able to analyze them from both musical and extra-musical viewpoints.

To this end, in addition to possessing initial and essential personality traits, the therapist must learn to form an integration between music, medicine and psychology, and must undergo supervision in a clinical setting as well as in verbal therapy or any other psychotherapy through art-modality.

THE PATIENT COMMUNITY

Since D.I.M.T. operates on a variety of levels of insight and employs music for a wide range of aims, I would like to stress that in the realities of therapy, in addition to the question of which patient is suited to music therapy and in what form, there is also the personality of the therapist to be taken into consideration. Not everyone can necessarily deal effectively with the retarded, the psychotic, or with the sufferer from severe neurological damage, just as not everyone can work in a significant manner with neurotics. It is my experience that D.I.M.T. is most suited to those applicants who during their initial interview and observation show a genuine interest in experiencing the medium, even if this is limited to certain aspects of it.

This opens the door for the treatment of those patients who suffer from verbal communication problems (either psychological or organic), from various levels of retardation, neurological problems, the psychotic, the neurotic, and even the healthy. The music therapist must, however, be cautious with schizophrenics who suffer from auditory hallucinations, patients with musicogenic epilepsy, hypersensitivity to sound, echolalia, and certain respiratory problems which can lead to fainting (a symptom which dictates extreme care when employing wind instruments). Such cases can in fact be treated by D.I.M.T., but only on condition that the problems and the musical resources are fully understood and appropriately dealt with.

D.I.M.T. believes in the study and application of verbal techniques combined with music or applied separately even when the patient may be of extremely limited insight, or even severely retarded. This is possible by matching verbal expression with the comprehensive ability of the patient. Even in the treatment of organic problems D.I.M.T. believes in explaining the motor action to the patient, in mirroring, summation, and in the active involvement of the patient in the entire process.

INTAKE PROCEDURES

Referral. As far as children are concerned, referral is generally instigated by a psychologist, school counsellor, occupational therapist, art therapist, physiotherapist, family doctor, neurologist, mental health center, social worker, and so on. With adults it may originate with the family, some other therapist or with the individual.

In the majority of cases such referral is indicated by difficulties in verbal communication, inhibition of emotional expression, or a rejection of verbal therapy. On occasions, when referral is made by a neurologist, the indication may include specific requests aimed at the treatment of the fine motor system, eye-hand and hand-hand coordination, defects of auditory memory, speech problems, etc. In all such cases, therapy is devoted to the Whole Being, not to its separate parts.

Initial interview and observation. The initial interview can be conducted with the minimum of advance information about the applicant, and since this is mainly based on musical activity, it increases the chances of unprejudiced observation.

Apart from certain details which may be considered essential to the specific case, in this first encounter the prospective patient is given a free hand in selecting his own form of musical expression (even though the therapist may support by modeling and by transforming the expressive use of music into a norm). The temptations, or stimuli, available in the music therapy space, as opposed to those in the premises of the psychologist or psychiatrist, can be seen as a means of diverting the applicant's awareness from internal to external interests.

From this point of view, whether we are discussing the treatment of children or of adults, it should be recalled that we perceive the therapeutic space as an "Intermediate Area of Experience." Thus the musical equipment might serve to express inner content and to create a suitable atmosphere for the reduction of anxiety.

During the initial interview observation is carried out according to the D.I.M.T. evaluation procedure (see Appendix 3) motor development, sensory development, sensory-motor integration, vocality, rhythmicity, the use of musical instruments, hearing and listening habits, as well as emotional, cognitive and societal characteristics. All this through music and techniques which will be briefly discussed later.

With the applicant's agreement the initial interview is recorded in toto, as are all ensuing therapy sessions. After this interview the therapist summarizes his evaluation and submits it to the referral authority together with his recommendations regarding the suitability of the applicant/referred-patient for music therapy.

As already mentioned, these considerations are a direct outcome of the potential patient's readiness to express himself through music and sound, or for those incapable of active expression, their willingness to undertake receptive therapy (see Case Histories Rita and Eric, Chapter 2, Note 11).

During the initial interview the music therapist makes use of speech combined with music according to his or her own judgement, and the session concludes with a summary conversation matched to the potential patient's level of comprehension and insight.

The Therapeutic Contract. In his book, *Man Encounters Himself,* Eliyahu Rosenheim writes, "therapist and patient undertake a joint journey to the unknown regions of the patient. They are ready, with all mercy, to enter that forest of the soul in which the hidden is far greater than that which can be seen.... As they set out upon their way both sides are in need of an initial agreement of cooperation. Whatever they may discover (e.g., the meaning of inner content) is yet unknown, but the means of search demand clarification. It is worthwhile defining the basic principles of their work and behavior—in professional jargon, a Therapeutic Contract" (Rosenheim 1990, 44–45). It should be noted that this refers to a contractual agreement in psychoanalysis which deals in the main with neurotics.

The contract offered by D.I.M.T. differs in both content and phraseology as regards an applicant with physical complaints, a retarded person with a limited vocabulary, or a neurotic who possesses insight. While it is true that therapeutic contracts can be made with any client and under almost any terms, the D.I.M.T. contractual agreement takes into account the expectations of the applicant along with the clarification of possibilities on the part of the music therapist. Where minors are concerned, the parents must also be partners to the agreement. One of the most common misunderstandings made by parents, educational authorities, and occasionally by applicants themselves, is to ignore the therapeutic aspect and to relate to the healthy side of music. This tendency to view music therapy as music teaching is worthy of further clarification, particularly in respect to the emotional expectations which underlie it.

Effective therapy demands mutual agreement, understanding and goodwill on all sides, from the beginning. It should be clear to all sides that the contractual agreement embraces music as a means of communication, expression, clarification and elaboration. The same holds true for those physical aspects of therapy which are simultaneously concerned with more than mere improvement of movement, diction and so on, but also with the emotional aspects. Children must be taught the rules of what is "Permissible and Forbidden" regarding their conduct when handling musical instruments as the therapeutic space contains not only sturdy instruments which may be forcibly beaten with no restraint, but also delicate, fragile instruments which serve a different form of expression. Experience shows that even violent children swiftly learn respect for the instruments and understand that they have a special role to play which is important to the child.

Part of the contract clarifies the confidentiality of whatever takes place in the therapy room and that all recordings (which are standard procedure from the outset) remain there, unless the patient (particularly if this is a child) expressly asks for a copy of a certain piece so that he may listen to it again at home.

Another aspect of the contractual agreement which may appear purely technical but is extremely important in ensuring stability, and a mutual sense of responsibility and obligation is the definition of the framework of therapy (individual, group, pairs, family), fixed days and their frequency (once or twice a week), and the duration of sessions (an hour or hour-and-a-half.)

Naturally the terms of the agreement may well undergo changes according to the dynamics and development of the therapeutic process.

THERAPEUTIC CONSIDERATIONS

If after the initial interview, observation, the contractual agreement and initial conclusion, it is decided that the applicant is suitable for music therapy and a therapeutic framework has been planned, there now comes the stage of therapeutic consideration and assessment and the determination of short, medium and long-term goals. This does not signify any rigid adherence to a preset program, nor does it necessarily insure against possible mistakes in judgement on the part of the therapist, but any therapeutic consideration without clearly defined goals may well miss the mark.

Since music therapy is concerned with emotional disturbances, speech impediments, as well as sensory and motor problems, etc., the therapist must weigh carefully just what are the specific possibilities which the patient can be offered, and which cannot at this stage be provided by, for example, psychotherapy, speech therapy, physiotherapy or occupational therapy. Music therapy can be either the sole treatment, or part of a wider process. This should not be left to chance nor dictated by technical limitations; great attention should be paid to determine which would be the most advantageous.

The first stage of therapeutic consideration is concerned with those aspects which can lead to an understanding of the applicant's problem (previous theoretical and/or practical experience), the determination of therapeutic goals, a consideration of the techniques to be employed, a practical approach to the use of music itself (even if at this stage this is purely hypothetical), and the therapist's own personal preparation for his role.

The major problem involved in D.I.M.T. in the primary stages of therapeutic consideration, and indeed during the entire course of therapy, is taking into account both physical and psychological problems and determining an order of priorities. What can achieve a breakthrough to what? Should both physical and psychological aspects be treated simultaneously? Should there be a preparatory process?, Might it not be better to deal with these aspects separately?

The answers are seldom unequivocal and are dependent upon the individual needs of the patient. For example, in the case of Anat (see Chapter 4, 82–85) we shall see that whereas (1), (2), and (4) work on the body with no verbal instruction, (3) works on the body while demanding comprehension of such verbal instruction, (5) works on vocal expression, and (6) combines all of these with emotional aspects. Within such a program a wide range of variations can occur according to the current situation at any given moment, such as the overall progress of therapy, and the patient's own initiatives, which can include preferences and/or rejections.

The process of therapeutic consideration repeats itself according to the various stages of therapy. As therapy proceeds we have more and more documentation at our disposal (recordings, transcripts, summaries, reports and video tapes), as well as an overall view of the entire process. Therapeutic consideration and assessment facilitate the therapist's ability to examine the stage at which both the patient and the therapeutic process are situated, to verify or to annul the approach, as well as to discern various aspects of the therapist-patient relationship.

THE THERAPEUTIC ENCOUNTER

Despite the wide variety of possibilities which may occur during therapeutic sessions, the therapeutic encounter is structured according to certain principles and techniques of music therapy which are outlined below.

Framework. Due to the specific potential of music to create a suitable atmosphere, the actual therapy session is often characterized by a musical opening or closing, which can be with or without words and either vocal or instrumental. The opening can serve a variety of functions, the threshold crossed from the outside world into the therapeutic reality, also the prelude to a dialogue. Sometimes this prelude is relaxing, sometimes it serves as a stimulant. The opening aids both patient and therapist to concentrate on the job in hand, and frequently serves as a bridge between one session and another.[15]

The opening can be either recorded or performed live; the closing usually represents a summation of the particular session, according to the patient's degree of insight. It is occasionally purely verbal but might also consist of instrumentally accompanied song, in which both patient and therapist take part. In this way words and their meaning combine with music and its meaning, reinforcing one another. When the session has been a difficult one, raising problematic issues, the musical closing may serve to create a more relaxed atmosphere, something which has a positive effect, especially in the treatment of children. The opening and closing give the sessions a form of permanence and stability, despite their often varying content, and aid in the establishment of mutual trust within accepted boundaries (see all Case Histories).

Developmental therapy, as the term implies, means that the approach, the materials and the means employed, are determined according to a diagnosis of the patient's problems and stage of development in order to advance normal growth. On occasions, when the case concerns a severe physical ailment or disability, it is the therapist who initially determines the material and the means. However, after a certain period of individual adjustment the patient himself learns to select the most effective means for his own case and the therapist assumes the role of guide and empathetic companion.

I would like to present a few examples:

Treatment of organic problems. Orit suffered from Cerebral Palsy with severely spastic legs (at the age of seven she was still unable to walk), but her hands and arms were slightly less spastic. On the other hand she suffered from hypotonia of the pelvic muscles. She could not speak and had difficulty in vocalizing even single syllables. She was, however, an intelligent girl, something which accentuated the gap between her physical, as opposed to her emotional and intellectual development. Physically she needed to improve her motor skills (relaxation and motor planning), and her vocal potential. Emotionally it was necessary to deal with her physical handicaps, to strengthen her ego and her ability to confront her vast array of problems, and to bring her to acknowledge the fact that she possessed a charming personality and could in fact contribute something to the world around her.

The therapist's initial proposal was to make use of musical techniques which could develop a sense of equilibrium in order to facilitate her ability to walk, reduce the spasticity, and improve her vocality.

Orit swiftly adjusted to the opportunities being offered her and soon took the initiative in defining her own course of treatment. For example, she readily grasped the importance of prosody[16] and enjoyed working with it, since it led to repetition and an eventual genuine improvement of diction to the extent of actually voicing clear syllables and even simple sentences. Her steadily growing control over her ability to walk and express herself in speech helped her to overcome many of the frustrations emanating from her disabilities and to close certain gaps in her development. At this stage the treatment of her physical problems became a matter of routine, and the emphasis shifted to her emotional difficulties.

It should be emphasized here that one of the major advantages of music therapy in relation to speech improvement (particularly with children and the severely handicapped) lies in music's natural quality of repetition and variation which permits a pleasant neurological exercise which is both playful and creative. Further, the legitimization of free and primal vocal expression rewards the patient with a sense of ease and freedom in which he or she can enjoy an infantile experience with no sense of guilt or frustration.*

Examples of developmental therapy with emotional problems. During one single session similar in form to several consecutive years of therapy, Ron, a blind multihandicapped child (see Chapter 3, 68–69), passed through a "Prenatal" posture to independence, commencing with a "Quasi-Symbiotic" posture on the carpet, gradually rising in control of his faculties (movement, playing, singing), and achieving the creation of his own songs which expressed both his difficulties and the encouraging aspects of his life. In Ron's case, despite certain periods of withdrawal, each session was marked by a slow but steady process of growth. In other cases progress can be gauged only by an overall review of the therapeutic sessions. Examples include Rita (see Chapter 6), and the case of Noa.

Noa was hospitalized at the age of 35 due to major depression which was manifested by lack of appetite, insomnia, total apathy to her surroundings, lethargy in her daily actions, feelings of worthlessness and suicidal fixation accompanied by actual suicide attempts.

Noa underwent both psychiatric treatment and music therapy. Two entire weeks were devoted solely to respiratory problems with the aid of recordings made by a lip microphone. Such recordings of inhalation and exhalation can reflect both pathological and normal processes. In this case the recordings revealed a lack of continuity and a withholding of energy, but gradually greater relaxation which was expressed by a rhythmic unity and a fixed dynamic. After some two weeks of such exercises, there was a spontaneous outburst of modest vocality which eventually developed into a form of dialogue with the music therapist, and after a few months into a genuine cooperation between equals in which there was no leader or follower but rather a total musical equality between patient and therapist.

Noa would improvise tunes and lyrics which expressed great distress, and would ask the therapist to accompany her on the piano. In this instance, an analysis of the musical process both reflects and symbolizes Noa's own psychological development, while the musical interaction expresses the development of object-relation. Starting with breath control (and the consequent sense of self-control as opposed to a panic situation), as well as trust in the therapist, there emerged a voice, as well as a rhythmic-dynamic-melodic development within the framework of a musical dialogue. In this dialogue one could observe the transition from monophony

---

*A.B. Recording Archive, Cassette 5: "Music therapy with C.P Children"

to imitation, to a form of responsive singing, to monophonic singing, and in the end to the initiation of vocal and instrumental polyphony. Quite apart from the personal aspect, one can see in this growth a parallel to the philogenic development of music itself, from vocal solos with short rhythmic units, to complex polyphonic structures.

Psychologically this represents a passage through the phases of "trust, autonomy, creative initiative and identity" (Erikson 1960). Almost from the very beginning of a strict discipline of respiratory exercises, (20-minute exercises 3–4 times a day), Noa's posture became less yielding to the force of gravity, and her quiet unstable voice gained in volume as well as in a variety of rhythms and dynamics.*

The representation of stress situations in sound and in music is not necessarily immediate or spontaneous. There is usually a need for the investment of time, which varies according to the individual, in which the patient may freely experience music, both actively and passively, with the support of a certain modeling on the part of the therapist. Apart from making use of existing compositions, the most effective demonstrative technique is improvisation. This can be done on a variety of instruments, as well as vocally and with the aid of the piano, which is considered to be the key instrument due to its wide expressive range and symbolic qualities. The representation of stress situations in sound and music extends over an extremely wide range of possibilities, from the expression of overt emotional states such as anger, aggression or misery, to more complex expressions of conflict, passive aggressiveness, or anxiety.

It should be emphasized even here that improvisation and the individual's own creation of words and music at various levels of expressiveness are a part and parcel of all stages of music therapy, from the initial interview and first patient-therapist encounter, through the revelation of the problem (either consciously or unconsciously), its realization (and transformation from passive to active), its elaboration in music and/or words, its summarization, and in the closing of the therapy session.

One can employ various means in order to represent an emotion, a problem, or indeed any other issue during therapy: musical instruments, motifs, entire compositions, etc. A few examples may serve to illuminate this:

Example one: representation of "splitting" by way of musical instruments. Michael (aged 8) was diagnosed as a borderline personality and was referred for music therapy due to his limited ability to cooperate in psychotherapy. He was prone to sudden outbursts of rage (temper tantrums) which found their expression in extreme violence against children and adults alike (stone throwing, knife wielding, kicking and biting). During his initial interview Michael emerged as a true "Music Child" with a marked ability to express himself, and to be guided by, and respond to, musical interactions. During this interview, when it was made clear to him that the choice was entirely his own, he took a large drum and a cymbal on a stand, playing alternately on both with tremendous aggression and a chaotic structure.

---

*N.C. Recording Archive, Cassettes 1–11: "Contrapunctal Respiration"

After about ten minutes of this, his playing resolved itself into a variety of clear rhythmic patterns, the drum was gradually abandoned, the cymbal continued alone for a further few moments and then also fell silent. Following this, on his own initiative, he produced a structured, gentle tonal melody and used this to verbally describe the war between the cymbal and the drum, the cymbal's victory, and how the drum and the cymbal can never be friends. Michael had undergone a process of moving from chaotic outburst to catharsis, then to gradual organization, which eventually led to an expression of gentleness and a description of the subject represented. This question of splitting, revealed here in the very first encounter is defined by Melanie Klein (1946) as one of the earliest ego-mechanisms and defences against anxiety.

Klein saw the child's play as a symbolic expression of its experiences, fantasies and anxieties. Technically she used it in a similar manner to that of free-association as practiced in adult psychoanalysis. In play, as in music, one can give expression to archaic themes, project inner threats and dangers, gain control, and so on. Splitting is rooted in the early infant's concept of the mother's breast as the source of both gratification (Good) and frustration (Bad). Childhood fantasies can be either restored or distorted in object relation. Normal development depends on gratification being more dominant than frustration, and on a synthesis within the splitting mechanism.

At the intake stage, with the aid of two simple instruments, Michael had already succeeded in expressing a problem of splitting which appeared to disturb him, and at the same time, due to the physical activity involved in playing them, in achieving sublimation and a sense of satisfaction and reconciliation which were essential for his growth.

Example two: representation of characters by means of a leitmotif.[17] Naomi (aged 7) suffers from severe psychological problems resulting from brutalization during infancy, she also has a mild neurological disorder. Naomi has been undergoing music therapy for three years now and is capable of free musical expression in a creative and significant manner. During a certain period she felt threatened by a family crisis and had difficulty in talking about it. Instead, during one of her therapy sessions, she picked out three glove puppets, cast them in their roles (King, Queen, Monster), composed a leitmotif for each, and asked her therapist to provide suitable accompaniment.

She then improvised the roles in an operatic fashion, developing the motifs and the libretto on her own initiative. During this "performance" (with only very slight mirroring on the part of the therapist) she began to realize that she was in fact talking about, and staging, her own family situation. This served as the threshold for further ongoing elaboration.

This form of representation is much more advanced than the one previously described, since it involves both thought and preparation, as well as the composition and setting of the leitmotifs. It also seems to have led to a certain deeper insight.*

---

*N.M. Recording Archive, Cassette 9: "Role Playing in Music Therapy"

Example three: representation of an emotional state by means of musical elements.
Tal (age 30) is a clinical psychologist who decided to undergo music therapy in
order to enrich his personal and professional potential. Despite the fact that he is
not a pianist, he nevertheless chose to experiment spontaneously with the opportunities the piano offers. Within a short space of time, and on his own initiative, he
had already familiarized himself with various elements of the instrument and was
capable of freely exploiting them (chords, clusters, tonality, atonality, chromatic
scale, harmonic tension and release, and so on). For some time he was occupied
with chromatic structures with no verbal intervention on our part. At a certain
stage he linked these chromatic structures, which were characterized by increasing
volume, with relaxing solutions.

Since his was an essentially verbal personality, I decided to let him experience
music without any analysis or interpretation on my part for as long as possible. At
a certain stage he spoke of his ambivalent feelings about the emotional and musical
significance of the chromatic steps (which are devoid of direction or any anchorage
in a central tone) as opposed to tonal solutions by which he would conclude his
chromatic phrases. This sudden understanding opened a window to a critical problem in his own life at that time, and he was especially fascinated by this new way in
which his subconscious was speaking to him.*

In these few examples (selected from countless others) we see that in every case
music served as a representation of subconscious psychic material, aided in the
experiencing and development of such material, and in the achievement of a certain
degree of insight. In D.I.M.T. we approach such musical representation in terms
of personal symbolism; nevertheless there do exist certain musical structures whose
recurrence in various past and present cultures and styles point to the possibility of
"collective archetypes," to adapt Karl Jung's terminology (1966).

Where music is concerned, it would seem that such archetypes exist within us as
latent musical patterns [18] which are aroused into activity only by cultural or other
life experiences. Isaac Sadai (1988, No. 2) describes these as "precomposed
elements" and goes on to prove their existence, and the fascinating similarity
which exists between them from the most ancient musical heritage up to today's
avant garde.

On the other hand, "Highly complex musical composition is not generally based
on the primal symbolism of certain sounds" (Sadai 1988, No. 3) This would seem
to be the major reason why in the simple creations or improvisations of the
nonmusician patient, primary symbolism is quite apparent and can thus be perceived as an analogy of subconscious psychic experience.

In a similar approach to that of Sadai, Shulamit Kreitler quotes Rank, Sachs and
Jung, who view such symbols as "the subconscious imprints of a primitive means
of adaptation." These sources claim that the invention of symbols is a process which
involves the active participation of the human being during which he descends to
a lower level of "thinking in images as a result of partial abandonment (as in artistic

---

*Recording Archive, Cassettes 1–12: "Music Therapy for Therapists" ecstasy) or total abandonment (as in dreams) of any conscious adaptation to reality" (Kreitler 1986, 43).

As far as music therapy is concerned, the symbolic representation of psychic processes serves to fulfill a number of functions:

a) A temporary distancing from consciousness in order to link by way of music with feelings of stress and to comprehend them stage by stage.

b) The realization of distress and conflict by means of creative expression, and hence the possibility of channelling these into release and sublimation, and at the same time to transform them into an aesthetic product. In this we can perceive a combination of two psychoanalytical approaches to art, the Freudian and the Kleinian (Noy 1983).

c) Control: perhaps arising in the human inclination to organize those basic musical elements originating in the organism and thus overcome those hidden anxieties and conflicts which distress arouses.

Noy proposes a synthesis between three psychoanalytical approaches to the arts (Freud, Klein and Ego-Psychology): "Any artistic activity reflects both unconscious desire, internal taboos and the efforts of the Ego to overcome these conflicting forces and to organize them.… There are works of art in which the fulfillment of hidden desires and their almost openly displayed gratification is prominent, whereas in others the element of control and restrained satisfaction gains the upper hand" (Noy 1983, 352).

True, the subject under discussion here is complex works of art and not spontaneous free improvisation, but from a psychological point of view (as opposed to that of a musicologist) our attitude to the works of a nonmusician patient is identical with our attitude to the works of any famous composer.

THE ROLES OF THE THERAPIST

Even when the treatment is for a physical disorder, the music therapist does not present himself or act as omnipotent, as is sometimes the case in certain medical models, but rather as the patient's guide in a search for the best path for him to tread along the way to self-improvement. This requires a basic attitude of respect for and faith in the patient from two points of view. First attention to the personality of the patient which permits him to experience and express his own feelings in his own way, even if these may seem to be extremely distorted in the eyes of the therapist. He must nevertheless respect the patient's personality and trust his abilities. In any case personal independence, which is after all the primary aim of therapy, is not achieved by way of omnipotence or dominance on the part of the therapist.

Secondly and unique to music therapy, is the acceptance of the patient's musical efforts as they are, with no attempt at intervention in order to qualitatively correct or improve, and with no value judgements. The music therapist can respect the patient by adopting motifs he produces, however primitive they may be, and through them creating a therapeutic dialogue, as if they were equal to the finest musical pearls of Mozart, Mahler or Stravinsky.

During initial experimentation with the medium (which for us marks the beginning of the working through process), respecting the patient consists of accepting and containing whatever material he produces on all the various levels of his activity. Respect can also be given by composing a piece based entirely on the patient's own words and music, in whole or in part. For Naomi for example (see earlier), a special song was composed which summarized her dealing with her family crisis. It was based on the characters she invented, the manner in which she portrayed them, and the leitmotifs which represented them. Trust and respect can also be instilled by the therapist's close attention and exclusive interest in the patient. This requires both the physical and spatial conditions needed for the establishment of intimacy (as described earlier) and the concentration (as opposed to dispersal) of all one's energies on the patient. The key to such concentration lies in empathy.

"Basic human similarity allows the therapist to approach and absorb the patient's emotional world. This empathetic process is fed as much by the content of the patient's expressions as by the way in which he expresses himself. Empathy is based on a carefully controlled use of the projection mechanisms" (Rosenheim 1990, 90–91).

In D.I.M.T. empathy operates on two levels, the personal and the musical. In order to establish the framework which will permit a potential space for creation and self-expression, the patient must trust in his therapist's ability to accept and understand his own means of expression and at the same time to maintain ethical standards. Since it is routine practice in D.I.M.T. to record therapy sessions, the patient must be reassured that the tapes are confidential and will remain complete and unaltered under the therapist's care.

Such a confidence-building framework can also be reinforced by a musical structure. A characteristic example is the use of a tonal or modal theme (either adopted from the patient's own repertoire or composed by the therapist) upon whose continuity the patient can mold his or her own musical and/or verbal content. Such a tonal framework, or the harmonic accompaniment of a repetitive musical pattern, provides the patient with a sense of security, and in our experience reduces both anxiety and defense-mechanisms. It was on such a basis, for example, that Ron (see Chapter 3) began to talk freely and openly, without anxiety or denial, about his severe problems as a blind, epileptic, retarded and C.P. child.

The role of the therapist in such a case is to be supportive, both by musical and nonmusical means. Making music together, while adopting the patient's own themes, is one of the best ways of displaying empathy.

Accompanying and setting clear boundaries are of tremendous importance in treating children who suffer from anxiety and lack an awareness of limitations. It is often necessary to stress this verbally, as well as musically; or to draw up a possible time schedule for the child, and to use repetition in order to encourage self-confidence. As has already been stressed, D.I.M.T. works on the principles of elaboration and on the expansion of insight which take place in the treatment of both emotional and organic problems. Whatever the case, body-language and the various levels of body and movement experience should be observed and interpreted in order to locate the focal points of difficulties and emotional problems (Yonah Shahar-Levi 1989).

Insight means that a person has discovered something new about himself, discovering early subconscious processes which hindered any adaptation to new environmental experiences. Rita (see Chapter 6) underwent severe suffering as an infant. This can never be changed, but her perception of those events within a different perspective, and her grasp of the opportunities offered by present-day reality could be influenced. Change came about when such early memories were elicited and expressed (in her case through a variety of artistic modalities), and her ego and belief in herself were strengthened by the discovery of her creative energies. The role of the therapist was to serve as her "mirror," and to help her decipher and interpret her creations.

Such mirroring and its interpretation can be either verbal or musical and can on occasions shift from one artistic modality to another. This kind of mirroring serves to legitimize emotions.

Alon (see Chapter 7) started beating his drum with tremendous energy and the therapist joined in on the piano in a similar style. Once this musical mirroring had given him the feeling that his therapist had perceived his emotions, further verbal mirroring was added for purposes of clarification. It should be stressed that mirroring is more descriptive than explanatory and should therefore be accompanied, when needed, by translation and interpretation.

Translation and interpretation can also be expressed in music provided that this includes meaningful words.[19] For example, Alon improvised a musical narrative about an Animal School with a Snake Pupil and a Lion Headmaster. His voice was soft, weak and virtually unintelligible. During the narrative it became clear that he regarded himself as the snake and his father as the lion. The lion banishes the snake from the classroom, accusing him of being "Lazy and Crazy." The snake then takes his revenge by biting the lion and poisoning him with his venom. At this stage of the narrative Alon's voice rose and he began to display physical signs of emotion. At first, mirroring consisted of a simple reflection of his own musical expression. Later it was brought to his attention that when he allowed himself to be angry, his voice rose, and finally, in conversation, he himself arrived at the conclusion that he was the snake and that the lion was his father. At the end of this session Alon composed a song about the relationship between the Child Snake and the Father Lion, and then went on to devote several ensuing sessions to revamping and improving it until he managed to express his exact feelings.

Rehearsing a song is seldom an exact repetition. There are variations and changes of nuance, both musical and verbal. On occasions a song can achieve its full and complete meaning only after a long series of repetitions and variations. There is also the possibility that the words composed by the patient at the outset of the process can gain their full emotional significance only after the challenge of composing a melody, provided of course that in this the patient is left to his own devices with no intervention on the part of the therapist.

Daniel (age 18) was hospitalized after repeated attempts at suicide. During music therapy he wrote the following words (translated from the Hebrew):

Silence and stillness return twice to abide
Within that uproar where we walk side by side
Here on the street, amidst the pell-mell
Only that silence between us shall dwell*

He sat for more than an hour devising a tune for these words and eventually the melody he managed to voice emerged from a single tone and a quiet, inhibited vocalization, into a wide tonal range and a complete vocal expression:

The therapist intervened only when the patient had succeeded in defining the melody and asked for instrumental accompaniment.

It would seem, therefore, that development during music therapy frequently springs from those same accepted concepts which hold good for psychotherapy. The main difference lies in the medium employed, and the achievement of aims by its specific use (as well as by verbal means). Just as the psychologist must be sensitive to the positioning and timing of reflection and interpretation during the therapeutic process, so must the music therapist beware of musical and verbal intervention. It should also be stressed that music by its very nature invites a kind of mutual conversation by playing together, singing together (and even listening together), which can lead to an extremely emotional experience dimension within the patient-therapist relationship. An example of this is the case of Noa (see above).

All of the these developmental techniques are conducted by the therapist in an improvisational manner, indeed the ability to freely improvise is one of the main skills demanded of any music therapist in all active models of music therapy (Bruscia 1987). Improvisation can serve a variety of functions, all in accordance with the patient's various levels of development, and the progress of the therapeutic process: imitation, dialogue, simultaneous dialogue, supportive accompaniment, mirroring, reinforcement of verbal interpretation, time out for relaxation, physical stimulation, the establishment of a pretherapeutic atmosphere, eliciting free-association, the interpretation of feelings or the representation of issues, summation of therapy, and more.

These are only a few aspects of improvisation, but it would seem that even this brief definition of the roles of the therapist clearly shows that the music therapist must be first and foremost a musician, easily familiar with his medium, flexible in his approach, and capable of retrieving appropriate material from his musical knowledge whenever necessary.

---

*Recording Archive, Cassette 3: "Composing Songs in Music Therapy"

PROCEDURES FOR DOCUMENTATION, TRANSCRIPTION, INTERPRETATION AND EVALUATION

1. A recording of every therapy session.
2. Video coverage whenever possible.
3. Transcriptions of musical material at critical stages of therapy.
4. Musical analysis of such material.
5. Analysis of extra-musical activity and its relevance to (4)
6. Registration of the focus of each therapy session: The problem, the dynamics, etc., and the approach and techniques employed.
7. Maintenance of a continuous therapy report.
8. Editing down a summary recording of any specific patient.
9. Editing down cross-reference recordings.
10. Regular self-examination on the basis of these recordings: The therapist's vocal ability, the guidance provided, his improvisations, the musical and verbal techniques employed, processes of transference and counter-transference.
11. Utilization of observational and assessment documentation during the entire course of therapy (see Appendix 3) for the purposes of both interim and final reports.

CONCLUSION

This chapter has presented the basic principles of the Developmental-Integrative Model in Music Therapy (D.I.M.T.) emphasizing the following aspects:

1. It concentrates on physical and psychological problems in accordance with priorities which are determined by the needs of the individual patient
2. It is suited to a varied patient-community in relation to the patient's problems: age, insight and intelligence, and stage of development.
3. It is a combination of music, medicine and psychology, in which music serves as the direct and primary language of therapy, medicine as a basis for understanding the human body, and psychology as a secondary language for the treatment of emotional aspects.
4. It perceives the basic parameters of music as a product of the human organism, and hence music itself as activating that organism's vital functions, this being the source of the medium's therapeutic potential.
5. It makes use of any musical means at its disposal, according to the individual choice of the patient, together with the therapist's assessment of the patient's cultural background, skills and insight.
6. It recommends flexibility within a supportive framework (both musically and otherwise) in order to encourage growth and development.
7. It approaches music as a powerful artistic medium, which is nevertheless open to a variety of interpretations, and hence concentrates on analyzing its influence on each and every individual patient, as well as on the relationships established between patient, therapist and music itself.

CASE HISTORIES
AND
CLINICAL ANALYSES

The following five chapters are devoted to individual case histories, each of which serves to clarify the various theoretical and practical aspects of D.I.M.T.

All names are fictitious in order to protect the privacy of the patient.

III

RON

MUSIC – AN EYE FOR THE BLIND

D.I.M.T. with a multihandicapped child (cerebral palsy, blindness, epilepsy, mental retardation and emotional instability)

RON: PATIENT PROFILE

Ron, the firstborn son of a large family, was referred for music therapy when he was twelve years old. A few months after a normal birth he began to display disturbing symptoms. When he was examined it became clear that he was almost totally blind, able to distinguish only between light and darkness, and he also suffered from both grand mal and petit mal epilepsy. Soon afterward he was diagnosed as suffering from right hemiphlegia (Cerebral Palsy),[1] spastic type.[2]

Ron had undergone physiotherapy from the age of ten months, and later special treatment for the blind. At the age of nine he entered a program for blind multi-handicapped children.

During the intake process I discerned limping on the right leg, a clenched right fist, flexion and pronation of the forearm, retraction of the shoulder and contracture of the elbow. His gait appeared unsteady, probably as a result of his blindness and spasticity. He was ignoring the disabled right side of his body, avoiding contact with it, and preferring not to make use of either his right arm or leg.

Movemental activity with music revealed that he did not even know the various parts of his body.[3] Although he displayed an obvious tendency for music, his singing and playing on even the simplest of musical instruments lacked both rhythmic continuity and expressive ability, despite the fact that he was making use only of the left (unaffected) side of his body.[4]

Verbal communication was extremely limited, and on hearing even the simplest of questions Ron would go into a state of extreme anxiety, expressed by increased spasticity, arm flapping, confusion and a lack of concentration.

He seemed to be unaware of his disabilities and had probably not achieved a sufficient degree of body-awareness or self-awareness, thus the majority of his comments and declarations were divorced from reality, such as, "Next time I'll come by myself, on my motorbike."

THERAPEUTIC CONSIDERATIONS

The complex combination of Ron's problems led to great difficulties in planning priorities for effective treatment. In addition there was a combination of primary retardation (which can accompany brain damage), secondary retardation (as a result of his blindness and spasticity), as well as the emotional liability which characterizes C.P. spastic children.

It was apparent that initial therapy must be concerned with a reduction of spasm and hypertonia in the right half of the body, in order to permit him to experience sensations in those denied areas and create a precondition for relaxation and trust. It should be recalled that at this time Ron was still undergoing group music therapy at an educational institution; individual music therapy was an extracurricular program.

Due to his blindness and epileptic seizures, Ron often found himself in a state of alarm and confusion. As a result, loss of muscle tone increased and his body (which in any case lacked balance) would lose control. Such loss of control would lead to anxiety and other reactions of the autonomic nervous system. Feldenkrais describes this as "an instinctive reaction to the state of falling" (1949, Chapter 10).

Ron also tended to enter into a state of anxiety in those situations which he perceived as being "under examination." Whenever being questioned (as was customary in his traditional upbringing) his spasticity would increase and he would complain of pains. Because of his retardation and limited awareness he was unable to describe his feelings in words, or to cope with them in any other way.

Since C.P. consists of irreversible brain damage, the question arises as to whether spasticity can in any way be decreased. If so, in what way can this be achieved by music therapy?

Schneider mentions that among the various positive effects of music on the C.P. patient, music can in fact influence spasticity and bring about a certain degree of relaxation (in Gaston 1968, Chapter 10). This may be only temporary, and the basic brain damage cannot be cured, but there are however some advantages in this:

1. Relaxation can lead to a corrective experience for the spastic child.

2. It might also reduce anxiety and improve function.

3. It might help to prevent the subsequent development of abnormal patterns of movement.

In the light of all this, the short-term aims of therapy were defined as follows:

Each weekly session would begin with musical movement-stimulation aimed at maximum release and relaxation, as a basis for further activity. The patient would be encouraged to reach a greater awareness of his body. Should such awareness be achieved through sensory-motor activity, there would be the chance of a corrective experience for the Body-Scheme.

In addition Ron had to be taught how to breathe properly, something which could also lead to an improvement of his vocality and the possible opening up of a vocal channel through which he might express his emotions (see also Chapter 4).

In music therapy, as already mentioned, the cognitive abilities can improve as a by product of the groundwork invested in both body and mind. It seemed there was a chance that if Ron's physical and mental tensions could be reduced, leading to an improvement of his breathing, vocality and body-scheme, he would eventually find it easier to express himself verbally, and perhaps even to enrich his creative abilities.

MUSIC THERAPY (Over a Three-Year Period)

Before going into details regarding Ron's therapy, I would like to refer back to the hypnotic model of traditional healing rituals. We have seen (in Chapter 1) how the traditional Indian healer in hypnotic ritual employs methods aimed at creating an atmosphere of relaxation and maximum concentration. To this end he establishes a soothing atmosphere devoid of excessive stimuli, speaks and sings quietly, and makes use of rattles or drums in a repetitive and moderate tempo. His patient remains passive, either lying on his back, or seated in a crouching position facing the healer. We had seen one impressive example of hypnotic ritual in eastern

Equador which was both filmed and recorded in its entirety and enabled us to scrutinize the therapeutic process and reach our own conclusions regarding present-day music therapy (see Chapter 1).

There the patient lies on her back while the healer sings and plays for her during a full ten hours with the aim of discovering, contacting and banishing the evil spirits responsible for her malady. All this time the healer maintains a repetitive unity of rhythm, dynamic and melody. The range of voice he employs in his singing is limited, reaching only a sixth in moments of climax; the singing moves from high to low and is always relaxed, the words or syllables are evenly paced and accompanied by the soft rustling of palm fronds. These principles of repetition which characterize such rituals, in music, movement, the healer's actions and speech, are shared by today's music therapist, however, the therapeutic rationale is different. The Indian healer's efforts are aimed at seeking out the evil spirit responsible for his patient's suffering. In doing so he leads his patient into a prolonged state of utter relaxation, but this is not the healer's avowed aim, it is more of a side issue. As opposed to this, the music therapist regards the inducement of such relaxation as an interim stage which enables the continuation of therapy. The music therapist's "Ritual" is brief, but is repeated over a lengthy series of sessions, whereas that of the traditional healer is a prolonged, one time event.

Indeed it is recommended that in a case such as Ron's the music therapist re-create such a relaxing atmosphere at the start of each and every therapeutic session.[5]

The basis for any relaxation exercise is a permanent and repetitive beat. The Japanese gynecologist Dr. Murooka (1976) conducted a series of experiments with a thousand month-old infants, using the sound of the heartbeat as it is heard in the womb. His report conclusively shows that a continuation of the in utero auditory environment serves as a relaxing influence. Four-hundred-three infants ceased their crying, 161 fell asleep after an average of 41 seconds, while the rest responded more slowly. In an attempt to further realize Murooka's conclusions, as well as similar results obtained by Salk (1973) and others, Vogel (1984) designed an ovoid-like structure similar to the womb within which the patient would lie on a water bed and listen to recordings representing womb sound while being given a massage according to the Shantala approach (Leboyer 1976).

In Vogel's technique, designed for brain damaged and retarded patients, special attention is paid to repetition and continuity. The "Walking to the Womb"; temperature, lighting, sound and vibrations; the division of therapy into well-defined stages; the massage and the deliberate fading out of such stimuli towards the end of treatment—all these constitute a relaxing and therapeutic environment. Recent reports from this German clinic show a significant improvement in the condition of patients who were previously in need of a high degree of medication in order to reduce their aggressive tendencies; in fact the changes were so radical that some of the patients were released from medication altogether. It should be stressed that there are very few institutions in today's world devoted to a therapeutic approach which closely follows the results of such research into the auditory womb sensation, which is aimed at regression in order to stimulate development.

My own clinical experience has taught me that the simulation of a womb-like heartbeat in order to achieve relaxation can be extremely effective, either by use of a metronome, or by soft rattling or drumming. In practice it is done as follows:

The spastic patient lies supine on a carpeted floor in a quiet room, exposed to the minimum of stimuli. The therapist is at his side, but remains silent. A recorded tape reproduces heartbeats whose tempo is dictated by the patient's condition (ranging between largo—56, and andante—76). After a while the therapist assists the patient to start moving his limbs, according to the natural stages of infant development: head movement, shoulder to fingertips, hips to legs and feet. This includes rotations in order to decrease spasticity.

Stage by stage the therapist inserts suggestions based on the characteristic elements of the lullaby which is being sung to the patient.

In Ron's case, this singing succeeded in transferring to him certain information regarding his physical actions, how this might help him, as well as a mirroring of his own physical and emotional condition. It should perhaps be stressed here that lying on the floor eliminates the effort to overcome the force of gravity and thus leads to greater muscular relaxation.

From lying supine we turn to lying prone, and from there stage by stage, progress through all the processes of motor development up to and including standing and walking. During this, the patient becomes more and more independent and in control of his functions, while the therapist provides him with musical support.

In other words, just as the patient progresses through various developmental stages (from simple to complex activity) so the music develops from basic beat-units to possibly complex textures. However, the repetitive beat-unit and tempo remain steady, the dynamics moderate, the melodic line is based on tonal or modal structures, and the harmony is traditional (although not necessarily primitive or dull).

This kind of music must be improvised and cannot be prerecorded. The therapist follows the patient's activity and improvises music and lyrics according to whatever develops, while at the same time preserving the above-mentioned musical framework.*

This process of matching music to patient while responding to his needs, resembles in a way the early development of object relation as viewed by Winnicott (1965). The infant experiences its mother as its primary environment, in which both of them progress stage by stage from dependence to independence. Since at birth the ego exists only as an unopened bud, the mother serves, in the initial stages of infant life, as an auxiliary ego and must adapt herself to the ever-changing needs of her infant. She must emphasize the joy of living and what Freud defined as "the pleasure principle"; or as Winnicott puts it she is supposed to act as "a good enough mother" in order that her infant will develop emotionally stage by stage and experience the continuum of existence.

Generally, a mother looking at her infant mirrors its own sensations (in movement or mimicry, in speech or in song), and in so doing facilitates holding and

---

*Recording Archive 1–20: "Music Therapy with C.P. Patients"

contact with the infant's feelings. In other words, the infant needs motherly response to his actions and emotions in order to experience their significance.
Winnicot also stresses the importance of psychological and physical holding as
factors in the infant's natural development. Such holding gives the infant a clearly
defined framework, and serves to develop its sense of physical boundaries as well as
those of the ego.

According to D.I.M.T., musical improvisation matched to the patient's own
passing experiences can symbolize the dynamics of such object relation. This can be
crucial in the case of a blind child who has no visual experience. Music which is
suited to his needs will be perceived by way of a healthy sensory channel and can
therefore serve to protect, contain, reflect and support a sense of pleasure, and at
the same time to facilitate the continuity of motor and emotional activity.

During his first year of therapy Ron underwent a weekly one-hour session as
described below. The various stages were repetitive, but they gradually changed
their time proportions. Relaxation soon took only ten to fifteen minutes and the
remainder of the session could be devoted to physiological and psychological problems as they emerged during therapy.

Sample Hour of Therapy (Sequence Chart, First Year)

Equivalent Stage of Natural Development	Therapeutic Activity	Agents of Sound
6–9 months gestation:	Patient lies passive on the floor, listening to moderate beat-units. Therapist remains silent, does not intervene.	Recordings: metronome, rattle muffled drum, tempo similar to heartbeat as heard in womb.
1–6 months after birth: (1–4 symbiosis, 4–6 start of differentiation and individualization).	Patient begins passive, but gradually becomes active. Therapist assists in limb movement according to order of development, until patient can move them himself. Accent on both sides of the body. Therapist adds supportive mirror-singing	The recording continues, and is supplemented by soft singing on the part of the therapist, matched to the patient's physical and emotional state.
6–8 months: (same stage continued)	Patient rocks from side to side; reaches out for objects to touch and identify. Therapist continues to mirror and lead with song accompaniment.	Piano, guitar, or any other suitable accompaniment for song. Background beat continues.

Equivalent Stage of Natural Development	Therapeutic Activity	Agents of Sound
8–10 months: (same stage—development of curiosity and space investigation)	Patient progresses to crawling and investigation, sitting up and attempting to play various instruments laid out within reach. Stress on bilateral body development.	As above. Once the patient achieves a sitting position, therapist plays or sings "Activizing Song" mirroring emotional content and stressing "object permanence"
10 months–2 years: (continued space investigation and exploration of body and self limitations.	Patient stands and walks. Emphasis on space orientation, intermittent two-handed activity, reinforcement of physical confidence.	As above. The "Activizing Song" is devoted to guiding movement, mirroring in song, issues concerning space orientation, feelings of anxiety and "seeing" through touch and sound.
2–3 years: Developing verbal communication, control and autonomy, consolidation of earlier systems.	Patient seated, facing therapist: exercises to regulate breathing, free improvisation of sound which gradually becomes more fluent. The reinforcement of a sense of body and vocal control.	Unaccompanied song, varied interaction in both singing and regular speech between patient and therapist.
3–6 years: (conflict between ego and superego)	Patient composes both melodies and lyrics based on his own themes. Therapist is supportive. Legitimization of feelings of jealousy, aggression and guilt.	Instrumental support while patient creates his song. Participation after its completion. Stress on music as an Intermediate Area of Expression
6–12 years: Ron's actual age (independence and creativity).	Independent initiative in movement, music, etc. Choosing recorded music according to his own needs or guiding the therapist to compose for him.	Recording, playing, singing, according to the patient's demands.
	Closing: a summary of the therapeutic hour, and a parting.	Patient and therapist together improvise a song to summarize the session.

I have deliberately not gone into details about the exact duration of the various stages within each session. The timing would change according to the child's development.

It should be emphasized here that Ron was at the same time undergoing physiotherapy and group music therapy, but not psychotherapy. It therefore seemed logical that individual music therapy could gradually be oriented away from his physical handicaps toward his psychological problems.

After about a year-and-a-half Ron was more and more inclined to talk about his paralyzed hand, his blindness, his anger, frustration and helplessness.* Some of these conversations were conducted by means of improvised song, some by direct speech. It took a full year until song could be replaced by normal conversation. It was clear that direct speech, without the soothing element of music, still aroused his basic anxieties, which were typified by increased spasm in the right side of his body, hand flapping, loss of balance and overall helplessness. Gradually, however, normal conversation took the place of song, with no external signs of anxiety.**

Step by step with his increasing awareness and acceptance of his severely handicapped condition, Ron stopped clipping off his syllables, both song and speech became more fluent, and his vocal dynamics began to match the emotions he tried to express.

A therapeutic approach based on the constant recording of all sessions and the consequent results of studying these playbacks, can be extremely advantageous when it comes to internalizing the process and progress of therapy. This was indeed the case with Ron. In his third year he began to compose songs on his own initiative, most of them simply described the atmosphere of the neighborhood in which he lived, some of them were devoted to his own personal experiences, while others served to sum up his emotions.‡

From this period I would like to present an example of Ron's verbal ability, and his capability for internalizing emotional matter.‡‡

> A child is born and his eyes don't see
> Because those eyes are blind
> A child is born and his right hand's no good
> And that can drive you wild.
> But still you can feel
> And touch things
> But still you can hear
> All those voices if only
> You lend them an ear.
>
>   (from the Hebrew)

---

*Recording Archive: "Treating Emotional Problems with C.P. Children"
**Recording Archive, Video 2, 1986
‡Recording Archive, Video 3, 1987
‡‡Recording Archive, Cassette 40: "Songs Composed by Patients as Part of the Elaboration Process in Music Therapy"

CONCLUSION

In detailing this case of a multihandicapped child I have attempted to demonstrate the importance of the developmental process through music.

Over a three-year period of weekly sessions the patient passed through the various stages of the developmental process, expressed on a variety of levels: sensory and motor activity, the expression of emotion, independence and initiative, comprehension and cognition.

The long-term goals of this therapy were to furnish Ron with strategies by which he could protect himself in a state of anxiety, to increase his self-confidence, both physical and mental, and to teach him to confront his disabilities both in actions and in words. The improvement was more apparent within the therapeutic space than within the educational institution which he attended, or within his own home.

It was therefore recommended that the approach and some of the techniques employed in music therapy be adopted by other therapists and educators, and that both group and individual therapy be continued.

IV

ANAT

A BODY AWARE
A SOUL ALERTED

D.I.M.T. with a hypotonic Down's Syndrome child

INTRODUCTION

I n the previous chapter we discussed the ability of music to reduce both physical and emotional tension in order to establish a prelude to therapy: the example was that of a child suffering from spastic C.P. and multiple handicaps. The following chapter is devoted to a patient suffering from Hypotonia,[1] and in order to improve this, was treated with music of a stimulative character.[2] As a result, whether this be a spontaneous reaction without any extramusical encouragement, or with the addition of verbal guidance, the patient is liable to start moving in a manner which will increase muscle tone and enhance overall alertness.[3]

The observations, test methods and therapeutic programs of various developmental schools (Kephart 1960; Kohen-Raz 1970; Ayres 1972; Piage 1974; Prechtl 1978), display an identity of views on a matter which is crucial to our main subject consideration. The earliest stages of life serve as a sensory-motor basis upon which the vital and complex processes of learning, emotionality, and socialization can develop. The greater the maturity of intersensory, intrasensory and sensory-motor integration, the greater the ability of the child to develop those complex systems so essential to healthy functioning.[4]

Infants born with Down's Syndrome display many symptoms connected with primary retardation.

Before going into therapeutic details, I should like to focus on this particular group in order to demonstrate the stimulative influence of music, and the physiopsychological changes it can bring about as a predisposition for continued therapy. The reason for choosing Down's Syndrome children as an example is based on the following statistics:

1. 77% are born with muscular hypotonia
2. 84% have weak initial reflexes
3. 82% lack the Moro reflex
4. 77% suffer from hyperflexibility and hyperextensibility.

Such birth symptoms undoubtedly serve as handicaps for infant development. To this day we do not know the basic causes of the Down's Syndrome child's retardation, but one can assume that the above mentioned factors contribute to primary mental retardation, and secondary developmental retardation. For these and other reasons it is essential to intervene and alter these factors as soon as is feasibly possible. In order to further understand this we shall first discuss the Down's Syndrome child's potential for secondary retardation, and the stimulation programs available today in various institutions throughout the world.

THE DEVELOPMENT OF DOWN'S SYNDROME CHILDREN

During his lifetime the human being expends a great deal of his energy in countering the natural force of gravity: this is an ongoing dynamic process which commences at birth. An infant who for whatever reason maintains a prone position and finds difficulty in countering the force of gravity is liable to be handicapped in his or her overall development, adversely affecting the potential for independence and limiting the concept of the surrounding world.

As already stated, the sequence of movement and posture is partially hereditary and partially the result of practice in gaining control. In this respect we should perhaps recall the initial reflexes which serve as a model for potential voluntary movement. For example the Moro reflex, which is lacking in a high percentage of Down's Syndrome infants is regarded as a vestige of Man's apelike past when grasping the branch of a tree was essential for survival. It is this reflex which serves as a basis for developing extension movements and overcoming the force of gravity. Another example is the weak Tonic Neck Reflex whose function is to teach the infant how to make use of each half of the body by itself, or the weak grasping reflex which serves as the basis for voluntary holding movements. Such cycles of learning extend beyond mere movement and, as previously stated, determine the infant's concept of the world around him as well as influencing his emotional state. Between the ages of two to five or six months the infant generally lies facedown on its stomach, raising its head when it hears its mother's voice and turning in that direction. This simple action, which is generally taken for granted, has in fact great psychophysiological significance. The infant extends the neck muscles in order to overcome the force of gravity and expand his field of vision. This is the first step in controlling his world by means of integrating and combining auditory stimulation, motor reaction, and visual and proprioceptive information. Proprioceptive information leads to a vestibular reaction in order to deal with a new state of balance, and at the same time the infant's concept of his surroundings is enhanced and enlarged. By this process the infant gradually learns the sound of the mother's voice with her visual appearance, thus reinforcing confidence in her actual existence.

As opposed to the healthy infant just described, the Down's Syndrome infant moves little and lethargically, apparently devoid of energy. Despite the fact that he is capable of hearing his mother's voice, hypotonia leads to clumsiness, and the lack of, or weakness in, initial reflexes hampers the development of basic motor patterns. In addition, the mother is liable to interpret his lethargic reactions as if he were "fragile." Thus she may be liable to treat him too delicately and so deny him the very tactile and movemental stimulation which enhances sensory-motor integration, defines the body's boundaries and makes motor planning efficient.

Such an example demonstrates just how hypotonia and a lack of, or weakness in, initial reflexes can lead to a chain reaction of disabilities from birth. The achievements of a normal infant, exposed to normal stimuli, will never be equalled by the Down's Syndrome infant unless he is encouraged and guided in the right direction.

For these reasons, in various institutions around the world, programs have been developed whose purpose is to provide the earliest possible stimulation in order to achieve the greatest narrowing of the gap between the normal and the Down's Syndrome infant. These programs focus on physical development (Zausmer & Peuschell 1972; Brinkworth 1975), as well as on the development of speech and language. (Buckley et al. 1968; Weistuch & Lewis 1985).

This consists of joint instruction of both parents and child from birth until the age of four to five years. Parents and children benefit from this in equal measure. A consistent and continuous series of encounters with professional advisors helps the frustrated and often resentful parent to channel his or her feelings toward more productive and practical aims. Above and beyond the exercising of the child's senses, movement, speech and intelligence, it is the constant parent-child contact which creates that essential interaction which aids emotional development.

Eye contact can serve as a good example. Cunningham & Berger (1981) showed that the eye contact of a Down's Syndrome infant is different and slower than that of a normal child. Thus a special sort of encouragement is needed in order to develop a swifter, more normal eye contact between infant and parent.

The following sketches serve as examples of normal and abnormal infant posture:*

First flexor stage (semiflexed position)

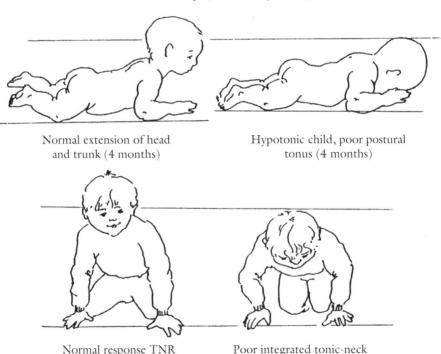

Normal extension of head
and trunk (4 months)

Hypotonic child, poor postural
tonus (4 months)

Normal response TNR
integration (18 months)

Poor integrated tonic-neck
reflex (TNR) (18 months)

*Sketches by Chava Sekeles and Marek Yanai, made during observation of Down's Syndrome children.

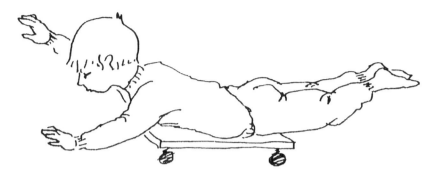

Normal postural response when riding wheel board in prone position (4-year-old boy)

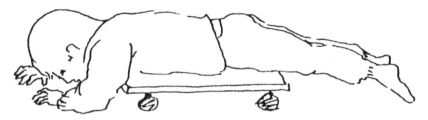

Poor postural response (the Tonic Labyrinthine Reflex is poorly integrated)
(4-year-old boy)

The different categories of Down's Syndrome which affect the child's development potential must also be taken into account. Certain stimulatory programs have revealed that Down's Syndrome children in various categories who were given early and controlled treatment made good (albeit relative) progress according to Gesell (1974) in four areas of examination: motor coordination, development of speech, adaptability, and personal and societal behavior (Fishler et al. 1964).

Among the achievements of such controlled stimulatory programs, one must stress the lessening of the stigma attached to a Down's Syndrome infant and his chances for progress. In the past he was generally looked upon as severely retarded and destined to spend his whole life in institutions. Today most Down's Syndrome children are able to learn and develop if given adequate treatment both at home and in school. It is only a minority who are in fact severely handicapped and dependent (Peushell 1984).

Scientific research into Down's Syndrome is still unable to define the exact source of retardation[5] or to indicate treatment. Similarly, research into the results of stimulation with laboratory animals, while demonstrating improvement, is as yet unable to prove the relevance of such experimentation as far as human beings are concerned. For example, examination of the results of controlled experiments in sensory stimulation of rats over a thirty-day period (Rozenzweig et al. 1972) revealed that in addition to an improvement in their motor function, there were also morphological changes in the brain, an increase in brain weight, a thickening of the cerebral cortex, and an increase in the level of acetylcholinesterase.[6]

Whatever the case, basic maladjustment of the cerebral cortex in Down's Syndrome children can serve only as an indirect explanation of the existence of mental retardation. Rahmani (1981) voices criticism about the capability of any sensory-motor integration program's capability to advance learning potential, particularly in cases of learning disability. It should be emphasized, however, that no claims are made by the advocates of stimulation programs that they are directly capable of advancing academic skills, but that they serve to improve the patient's day-to-day functional ability, enable him to experience positive sensations, bolster his self-image, and thus reinforce the basis for learning.

Rahmani also warns against any rigid or arbitrary interpretation of the hierarchy of developmental continuity, since many of these stages overlap one another. The young brain is still flexible and capable of developing alternative skills which can assist the process of learning (ibid.).

MUSIC THERAPY AND DOWN'S SYNDROME

Early stages of stimulatory programs for Down's Syndrome children include musical activity, especially rhythmic. Peushell (1987) stresses the need to encourage and develop verbal communication and improved motor skills, to facilitate emotional expression, teach socialization and encourage overall motivation.

When one considers the multifaceted difficulties of the Down's Syndrome child, Peushell does in fact propose a variety of therapeutic possibilities. Even though the actual causes of retardation, hypotonia, speech impediment, etc. are still unclear, clinical experience shows us that consistent and controlled therapy can lead to positive results. Such a program can, as already stressed, involve music due to its inherent links with, and influence on, sensation, movement, vocality, emotion and cognition.

A review of professional music therapy literature reveals that the general attitude toward Down's Syndrome children is similar to that adopted toward other categories of retardation. Until the 1950s or thereabouts, music was employed in the treatment of the retarded mainly as an instrument for the improvement of learning abilities, due to the fact that music can be absorbed in a concrete manner which does not demand any great intellectual ability (Howery in Gaston 1968, Chapter 3). From the 1950s the aims of music therapy expanded and became directed toward observation and diagnosis, the establishment of contact, adjustment to extra-institutional surroundings, the acquisition of day-to-day skills and abilities (A.D.L.),[7] development of speech and language (Somerville 1958), the learning of body concepts by means of Activating Song (Lathom in Schneider 1963, 115–121), and more.

Since there does not exist any specific approach to this syndrome, I should like to describe the role music can play in the treatment of the basic developmental problems it presents: movement, posture, sensory-motor integration, vocalization, and the child's emotional world.

Such an approach can become a part of developmental therapy from a tender age, and can continue through schooling, at which stage the child is usually compelled to mainly concentrate on academic studies. From the various Down's Syndrome children I have treated, I have chosen Anat as an illuminating example.

ANAT: PATIENT PROFILE

Anat was born retarded in 1974, the first daughter in a family of three; her mother was then twenty-nine years old. Both parents are academics and have undergone professional instruction and guidance since Anat was born. At the age of eighteen months Anat began to attend a kindergarten within the Institute for Child Development, and underwent treatment by a multidisciplinary team of therapists. From the age of three to six she was in a special kindergarten for the retarded, although for a certain period there was a time-sharing arrangement with a kindergarten for normal children.

During compulsory kindergarten attendance she was integrated into a regular study program, with the acquiescence of a kindergarten teacher who was totally devoted to the child's development. From the age of seven to thirteen she studied at a special school for those with learning disabilities, and recently completed her studies in its high school. She benefited from three years of individual music therapy, an additional two years of group music therapy, cognitive enrichment, and psychological support during those years.

She has also undergone plastic surgery in order to improve the chin and the eyes, and to shorten her lolling tongue.[8] Clearly, Anat has since birth been given the best possible treatment from every point of view.

I have followed Anat's development since birth, and first began individual music therapy with her when she was five years old. The first two months of observation revealed the following:

1. Low muscle tone despite her active participation in earlier stimulation programs. Basic movement existed but its quality was poor due to still extant hypotonia. The hips and pelvis were unstable, and could not sufficiently resist the force of gravity. The muscles of the face and tongue were hypotonic, arms dangled, and walking was clumsy. There could be no doubt that such physical postures betrayed a state of retardation and demanded continued treatment.

2. Trying to listen to music or a vocal narrative while lying down in a relaxed position, Anat would soon enter into a state of physical restlessness. Passive listening seemed to be impossible; later she was unable to recall the content of what she had heard. It seemed that intellectual perception in such a pose was ineffective.

3. Once given the choice, Anat supplemented her listening with energetic movement, a spontaneous acting out of what she was hearing. Later she would be able to recall such content more lucidly and with greater ease.

4. As a result of predetermined movement exercises dictated by music of an ecstatic nature, a number of features could be noted:
   a) Increase in muscle tone
   b) Improved antigravitational posture
   c) Overall alertness and improved perceptive abilities
   d) A better ability to recall and repeat verbal content.[9]

In the course of time it became clear that after an initial exercise devoted to movement and posture, not only her overall input and output improved, but also her willingness to confront emotional problems.

Such observations have no scientific foundation. Furthermore, despite the fact that hypotonia is mentioned as an integral part of Down's Syndrome, I have yet to find any research which can explain its origins, or even its connection with difficulties of attention.

The assumption was that despite the fact that the majority of Down's Syndrome children are able to control basic motor function from kindergarten age (Peushell 1987, 15–52), hypotonia nevertheless continues to sabotage any complex movemental development (Sekeles & Cohen 1988).[10]

It would seem that the infant lying on the rug and simply listening, while reducing his muscular tone to the minimum, for some reason is limiting his powers of concentration. In such a state he indulges in "self-therapy" by means of excess movement which might indeed increase muscle tone.

A further example of such self-help can be seen in the video documentation of "Piano Lesson for Hypotonic Down's Syndrome Child"* under the guidance of Yael Barnet.

Whenever the pupil had to play normally with flexed fingers he encountered difficulty due to the fact that the flexed posture decreases muscle tone, or a worsening of the basic condition. The spontaneous solution discovered by the pupil's instincts was to stretch the fingers while playing. In this way muscle tone was increased and he was able to play in rhythm and with a quality which was comparatively quite good. This shows us how a change of movement and posture can, as a side effect, contribute to change and improvement in learning ability. However, the music therapist's prime consideration is not to improve the patient's learning skills, but rather to help change basic disabilities, particularly physical, vocal, and emotional, with the aim of creating a situation for the improvement of learning ability and societal adjustment.

With this in mind I devised (in 1982) a program of auditory stimulation for Anat and for other Down's Syndrome children. For the first three months this occupied the entire therapy hour, but eventually became half of that, leaving more time to deal with any aroused emotional content (Sekeles 1988). During the years 1985–87 I joined forces with movement specialist Einya Cohen, and the emphasis shifted from spontaneous movemental reaction to music, to guided and predetermined actions designed to enrich and expand the movemental repertoire, to reinforce physical awareness and to promote integration between emotion and cognition by means of the unique contribution afforded by the combination of these two art forms.**

Let us now detail the program developed for music therapy with Down's Syndrome children, as described in the following charts.

---

*Barnet Recording Archive, 1982
**Cohen & Sekeles Recording Archive: "Combined Music and Movement Therapy for Down's Syndrome Children" Video, 1987

THE THERAPEUTIC APPROACH*

Musical Elements Employed	Therapeutic Aim	Anticipated Reaction to Musical Stimuli, Occasionally with Verbal Guidance.
1. Accentuated beat-units, graded acceleration, harmonic tension, wide range, crescendo. Drums, oboes, cymbal, piano.	Direct stimulation of vestibular system to increase muscle tone (5 Minutes)**	Energetic whirling, spinning and rolling movements dictated by music
2. Free flow and arrest improvisation using the same components and instruments	Anti gravitational muscle control (10 minutes)	Free improvisation of flow and control, as guided by music
3. Activity songs (sung by Therapist to piano accompaniment): flow and arrest	Increase of muscle tone (in sudden arrest) (5 minutes)	Jumping on Physio-Ball, arrest in tense postures, activity dictated by words and music.
4. Therapist and Patient play together on instruments graded from global motor hand function (huge drums), to fine movement (strings), and hand-mime based on movement and arrest.	Improvement of fine motor function in balanced posture: preferably kneeling or standing (10 minutes)	Free and guided improvisation on musical instruments, as well as in movement.
5. Clear rhythmic patterns on drums: fast & slow. Accelerated and decelerated singing, either accompanied or unaccompanied.	Control in sound production, improving elocution in both speech and song (10 minutes)	Vocal exercises and games, with musical or movement accompaniment, to express a sense of time

*Sekeles Recording Archive 1, 1983
**These timings are variable, depending upon the progress of therapy

Musical Elements Employed	Therapeutic Aim	Anticipated Reaction to Musical Stimuli, Occasionally with Verbal Guidance.
6. As in 1. with low-range sudden clusters, nonresolved diminished chords and harmonic tension. Variety of musical instruments, music drama.	Indirect increase in muscle tone. Transition of therapy to emotional problems. Elaborating emotional issues. (20 minutes)	Music drama by means of voice, movement and the playing of instruments. Discussing and developing the issues raised by the patient during therapy

THE PROGRAM

1. The most direct way to increase muscle tone is by *stimulating the vestibular system*. The influence of the vestibular system on muscle tone is mediated by way of the lateral and medial vestibular nuclei in the brain stem, through efferent transmissions down the spinal cord.

Kampinsky & Ward (1950) found that individuals with insufficient afferent flow, or integration from the vestibular system, must work harder in order to perform certain movements. This is also true with slow hypotonic children.

The vestibular system enables the organism to follow a movement, in particular regarding a change toward gravitation. It helps the organism to distinguish between sensory stimulation connected with the external world or in body motion (e.g. do you go around on a roundabout, or does the roundabout go around you?)

The vestibular system transmits stimuli to the cerebellum and to the pons, thus causing excitation, or inhibition and relaxation. This depends upon the character of the stimulation: slow rhythmic stimulation while moving the limbs of a passive patient leads to inhibition and relaxation; fast rhythmic stimulation accompanied by fast energetic stimulation leads to excitation (Ayres 1972).

As opposed to the well-recognized links between the vestibular system and the visual system, it remains unclear whether the auditory system has any similar connection with the vestibular system, apart from the fact that both are located within the inner ear.

The linkage is probably indirect. Music of a stimulative nature leads the patient into spontaneous motor reaction in the same way it affects the participants in ecstatic healing rituals—rapid motion, whirling, spinning, leaping, etc. Depending upon the functioning of the vestibular system, changes of head posture influence the sense of balance; hence it is the vestibular system, once activated, which influences muscle tone, and muscle tone in turn increases and changes body posture.

Ayres suggests that there appears to be a two-way connection between the auditory and vestibular systems at the brain stem level. She emphasizes, as a result of clinical observation, the links between vestibular stimulation and the hearing process, particularly the improvement of those vocal skills connected with hearing ability (Ayres 1972, 27). It should, however, be stressed that Ayres' programs for sensory-motor treatment do not refer to auditory stimuli unless these are relevant to the development of language. At this stage I would propose the use of ecstatic musical styles which have over the millennia served as stimuli for movement and postural change: since their influence is on a subcortical level and demand a simple spontaneous response which can be easily achieved, the patient has no need of a cognitive effort in order to react. The music assists him to maintain a motor continuity; the activity is pleasant, releases negative energies if such exist, and this can be effective in both individual and group therapy. In addition, such activity can easily be transferred to the home or to any educational institution.[11]

In this context the means at our disposal assume great significance. We can use recordings of traditional ecstatic healing rituals in which drums (occasionally oboes) play a central role. On other occasions we can improvise the music ourselves, and when necessary add instruments which might suit the therapeutic situation and are an integral part of Western culture (piano, cymbals, electric guitar, etc.). Apart from authentic recordings of healing rituals, we might also make use of rock, break dance, and so forth. It should also be pointed out that style is less important than the musical elements involved and the accumulation processes which typify them. This stage of free movement with excitatory musical stimulation will usually last some five to ten minutes. In the case of Anat (and others) all these stages of music-movement activity became shorter after about three months of therapy, thus allowing more time for psychological treatment.*

2. Flow and control: *movement and arrest* is another way of increasing muscle tone and the patient's body control. Over the years I have been observing both patients and nonpatients from the ages of three to sixty, and have discovered spontaneous reactions which are common to all. Without any verbal guidance each and every patient (depending on his own motor ability and freedom of movement) would respond by moving or stopping according to the following musical elements: repetitive beat units, acceleration or deceleration, excessive changes in volume, the expansion of vocal range, and the continuation or cessation of the music.[12]

Here it is worthwhile stressing that since it is important for movement to be arrested in a balanced posture (without decreasing muscle tone), it is the role of the therapist to guide the actions by his music. This means before the break there should be no deceleration, diminishment of vocal range or decrescendo—quite the opposite, the music breaks off at a climax. There is an advantage here in that it is the therapist who creates the music, since this enables him to observe the patient or patients and to dictate and balance their movement and posture as required. In Anat's case, although she responded spontaneously to rhythm, intensity, continuation and cessation, she had difficulty in combating the force of gravity and thus retaining her balance. This condition improved during the course of therapy, particularly after the movement specialist joined the program and made her own contribution.**

---

*Sekeles Recording Archive 2, 1983
**Sekeles Recording Archive, as above

This improvement of swifter reaction to such musical components as tempo and intensity came as a direct result of an increase of muscle tone (as described previously). After about two years of therapy her ability to move and arrest movement was almost identical to that of any normal child with no motor problems, but with no special training in movement.* This also found expression in her interactions with her companions, thus aiding the development of societal relationships and overall self-confidence.**

3. The employment of the usual *activities of physical rehabilitation*, such as sitting and bouncing on a Physio-Ball led to increased muscle tone and an improvement of posture. Music therapy's additional contribution to this process consisted of activation by means of song. The melody and the manner in which it was performed dictated rhythmic movement, while the lyric clarified and reinforced the message. The song itself was composed of movement and arrest and through a play situation suited to the child's world supported the activities defined above (1. & 2.). It should also be noted that when the aim is to reduce muscle tone, the patient lies prone across the ball and propels it very slowly.

In this case the song components and the verbal instructions were obviously variable.*** Anat reacted to such singing extremely well, and after a few weeks began to control movement and arrest and even to supplement these with complex movemental variations as she exercised on the ball. In other words there was not only an improvement in muscle tone, in movement and in posture, but Anat was also gaining self-confidence in order to independently develop more complex patterns of movement.

We should now consider the fact that in all stages the child is enabled to be creative and to develop his own movemental repertoire through his own experience and functional improvement.

4. Such activity is aimed at *improving the fine motor skills* by means of both playing music and/or by reacting to it in movement. In both cases the principal factor is the increase and acceleration of all musical components, and their cessation at a climax. At the start it is preferable to make use of a full drum set and to activate global arm movement. This is transferred by degrees to smaller percussion instruments, drums and xylophones for example, and eventually to plucked instruments, such as an autoharp, and thence to keyboard instruments, piano, organ or synthesizer. Such graduated activity allows the hypotonic child to exploit finger flexion (or semiflexion) for maximum efficiency without resorting to hyperextension in order to increase muscle tone.

It is important to bear in mind that, as opposed to other forms of physical exercise, music activity creates an immediate auditory feedback which can be linked to emotional matters aroused during therapy. These are a few examples which reveal Anat's concerns:

---

*Sekeles Recording Archive, 1984
**Sekeles Recording Archive, 1985
***Recording Archive: "Motor-Activating Songs," 1962–1990

"When I'm scared when Dad goes out to work" or "I got all het-up today on the bus on the way to school." These were themes that she raised on her own initiative while playing on the full drum set in the accumulative manner already described.

There would appear to be a natural analogy between accumulative playing toward a climax and the accumulation of anxiety, excitement, anger and so forth. The physical sensation of emotion, experienced through music and movement, is transmitted by the patient (in this case as well as in others) and merges with his own feelings. This is something which opens up the possibility of working on these emotions, and expressing them through music in order to achieve release, moderation, and sublimation.

An example of such a link between musical action and emotion is a poem which Anat composed at the age ten:

> The drum gets angry when I am cross
> The drum is a thunder beating at my ears
> When you are angry and at a loss
> It's best to beat the biggest drums.*

5. Down's Syndrome children generally speak unclearly, in low, hoarse voices and their speech tends to accelerate. This can be partially explained by the hypotonia of the tongue, lips and muscles employed in voice production. By making use of a *combination of vocality and movement*, or of vocality and instrumental playing, it is possible to treat problems of articulation, rhythmic exactitude, and the control of the duration and acceleration of voice production.

Voice production exercises are preceded by guided self-massage of the mouth and lips and other facial features. Later on the enunciation of various syllables is combined with contracting and relaxing the facial muscles in accordance with the therapeutic approach of Paula Garbourg (1982).

From here we progress to the elocution of complete words and sentences, accompanied and reinforced by individual movement on the part of the patient and music played by the therapist. It should be noted that although Anat's diction improved in regard to certain syllables with which she had previous difficulty, not only in speech but also in song, her singing showed no marked improvement as hoarseness and limited vocal range remained unchanged. In general, as with other patients, this is an aspect which does not make satisfactory progress and is worthy of further study and a new approach.

6. At this stage of therapy, which links sensory, movemental and vocal treatment with the *emotional aspects*, the therapist composes a story with dramatic emphasis, reinforced by playing and singing (see charts). The themes of such a story derive from the patient's own personal world, either directly or by inference. The patient acts out the story by means of movement, voice, instruments, or the use of any other property available in the therapy room. In this way, depending upon personal ability and willingness, he or she confronts all of the above mentioned aspects.

---

*Recording Archive 3–7–8: "Emotional Songs Composed by Down's Syndrome Children." Translated from the Hebrew.

Themes raised and elaborated upon by Anat during therapy included such subjects as:

"Why do they call me retarded?"

"Grandma fell ill and died."

"Mummy bore me a sister," and so on.

As we shall see, such themes were without doubt extremely significant in Anat's private world, just as they are central to life in general. During the process of adapting such themes, Anat composed a number of little poems, two of which (also written at the age of ten) I would like to quote here:

> 1. I'm sad today
>   In my neighborhood they called me retarded
>   Mommy said that I shouldn't be hurt
>   What do you think—that I haven't any feelings?*

> 2. I visited Mommy in the hospital
>   Mommy was lying on a white sheet with blue stripes
>   She explained to me that she's not sick
>   She explained to me that a new baby isn't a disease.
>   I saw the baby and they told me that it's my sister
>   What do you mean sister? They didn't even ask me!
>   I felt angry and my tummy hurt
>   I don't want a baby and I don't want presents
>   I just want to be sad and to cry.**

These poems reflect Anat's ability for self-expression and the manner in which she was capable of confronting and discussing her feelings. This serves as a confirmation of the potential for psychotherapy with children suffering from moderate mental retardation, of the level of verbal expression which can be achieved, and of the value of integrated therapy between body and mind.

CONCLUSION

In this chapter I have presented a program of developmental therapy which employs music as an intermediate agent. In this program sensory-movemental exercises and games are aimed at improving the patient's physical ability to function as well as encouraging her to expand her awareness of her psychological and societal situation.

We still lack definitive scientific research concerning the links between physical posture and mental receptivity, or the influences of improved physical stability as an encouragement to learning ability. However clinical observation in all spheres concerned with developmental-integrative therapy demonstrate that in practice there does exist a positive connection between both of these.

---

*A.B. Recording Archive 3: "Emotional Songs Composed by Down's Syndrome Children"
**Recording Archive 8, as above: Both poems translated from the Hebrew.

In this context the acknowledged contribution of music to the various fields of developmental therapy (occupational therapy, physiotherapy, speech therapy, psychotherapy, etc.) emerges from the following aspects:

1. The inherent potential of music to evoke movemental reaction, and the ability to direct such movement by means of specific musical components, mainly tempo, dynamics, tonal range, continuation and cessation.

2. The natural combination of vocality with instruments, and/or movement, which permits both creative and playful treatment of vocal problems.

3. The natural links between music and emotions which enable the patient to make contact with repressed feelings and subjects.

4. The possibilities presented by playing on a variety of instruments for the development of fine motor skills in an enjoyable and satisfying manner.

5. The sensory-motor integration which optimal musical activity facilitates.

As an example of a music therapy process, first aimed at the creation of awareness and the overcoming of hypotonia, we took the case of Anat, born with Down's Syndrome (Trisomy 21), who also suffered from pronounced hypotonia. Despite the fact that she underwent an impressive series of treatments, her hypotonia continued to sabotage her movemental abilities, above and beyond the basic movements demanded by day-to-day existence. According to observation by others, as well as by me, there seemed to be some connection between her physical alertness, concentration and intellectual responsitivity.

Based on many months of observing Anat as well as other Down's Syndrome children, I drew up a plan for a therapy session which would include various stages and aspects of motor-integration by means of music.

Over a three-month period the sensory-movemental phase was reduced to about half an hour, thus allowing more time to deal with the emotional matters which Anat would raise. As her skills developed, she was more and more capable of increasing muscle tone and improving her overall Body Alertness in a very short space of time. It is worthwhile mentioning here that despite differences of category, natural potential, and therapeutic and family history, clinical records show a relative degree of progress in all those Down's Syndrome children who for at least a whole year were subjected to continuous music therapy, as described above.

I should like to stress that a combination of movement and music therapy administered by two specialists is to be highly recommended as it enables a higher level of awareness of the body and its repertoire of movement.*

There can be no doubt that as long as the child continues his development and is capable of a more conscious confrontation with the various aspects of body and mind, he can better confront his own congenital problems. And so, Anat became a member of a local dance group composed of normal boys and girls of her own age. She excels in her spinal posture and head holding. We believe that this contributes to better perception and reception of her surroundings, and at the same time to a lessening of the external impression of her being retarded.**

---

*Cohen & Sekeles Recording Archive, 1986–1987

**Since 1990, when this research was first reported, Anat has completed her high school studies and carries out her National Service as an assistant kindergarten teacher.

V

JACOB

REVIVING PRAYER THROUGH SONG

D.I.M.T. in the rehabilitation of a brain-damaged cantor

Introduction
The Brain and Its Musical Functions
Jacob: Patient Profile
Therapeutic Considerations: Restoration of Musical Skills
Summary of First-Year Therapy
Therapeutic Considerations: Emotional Rehabilitation
Epilogue

INTRODUCTION

T he two previous chapters were concerned with music therapy for children with congenital deficiencies. As opposed to this, we shall now discuss the loss of musical abilities by adults as a result of brain damage. As an example I have selected the case of a cantor who suffered a cerebrovascular accident[1] in the right hemisphere.

At the outset we shall briefly describe various research concerning the location of musical function in the brain. Later we shall present an example which demonstrates the need for music therapy in order to rehabilitate specific musical skills, as well as to elaborate on relevant emotional issues.

THE BRAIN AND ITS MUSICAL FUNCTIONS

The cerebrum is divided into two hemispheres, linked by nerve fibers which serve as channels of communication between these two halves. Each hemisphere serves as a mirror image of its opposite partner, just as do the two sides of our body. The sensory and movemental control of our body is divided between these two hemispheres in a contralateral organization. It is already generally accepted that both hemispheres contribute to complex (high) mental activity but are different from an organizational and functional point of view. For example, a simple check of hand skills will reveal a difference between right and left. Statistically some 90% of human beings use their right hand for writing, others prefer the left, while a small minority are ambidextrous. Among right-handed people it is the left hemisphere of the brain which dominates not only the right hand and arm but also speech. Left-handedness or right-handedness is only one of many aspects which can teach us about the asymmetry of the brain hemispheres. Reports concerning the differences between these hemispheres date back about a hundred years or so, but systematic research and a growing interest in this subject began only in the 1960s. Research into auditory perception and performance divides into two major approaches:

1. Lateralized stimulation in which only the left or right ear is subjected to stimuli, in order to examine the way in which it is processed by the opposite hemisphere.

2. Dichotic stimulation in which the subject listens to two different and simultaneous auditory messages, each of which is directed to a separate ear. It is the subject's task to differentiate between the two.

Research undertaken by Kimura contribute the following observations:

a) Verbal stimuli are processed by the left dominant hemisphere.

b) Verbal activity leads to an increased blood flow to the left dominant hemisphere, whereas music activity increases blood flow to the right minor hemisphere.

c) The right minor hemisphere takes precedence in perceiving and processing musical stimuli.

d) The right hemisphere also has a preferential ability to memorize pitch and nonverbal continuity (Kimura 1963; Kimura and Archibald 1974).

In their research, Bever and Chiavello (1974) stress the difference between perceiving and processing music material among musicians and naive listeners. The professional displays an advantage in receptiveness and memory through the right ear, apparently due to his ability to absorb music both structurally as a gestalt as well as analytically. The greater the degree of musical education and practice, the better the integration between analytical and gestalt perception, whereas with the nonmusician musical perception is almost totally gestaltic.

Regarding musical disabilities, it appears that excision of the left or right temporal lobe[2] causes a variety of deficiencies. Excision of the right hemisphere leads to errors in perception and performance of melodic structures, intensity, rhythm and timbre. In terms of melody, the major damage was in the ability to control pitch; the sense of rhythm was less impaired. On the other hand excision of the left hemisphere led to no music disabilities whatsoever (Bogen & Gordon 1971).

Even more fascinating information can be gleaned from research into song birds. Fernando Nottebohm shows that the canary's syrinx is divided between the left and the right hypoglossus nerve. The majority of the adult canary's singing ability is controlled by the left hypoglossus, hence Nottebohm speaks of "The dominance of the left hypoglossus," damage to the bird's left hypoglossus results in severe impediment of its singing ability. Sectioning of the right hypoglossus, however, has virtually no effect on its song.

We should recall here that the canary's singing does not serve a purely musical function. It is in fact a means of vocal communication, hence the dominance of the left side—as in man. Nevertheless it would seem that man's development of speech has led to greater polarization between the two hemispheres of the human brain. (Nottebohm, in Rahmani 1984).

Rahmani (ibid.) stresses that the more man grows and develops, and his verbal abilities improve and expand, so does the asymmetry between the two hemispheres of the brain. This asymmetry finds its initial expression at the start of embryonic life. Seventy percent of embryos only a few months old were found to have a left temporal lobe larger than that on the right; the pyramidal tract was more extended on the left than on the right; on the other hand the angular gyrus was larger in the right hemisphere.

In general, the left hemisphere specializes in language functions, due to its analytical abilities, whereas the right hemisphere specializes in visual and spatial functions, as well as in nonverbal sound, due to its superior ability to deal with information in a holistic manner.

Since we are concerned here with music, perhaps a more definitive clarification is called for:

1. The right hemisphere is responsible for memory, tonal and modal performance, recognition and reproduction of melodic patterns, sound duration, and performance of timbre and intensity.

2. The left hemisphere is responsible for judgement of duration, temporal order, sequencing, music reading, composition and analysis (Springer & Deutch 1985).

It would seem therefore that as far as music is concerned, as in all other fields, there is a significance to this hemispherical system inasmuch as it can lead to mental unity. Rahmani describes it thus: "The linkage between the two hemispheres serves as a mechanism through which is created the illusion of a single and perfect psychological space" (Rahmani 1984, 17).

This is of primary importance in understanding any attempt at musical organization which combines words and singing, or those intermediary forms between singing and words: vocalization, incantation, recitation, etc. If there did not exist such a psychological space which Rahmani describes, it would be impossible to treat someone whose singing ability had been damaged (the right hemisphere) without being aided by the nonaffected left hemisphere using combined and integrated techniques.

The following case of a professional musician who suffered a stroke in the left hemisphere can increase our understanding of the hemispheres' musical functions. Maurice Ravel suffered from Wernicke's aphasia (receprive)[3] as the result of such brain damage. Ravel was at the height of his musical career, but lost his ability to write music or play it. Nevertheless his musical mind remained unimpaired; he was able to distinguish any false note, and to continue to hum or play any of his own compositions as soon as he heard the first few notes. He was, however, unable to organize his thoughts and ideas into a musical grammatical form due to this aphasia, or even to name the notes (Alajouanine 1984).

Another example, from my own personal experience: as a music therapist in Holland I treated a patient who had once been a famous concert pianist; at the age of sixty-plus he suffered diffuse cerebral damage in both hemispheres. He lost his analytical music ability and it was clearly apparent that he could no longer maintain a constant rhythm, nor avoid acceleration or express dynamic change. Despite this he was capable of reading a score, and once I had played him the opening of any given work he could recall this from his audio-motor memory as a complete structure and play it reasonably well.

Here we see that in cases of diffuse injury the skill and ability loss is also multifaceted and so we must carefully consider therapeutic approaches and techniques.* Similarly, we must take into consideration the possibility of performing impaired activity by way of the undamaged hemisphere.

Such development has been clinically observed in numerous patients, who suffered from Broca's aphasia (expressive), but were nevertheless able to sing words in sequence.

Over and above the obvious emotional value of this, in which someone who has lost his power of speech is nevertheless able to give voice to meaningful sound, it is something which can be developed into speech through therapy, with music serving as an interim bridge.

An example, again from personal experience, is that of Anton, a forty-year-old patient who suffered from cerebral palsy (right spastic hemiplegia) and unfortunately had never developed verbal skills. However, after a certain period of music

---

*Recording Archive 10: "Music Therapy in Rehabilitating Musical Skills"

therapy he was able to combine music and song and to gradually go over to speech which was not dependent on musical melody.*

> Since high-level training of knowledge and music in the population at large seem to be the exception rather then the rule, it is probably justifiable to assume that dominance for general musical faculty tends to develop in the right hemisphere first. A gradient theory would explain how, as training progresses, dominance would be gradually transplanted to the opposite hemisphere for perceptual processing (Damasio & Damasio in Critchley & Henson 1977, 152).

Damasio & Damasio go on to discuss the phenomenon of words in song:

> The former process concerned with words within the framework of a song or poem operates out of an "oppositional" store and emerges in a global gestalt way. The latter, which is concerned with most regular verbal utterances, stems from a "propositional" mechanism, resulting from a more analytical construction.... In fact, one might propose that language and music do unite in the right hemisphere in order to escape interhemispherical rivalry (ibid.).

However, the development of speech independent of singing in patients who are able to sing but unable to talk, demands a systematic and well-defined therapeutic process and can not be expected to develop automatically.

Despite the fact that many open arguments still remain regarding the hemispheres and their musical relevance, we must nevertheless take into consideration all the aspects of current research when dealing with a patient suffering from brain damage in one of the hemispheres.

My chosen example is that of an elderly patient (over sixty years of age) who suffered a sudden cerebrovascular accident in the right hemisphere. As a result, he became severely handicapped in his ability to perceive, comprehend and perform music.

JACOB: PATIENT PROFILE

> Sometimes someone bends down to pick up
> something which fell from his hand
> and when once again he straightens up
> the world is not what it was.**

Jacob was born in the 1920s. He lectured in Jewish religion and philosophy, and was the cantor of his local congregation. He had no formal musical education, and his cantorial skills were attained solely by practical experience over many years.

One could say that in Jacob's life both hemispherical functions were integrated: professionally his was a verbal occupation, dealing with abstraction and analysis. It was his emotional inclinations which led him into his occupation as a cantor in an Orthodox Jewish Synagogue.

In late 1983 he suffered a stroke as a result of high blood pressure, which led to the paralysis of his left side. After some three months of hospitalization he attended

---

*Recording Archive 17: "Music Therapy with Brain Damaged Adults"
**"From Man Thou Art and to Man Shalt Thou Return," Yehuda Amihai (1985)

a day center for rehabilitation in which the emphasis was placed on physiotherapy as well as improving speech elements such as breathing, articulation, intonation and resonance.

It should be noted that the aspects on which the speech-clinician concentrated were the musical elements of speech. Jacob had not lost his ability to speak and was not suffering from aphasia, but there were certain musical deficiencies in his speech which led to a lack of verbal clarity. At this stage his ability to function in his capacity as a cantor had not been examined. We should also note that standard procedure for the examination and treatment of hemiplegic patients still does not include any examination of auditory and musical losses, even in cases where music plays a major role in the patient's emotional and professional life.

When Jacob discovered he was no longer able to sing properly, he sank into a mood of depression. It was this development which led his clinician to invite me (as an outsider) to assess the possibility of vocal/musical rehabilitation.

The initial examination consisted of two full-hour sessions which highlighted the following crucial problems:

1. Difficulty in recognition and performance of pitch.
2. Inability to maintain a steady beat-unit.
3. Difficulty in integrating on time and tending to accelerate when singing within a given tempo.

In other words the two most fundamental elements of music, perception and performance of tempo and pitch, had been severely damaged. At this stage Jacob was able to sing only within an approximate four-note range:

After examining recordings of cantorial music which Jacob had performed before his injury, it was clear that the damage was indeed serious.*

Emotionally, Jacob was depressed. His impaired singing ability was a critical factor for him. As he put it, "True, they can treat my body, but I've lost first and foremost my ability to sing—which means my soul."

It should be mentioned here that some 62% of hemiplegics suffering from damage to the minor right hemisphere tend to display emotional instability, whereas only some 10% of those suffering from damage to the major left hemisphere show similar symptoms. This has been proved by laboratory experiments based on the Wada Test.[4]

Recent research utilizing modern analytical techniques has revealed differences between the two cerebral hemispheres regarding emotional reactions after brain damage (Lishman 1987).

Whatever the case, Jacob displayed symptoms of depression, and during therapy further symptoms of emotional instability ranging from nervous

---

*I.R. Recording Archive, Cassettes 106–131: "Music Therapy in the Rehabilitation of Music Skills after Brain Damage"

laughter to uncontrollable weeping. Beside the organic causes, his depressions could also be related to the damage inflicted on his vocal abilities, which once served as the essence of his emotional world. On the other hand, even during the initial interviews for music therapy one could perceive an improvement of mood which gave both patient and therapist a certain optimism regarding the possibilities for improvement. Replay of the initial interview recordings revealed that whereas Jacob proved incapable of controlling pitch, imitating intervals or even performing a brief melody without any harmonic support, when this was supplied, from piano or electronic organ, his vocal exactitude and clarity immediately improved. When these tapes were replayed, Jacob became encouraged and his motivation for music therapy was enhanced. Indeed he displayed extraordinary self-will and determination which doubtless were of inestimable aid to him in facing the challenges he had chosen.

Here we must stress two intermediate, but extremely relevant points:

1. Musically accompanied singing is not acceptable in the Orthodox Jewish Synagogue. It was therefore an essential long-range goal of therapy to free the patient from any dependence on harmonic-chordal accompaniment. During the initial stages of therapy this was totally impossible because chordal support was the way of enabling him to hold a tune. At this stage it was also essential to keep the expectations of Jacob's family within realistic proportions.

2. That same year I examined another three patients who had suffered stroke in the right hemisphere and consequent left hemiplegia. A few years later I encountered a further four patients of a similar nature. Apart from the severity of the injury, the progress of each individual patient regarding musical ability and emotional stability differed from case to case.

There can be no doubt that the patient's progress was dependent on his individual personality and maturity, as well as on his ego-strength (see Versluys in Trombly 1977, 27). In Jacob's case, both his personality and the constant support of his family and community served to advantage.

THERAPEUTIC CONSIDERATIONS: RESTORATION OF MUSICAL SKILLS

As already mentioned Jacob never studied music as a profession, he simply acquired it through experience. Any analytical approach to music as a communicative language with its own rules of syntax was totally foreign to him. This meant that any rehabilitation of music skills could not rely on the functions of the undamaged left hemisphere. Unfortunately the intuitive perception and performance of music upon which Jacob naturally relied were the very functions which had been damaged. This is typical of injury to the lateral region of the right temporal lobe which causes musical agnosia. He was unable to differentiate between the acoustic nature of a sensation and its significance. Working with the support of musical instruments can often restore the linkage between a sound and its origin while taking into consideration the need to reinforce self-confidence and to encourage the patient's strength, I decided to devote a great deal of time to accompanied singing which would emphasize the harmonic potential of the melody. Such harmonic support could stimulate and reactivate inherent codes, similar to inherent verbal codes, on the assumption that such codes are the basis of melodic singing. Since Jacob had lost his sense of pitch and his ability to reproduce it, instead of working on single notes he began to practice on complete structures emanating from tonal codes. It should nevertheless be noted that the ability to repeat simple tonal or modal melodies could not guarantee the ability to perform complex liturgy such as the "Kol Nidre" sung on the Day of Atonement.

Start of Kol Nidre:

Along with the rehabilitation of his melodic skills, it was essential to deal with rhythmic ability. First and foremost this demanded developing hearing and response to constant beat-units and tempo.

At this point I should like to stress that while psychophysiological researchers can devote their time to discussing the sources of rhythmic behavior, proposing and deposing various theories (instinctive, physiological, motor, acquired, etc.), the music therapist must approach the problem directly in order to facilitate the patient's growth.

According to D.I.M.T., reconstruction of beat-units is done through a combination of auditory and locomotive functions as they occur in natural development. This involves auditory stimulation of repetitive beats in utero, its transfer after birth to passive movements of rocking and rhythmic touching and a gradual development into complex movement.[5]

Indeed, both exercise and rhythmic treatments were conducted according to the above-mentioned principles, even though the patient himself was more than sixty years old. At the same time these exercises also had their effect on both the relaxation and stabilization of breathing, something which is essential for any patient who lacks both physical and emotional control.

Jacob's initial physical response to a strict rhythm which matched the rate of an average human heartbeat consisted of activating various limbs in response to metronome beats accompanied by the piano. The music was tonal or modal, and hence reinforced his own loss of tonal and modal ability.

Next, Jacob went on to rhythmic exercises on a variety of instruments, with a gradual but steady improvement. The use of various instruments served to develop and restore fine motor skills. We made use of various sized drums, xylophones, metallophones, an autoharp, a dulcimer, psaltery, a variety of bells, etc.

The tendency to react with movement to audible rhythm has been subject to vast research. Boring stated as early as 1942: "Only after a rhythm has been actually played, can it be perceived and internalized." This theory, proven over and over again in various recent research (Deutsch, Fraisse, Sternberg, et al. in Deutsch 1982), can help us as music therapists. After two to three months of intensive therapy Jacob's receptiveness and performance regarding rhythmic units had improved to such a degree that he was able to progress to more complex structures and to better combine melodic and rhythmic activity.

From an emotional viewpoint it was essential to take into consideration the patient's own educational background in order to understand his limited freedom regarding both physical and vocal expression. In the case of an introverted personality such as Jacob's, emotional inhibitions (due in part to education and life-style) are liable to limit or even block physical expression. In such a situation a step-by-step approach must be adopted: controlled exercises whose rules are limiting but nevertheless inspire self-confidence, vocal and instrumental improvisation which graduates from the well-known and familiar to the freely imaginative, and eventually guided fantasizing in music.

From my point of view as a therapist, the fact that I am a woman could have created difficulties. A religious Jew is actually forbidden to listen to a woman singing: "The voice of a woman in song, is tantamount to self-exposure" (Benedictions: Babylonian Talmud).

Despite being of an orthodox background Jacob was able to regard my singing as an integral part of his therapy, and soon displayed the ability to enter into the musical experience and to respond in movement and vocality with a sense of enjoyment. The first stage of therapy lasted a full year, with stress on the restoration of musical ability and skills and the encouragement of self-confidence.

SUMMARY OF FIRST-YEAR THERAPY

Goal	Technique	Means	Duration of Therapy	Progress Versus Pre-Injury Condition[6]
1. Rehabilitating beat-units	a) Listening to rhythmic stimulation b) Self-performance	Metronome drums percussion dulcimer autoharp organ singing	1½ hrs + practice at home for 3 months	40–50%
2. Rehabilitating rhythmic patterns	a) Perception (listening) b) Vocal and instrumental imitation and performance	As above Religious and secular songs and poetry	1½ hrs + practice at home for 10 months	60–75%

Goal	Technique	Means	Duration of Therapy	Progress Versus Pre-Injury Condition[6]
3. Tonal/modal rehabilitation	a) Listening b) Repeating single sounds, intervals and melodies	Singing with harmonic accompaniment	1½ hrs + practice at home for 3 months	40–50%
4. Tonal/modal rehabilitation	a) Listening to musical compositions especially religious songs b) Singing melody and parts of melody c) Singing, with transpositions	Accompanied singing Composing songs Singing with self accompaniment	1½ hrs + practice at home for 10 months	60–75%

At the end of his first year of therapy, Jacob was able to return to his previous position at his local synagogue as a cantor and in coaching boys for their bar mitzvah (coming of age) ceremony. True, the restoration of his musical skills was as yet incomplete, but was functionally satisfactory, and had restored his self-confidence as well as a sense of achievement and compensation in the face of loss.

THERAPEUTIC CONSIDERATIONS: EMOTIONAL REHABILITATION

During his first year of music therapy Jacob, who was mostly used to cantorial and liturgical music, encountered musical and verbal material which was completely foreign to him. This included unfamiliar musical instruments, free-style singing, a variety of vocal and instrumental improvisation, the associative verbal response to music, freedom of movement, and so on.

Early in 1985 he wrote about this new awareness of openness:

I do things in this room which emerge from layers inside me of which I know nothing. Invisible worlds. I feel as if the paralysis and the loss of the physical body serve as the gateway through which an ailing existence went in, and from which a regenerated musical entity emerged. As you know, I come from a different musical tradition, aware that Western music has its sources in Christianity. However, as a result of this new experience I learn that it is not the literal, religious, philosophical roots which are of the essence, but rather the pure music—which can touch agony and transmute it into pleasure.

These words summarize a period which was mainly devoted to functional rehabilitation and the opening up of a new stage in which it would not only be necessary to encourage and preserve these achievements, but also mostly to elaborate the emotional aspects involved. The more the patient's musical organization improved, the easier it became to devote additional energy to confronting emotional matters which he would now raise quite freely. Linking his love of music with his love of words, Jacob began to compose his own songs. His two central motifs were, on the one hand loss and death, and on the other hand love and eroticism.

These were themes which were easily aroused during free-association sessions in which he could verbally interpret musical motifs or passages from musical works. For example, a descending chromatic passage in an adagio tempo on the lower part of the piano was interpreted by him as an embrace. Choral sequences were seen as a kiss; a diminished chord and its solution meant a tragedy ending in love.*

At this stage Jacob's playing was endowed with rich dynamics which expressed a variety of emotions. It should be noted that during the first year of therapy this dynamic variation emerged quite spontaneously with no overt guidance on the part of the therapist. In music, changes of intensity (dynamics) constitute one of the most significant elements of emotional expression and its transmission to others. It would seem that the more the patient was able to identify with his own inner feelings, the better he could express them in music.

In the art therapies in general (and in this case music therapy in particular) as opposed to psychodynamic verbal therapy, it is at least partially possible to deal with emotional subjects by means of the artistic modality itself. By arousing musical associations, by composing tunes and lyrics, by choosing poetry and narrative and setting them to music, by verbal conversation emerging from guided imagery with music, we can help to elaborate emotional content and to open up the emotional world for the patient.

In addition, these love songs which he composed and accompanied enabled a process of sublimation which suited Jacob's religious upbringing, served as a personal compromise, and avoided any confrontation with his environment.

Through the realization of erotic fantasy in song (whether adopted from literature or self-composed) it was possible to identify the focus of transference. Love of woman? Of mother? Of child? Does his preoccupation with the themes of death and loss indicate the termination of therapy? True, at this stage music therapy gave birth to love songs to a woman, which later became lullabies to a child, and apparently to some kind of closing of a life-cycle. This brought an end of longing, of conscious return to childhood, to primal object-relation and to a better acceptance of physical loss.**

---

*Recording Archive 118: "Music Therapy in Restoring Musical Skills After Brain Damage."
**Recording Archive 117–131: "Music Therapy in Restoring Musical Skills After Brain Damage," accent on "Emotional Aspects of Therapy."

Jacob's choice of poetry made him more aware of his own affinity to certain subjects. We could now work on a chosen poem through music, and discuss musical metaphors as well as verbal content and meaning.

All of these led the patient toward a confrontation with his emotions, while reducing his guilt feelings and strengthening his sense of enjoyment. With this in mind, I proposed two books by Yehuda Amihai: *Hour of Mercy* and *From Man Thou Comest and to Man Thou Shalt Return,* on the assumption that the patient would be able to identify with poems concerning love, the relinquishing of youth, and departure from this world.

Jacob began to examine his choice of instruments not only from an iconographic and structural point of view, but also regarding their emotional-musical potential. He began to clarify his love-desires, and expressed this in abstract musical terms, in composing poetry which was not only direct but also made use of metaphor, and in conversation. During this entire process it seemed that Jacob had learned to see human instinctive urges as leading to a positive process of creativity.

During the last months of therapy, various existential questions were raised and expressed not only in his music but also in what he wrote. For example, this lyric written in November 1985:

> Why does the sea never end
> and only one's life ebb away?
> Why do the waves change themselves everyday
> and only the people die?
> Why does the mountain rear up like a rock
> And God's alone, silent, up there?
> The sun's scorching frown
> Lasts for ever and ever
> It's only one's life which bends down.*

EPILOGUE

Music therapy was concluded in 1985 and Jacob was planning a family visit to the land of his birth, something which was also an obvious attempt at "closing the circles." He never made it. Only a few days after the completion of his therapy Jacob suffered a heart attack and died.

---

*Recording Archive 131 (ibid.)

VI

RITA

FROM A BAD BABY TO A NEW BIRD

D.I.M.T. with a hospitalized adolescent
suffering from a traumatic childhood

INTRODUCTION

I n previous chapters I have presented and analyzed the therapeutic rationale which guides the music therapist in his use of music for both relaxation and stimulation concerning problems caused basically by physical (and/or genetic) disability. The theory, based on clinical experience, is that such relaxation or stimulation can lead to psychophysiological changes which will permit the continuation of therapy aimed at the patient's emotional needs.

Each instance of relaxation or stimulation was represented by a typical case history. These case histories were chosen in order to represent a certain patient group, and the music therapy approach previously defined as the Developmental-Integrative Model.

Ron, suffering from cerebral palsy was chosen to demonstrate the need for preliminary relaxation in order to lower spasticity, and at the same time to lessen anxiety. In the same way Anat, the Down's Syndrome child was chosen to demonstrate the need to increase muscle tone by excitation, since the majority of such patients suffer from overall hypotonia. Increase of muscle tone can be achieved through a combination of music and movement, with music serving as a stimulant, and movement as a reaction.

In both the above examples, the physical defects were present from birth.

In a later chapter I continued to stress the overall approach which takes into account both the patient's physical and emotional problems. In this case we were dealing with Jacob, a patient who suffered brain damage as an adult and was thus in need of professional and emotional rehabilitation.

In this chapter, which concerns treatment of a psychological problem, we shall demonstrate the advantages of relaxation by means of music when dealing with patients suffering from constant anxiety due to severe trauma in childhood.

For Rita physical relaxation served as an essential phase in psychotherapy, in two ways:

1. Music paved the way to physical and mental relaxation.
2. This very relaxation opened the way to the elaboration of emotional problems.

CHILDHOOD TRAUMA

Trauma is "an event in the subject's life defined by its intensity, by the subject's incapacity to respond adequately to it, and by the upheaval and long-lasting effects that it brings about in the psychical organization" (Laplanche & Pontalis 1985, 465). It is a term adopted by psychotherapy from medicine. In both fields it indicates penetration and injury and their influence on the psychophysical organization.

The term "Childhood Trauma" embraces many and varied aspects: loss, abandonment, hospitalization, an unbalanced family environment, mental and physical molestation, and more.

Vaugham (1957), Bowlby (1952, 1960) and others concerned with childhood trauma as a result of hospitalization, came to the conclusion that even though, since the 1950s, parents are permitted to accompany their children in hospitalization, and even sleep at their bedside, many of these children suffer from deep emotional scars and constant anxiety. This is especially prominent in children under the age of four. Such anxieties are liable to increase at moments of crisis such as parting, the death of a parent, or any other significant loss.

As far as child abuse is concerned, the typical behavioral dynamics of such children may vary:

1. Acceptance, passivity, and self-negation
2. Resignation, acceptance and introversion
3. Aggression, demand and struggle (Zimrin 1985).

In the first example one could say that the abused child develops a kind of "false self" (Winnicott 1965). When suffering and frustration become unbearable, and the child repeatedly undergoes hunger, beatings and deprivations, he ceases to weep or to demand, giving up on his present, and apparent future needs. Instead of developing an authentic personality he succumbs to the parent's demands. Such a "good boy," who later on in life encounters a serious crisis, may respond with a psychotic outburst.

In the second example, the resignation and acceptance are aimed first and foremost at minimizing any dangerous encounter with the aggressive parent. Such children develop an introverted physical stance, on the alert and always defensive. They are tense, display passive aggression, misery, a negative body image, and basic insecurity.

In the third example, when the child is still able to resist and demand, he stands a better chance than the aforementioned two. His struggle displays a certain strength, and he shows blatant aggression rather than surrender.

Abused children generally lag behind their peers in class achievement at school since their traumatic development sabotages their "initiative, creativity, curiosity and all those other essential elements of intellectual development" (Zimrin 1985, 45).

Professional literature concerned with the dynamics of child-abuse offers various classifications (Resnick 1969; Rutter 1972; Scott 1973; Zimrin 1985; Dale, et al. 1986). Among the major causes they stress paternal behavior patterns passing from generation to generation and originating in childhood trauma which was not treated in time. The same parent who suffered neglect and abuse as a child bears a certain image of parent-child relationship which he reenacts with his own offspring.

Another possibility is that of a parent convinced that his child is endowed with negative qualities and is thus deserving of punishment. Such a parent is in fact confronting his own evil (which causes him anxiety), and projecting it onto his child. This, by the way, is typical of psychotic parents.

There is also the phenomenon of abusing a handicapped child because it serves as a blemish on the parents, signifying their inability to give birth to a perfect human being.

Other parents emerge as childish, with exaggerated expectations of their offspring. The moment the child does not fulfill these he turns out to be a disappointment, and therefore deserves to be punished. In other cases, children are seen as substitutes who serve as targets for aggression aimed at another member of the family. Thus a frustrated wife might displace her hate for her husband and beat her child, who serves as a handy and convenient target for her own antagonisms. In certain families it is the child who serves as a scapegoat, thus preserving family union.

Hanita Zimrin, enumerates various secondary causes for child-abuse which include lack of parental ability, mental retardation of the parent, alcohol or drug addiction, and other psychiatric causes. She also mentions additional pressures such as inferior socioeconomic status and family crises (ibid., 23–38).

In my experience over the years, out of thirty music therapy patients who suffered childhood trauma, fourteen were hospitalized for periods which varied from a few weeks up to three years. Ten underwent various forms of surgery—internal, orthopedic, neurological, plastic, etc. Sixteen of these were designated as victims of child-abuse at an early age. Of these, eleven were born into unstable families (psychiatric hospitalization of a parent, being an orphan, illegitimacy, divorce, severe illness, etc.). Five of these suffered, in infancy, from various serious injuries due to parental negligence.

From all of these cases I have chosen as an example of music therapy the story of an adolescent girl.

During her first three years, this young lady underwent severe traumatic experiences at the hands of her natural mother. After being badly injured she was hospitalized, and later adopted by a childless family.

When she was seventeen years old her adoptive father died, and she went into a psychological crisis. After attempting suicide she was committed to a psychiatric hospital. There she was treated with individual music therapy for about a year, and for a further year and a half with individual and group therapy as an outpatient.

RITA: PATIENT PROFILE

Rita was born as an illegitimate child; her mother was then aged about eighteen, and her father had long ago vanished from the scene. Rita's mother grew up in a working class family with six children. She finished primary school but dropped out of high school. When she became pregnant she clashed with her parents and severed all contact, even after she gave birth to Rita.

During her first three years the infant was raised by her mother, who was supported solely by Social Welfare. During this period the mother twice became pregnant from casual encounters, and underwent abortions.

The social worker's report described the mother as childish, aggressive, given to unpredictable emotional outbursts, lacking any motivation for study or employment, and reluctant to accept help. During the three years in which Rita's mother "cared for her" the infant suffered from severe neglect, beatings and bruises, cigarette burns on her body, broken limbs and severe undernourishment.

At the age of three Rita was hospitalized with broken arms. A court order retained her in hospital and denied her mother access, or parental rights. Later, Rita was adopted by a thirty-year-old childless couple. The father was a laboratory technician, the mother a housewife.

During the adoptive process the prospective mother described Rita as an intro-verted child alarmed by any sudden changes around her, such as loud noises or shouting. Her motor development was delayed, and she suffered from malnutri-tion. The adoptive parents, under the guidance of a social worker, invested a great deal of effort and affection so that the child might overcome her nutritional defi-ciencies, as well as her motor and linguistic handicaps.

By the age of six she was defined as a comparatively calm child, even though the adoptive mother spoke of constant anxiety, mother dependence, difficulties in making contact with children of her own age, introversion, and sudden temper tantrums accompanied by weeping and screaming, particularly while taking a bath.

Rita's adoptive parents sent her to the Montessori kindergarten, and she contin-ued there until entering primary school.[1] It seems that the Montessori system, with its emphasis on the needs of the individual and a supportive approach to the pupil, enabled Rita to achieve a fair degree of organization: her temper tantrums gradu-ally ceased, and her difficulties in concentration lessened. After completing primary school she was enrolled in a vocational secondary school which suited her natural tendency for handicrafts.

When she was seventeen, toward the end of her third year of high school, her adoptive father contracted a fatal disease and died a few months later. The loss of the father, who had been a stable and pleasant personality, was a severe blow to the family balance. Rita began to lose her powers of concentration, to absent herself from both home and school, wandering around the streets with no clear aim, and returning home unkempt and confused. At the age of seventeen-and-a-half she was referred for psychological treatment by the family physician, but found it difficult to cooperate. After a suicide attempt she was committed to a psychiatric hospital. During intake she appeared thin, unkempt, introverted, depressed and anxiety ridden. In conversation she barely responded, displaying an ambiva-lent attitude toward the adoptive mother while completely ignoring the death of the father.

This psychiatric hospital had a very extensive staff of psychiatrists, nurses, psy-chologists, a rehabilitation center (workshops, etc.), and also treatments which were considered innovative in the 1960s: music, drama and visual arts therapy, as well as movement and physiotherapy. As a part of this framework, Rita was sent for observation to music therapy in order to determine her suitability, and potential for expression in music.

In initial observation her reactions were extremely limited. She showed hardly any initiative, but revealed extreme anxiety. Nevertheless she would regularly and punctually attend music therapy sessions, and began to gradually discover the "music child" within.[2] Despite the fact that at this stage she was capable of no more than simply listening to the music she chose, and showed no initiative or ability to respond creatively, it was deemed worthwhile to schedule her for individual music therapy alongside psychotherapy. And indeed Rita spent about a year in individual music therapy as an inpatient, and a further eighteen months in both individual and group therapy as an outpatient.

OBSERVATIONS AND THERAPEUTIC CONSIDERATIONS

Rita began life in deprivation, with no father, no family circle, and an immature mother who was incapable of accepting responsibility for raising her baby. During critical stages of her development Rita suffered from neglect as well as physical and emotional brutality. Bowlby (1952, 1960) maintains that among young unmarried mothers who are characterized by casual affairs with men and a lack of motivation for personal development, the infant serves as a safety valve against a total vacuum in their lives. This safety valve, however, is liable to steadily become an encumbrance and an object to be tormented. It should be recalled that we are not discussing a onetime trauma but an ongoing situation of severe physical and mental injuries and hospitalizations, with all that that implies, including separations from the mother, neglectful though she may have been.

The developing infant passes through various stages in which he comes to believe in the similarities between himself and some close figure, whose characteristics he believes he himself contains. This is true of both negative and positive figures. Such identification begins with the process of incorporation which endows an external object with one's own characteristics, and in the case under discussion the infant grasps the bad character of the mother as if it were her own, with no distinction between the two. This process continues with the introjection of such characteristics and is completed by a process of identification. In other words, there is no process of imitating external characteristics, but rather of subconsciously adopting and internalizing an entire emotional pattern. Identification with a negative role model (as occurs with a victimized child) can lead to the implanting of feelings of insecurity and anxiety because the identifying child comes to believe in the evil within himself.

In Rita's case such anxiety found expression during hospitalization (and according to the adoptive mother, in the course of her development), in her overall behavior, her introverted posture, and her inhibited movements, as if the defensive stance which almost certainly characterized her infancy had now become a behavioral norm. It was apparent that despite the fact she had been adopted by a devoted and loving family who had invested vast and sincere effort in caring for her, she remained heavily scarred by the traumas of her childhood. The sense of "basic trust" (Erikson 1950), which is instilled in the infant when its needs are met by a regular and reliable response, had been deeply damaged in Rita's case. Her school reports also revealed that despite support and encouragement, she had remained somewhat isolated, having difficulty in making friends. Being an only adopted daughter, even at home she had not experienced a variety of human relationships, apart from those with her adoptive parents. In addition, the team concluded that the adoptive mother developed an overdependent, and overprotective attitude toward Rita, partially due to the child's traumatic history, but in the main due to the adoptive mother's own personality. In this context Eliezer Ilan emphasizes that: "The adolescent who comes for treatment is precisely the one who has not succeeded in sufficiently distancing himself emotionally from his parents, and in finding a substitute in a friend within his own age group" (1971, 191). Similarly, the adolescent who denies his parents is subconsciously attached to them emotion-ally, and in need of psychotherapy in order to release such dependence.

During Rita's first period of hospitalization, the team reevaluated the degree to which childhood traumas and adoption had been worked through. It appeared that despite the fact that the adoptive family had enjoyed the constant and devoted attention of a social worker, the working through process had probably been insufficient.[3]

The process of imprinting, considered to be the most powerful during the first, sensitive year of infant life, was reinforced in Rita's case by negative and corrupting content over a further two years. The essential investment in infancy of love, dedi-cation, permanency and attachment, with no crises, was nonexistent during her critical formative years. Correcting this situation, it would seem, demanded greater resources than those that a normal home, the adoptive parents, and the educational system could provide. All of these could furnish only a kind of cover which easily blew apart on the death of the adoptive father and plunged Rita into a crisis and severe regression. The father died during her adolescence, which in any case serves as a biological and psychological crisis period.[4] Due to this unfortunate combina-tion of crisis within crisis we must now consider the problems of adolescence and their relevance to the case under discussion.

> Adolescence is viewed as the sum total of all attempts at adjustment to the stage of puberty, to the new set of inner and outer—endogenous and exogenous—conditions which confront the individual. It evokes all the modes of excitation, tension, gratifica-tion and defense that ever played a role in previous years—that is the psychosexual development of infancy and early childhood (Blos 1962, 11).

If we divide adolescence into interim stages, then at the time of her hospitaliza-tion Rita was in the mid-stage of both sexual maturity, and completion of high school studies.[5]

As already mentioned, she had had a traumatic childhood. The stage of latency, which serves as a preparation and encouragement towards adulthood, depended upon an ailing branch and at this stage of puberty she suffered a severe blow, the loss of the only stable and reliable human being she had ever known. As a result of Rita's constant difficulties in establishing human contacts, when her adoptive fa-ther died she had no strength to resolve her renewed Oedipal conflict and to direct her heterosexual instincts to her peers.

Peter Blos (1962), who devoted most of his research to the problem adolescent, claims that during adolescence there is a revival of the Oedipus complex and cas-tration complex. The adolescent must undergo a separation from the parents, self-identification, reorganization of the personality and the definition of the conflicts in a manner which will not interfere with, but rather combine with life.

> At the close of adolescence, conflicts are by no means resolved, but they are rendered specific; and certain conflicts become integrated into the realm of the ego as life tasks. This was described as the achievement of late adolescence. It remains the task of post-adolescence to create the specific avenues through which these tasks are implemented in the external world (ibid., 150).

Rita was incapable of undertaking adult obligations, and so instead of undergo-ing a process of self-identification she was overcome by loneliness and panic. She was incapable of making contact with past experiences due to their weighty and painful memories. In this way her personality crisis was perpetuated: she remained confused with her only refuge being "not to be."

According to Erikson, many adolescents who suffer from continual personality disintegration will prefer to be a nobody, a bad person, or a dead person (1959, 132).

This was the state in which Rita began her first year in the psychiatric hospital (individual music therapy in coordination with psychotherapy).

The general approach of the hospital concerning adolescents was:

1. Channeling, refinement and reduction of fear, aggression, and enmity by means of creative endeavor.

2. Increasing self-confidence by means of the creative process and its products.

3. Encouraging interpersonal relationships by means of creative artistic activity; and the opening up of society's appreciation of individual effort.

In this case the elaboration of content in music therapy was generally carried out through the artistic modalities and with the minimum of speech. On the other hand the patients' artistic material was extensively discussed by the team of therapists and served as raw material for dynamic therapy sessions (provided, of course, the patient-creator would agree).

The above-mentioned goals indeed served as aims in Rita's music therapy, over short and medium length periods. Rehabilitation was considered to be the long-term goal.

MUSIC THERAPY: FIRST STAGE
A LESSENING OF ANXIETY

As described above Rita suffered from constant and uncontrollable anxieties, was incapable of taking the initiative, and was extremely limited in verbal communication. Nevertheless she would arrive punctually for music therapy sessions three times a week. The only activity to which she would agree was to listen to music. She would make random choices from the record library which was placed at her disposal, listen in silence and leave after half an hour. During the first two months her preferences began to emerge. She would totally reject any vocal works and preferred stringed instruments such as the guitar or lute, later progressing to the harp and the piano. Her favorite period was the 16th to 18th centuries (the record library comprised a wide range of some hundred such recordings). When her choice of music seemed to become more shaped, I suggested that she sit on the carpet, rather than in her chair, and work on breath control while listening to the music.* It should be noted that lying supine, as necessary for certain breathing and relaxation exercises, is extremely revealing, and as opposed to a prone, semi-fetal position, exposes the most sensitive human organs. In Rita's case it was a fair assumption that a supine position would be liable to trigger childhood memories and increase her anxieties;[6] we therefore progressed carefully and gradually, guided by hints from the girl's own behavior.

---

*Recording Archive 1–20: "Recorded Music for Relaxation"

Slowly, while preserving the relaxed "Orphean" style of the music, we progressed to Active Relaxation Exercises as developed and described by Joseph Wolpe (1958).[7] His original system did not include music in such exercises, this was to be our own contribution. As already mentioned earlier in this book, music which is typified by soothing elements, by its very nature influences the spontaneous formation of breathing patterns and to a lessening of anxiety.

Physiologically, anxiety involves an extreme reaction of the sympathetic system, such as contraction of the peripheric blood vessels and hence pallor, an increase in pulse rate, in blood pressure, and swift, shallow breathing. All these lead to a decrease of oxygen in the blood stream, even to fainting. When the rate and depth of breathing can be moderated, the oxygen input to the bloodstream increases, resulting in a lessening of pulse rate, of blood pressure, etc.

In addition it should be noted that a focus on physical actions transfers concentration from the source of anxiety and assists in reducing its dominance. Furthermore, the clearly defined framework of hospitalization and biological therapy were of help to Rita in finding her way back to life.

In the 1960s the technique of guided imagery through music as developed by Helen Bonny and Louis Savary (1990), was still unknown, and this combination of Wolpe's relaxation methods with music composed of soothing sounds was the result of personal experiment on my part. Emphasis was placed on a combination of verbal guidance and suggestive sounds,[8] in accordance with the patient's reactions.

It is worth noting that even though Paul and Trimble (1970) had not yet published their research, clinical observation indicated that the presence of the therapist, and hence the possibility of adapting both verbal and musical guidance according to the reactions of the patient were what contributed to a sense of security, and the process of achieving relaxation.

Paul and Trimble examined thirty students who were subjected to three different systems of guidance by means of ready prepared recordings, hypnosis, and with a live instructor who would vary his verbal guidance for active relaxation exercises in accordance with the given situation. It was found that the prerecording was certainly the least desirable system, resulting in increased pulse rate, decreased muscle tone and other reactions comparable with a stress situation. Similarly there was little difference between this system and the results achieved by hypnosis.

I should like to emphasize here that the relaxation process should be seen as only one of the tools of therapy, not as a substitute for deep psychotherapeutic treatment. Hence it was decided that relaxation exercises by means of music should be employed as a prelude to sessions with the psychiatrist. In this way it would be possible to gauge their effectiveness in influencing Rita to be more cooperative in her verbal dynamic sessions.

About five months after Rita had been hospitalized, a new chapter was opened. After about twenty minutes of music therapy relaxation she agreed to discuss her sensations and experiences during the relaxation phase. She did this in a variety of creative ways: writing a short poem, sketching, sometimes composing music. Of these three, it should be noted that her only previous experience was in the graphic arts. Writing and music were new to her, and were incorporated in various ways into a medium with which she was familiar. It seemed as if this sudden outburst of creativity came as the result of a lengthy and indispensable period of incubation.

Out of a vast amount of creative effort over a period of two-and-a-half years of both individual and group therapy, I have chosen six examples for analysis.[9]

MUSIC THERAPY: SECOND STAGE. CREATIVE FLOW

For the first time during music therapy, Rita drew a sketch. She called it "Dead City" (see Plate 1). This was at a time when she refused to participate in visual art therapy. At my request, after she had completed her drawing, she described it in words and about a week later improvised a melody. It is interesting to note that she sang this while looking at her drawing, not at the words of her poem. The process seemed to be drawing, writing a poem, and then improvising music to picture.

> Crosses on the Dead City.
> The church is empty
> Empty is the church and the light in the windows is dark
> The man with the eyes
> The man with the blue eyes is dead
> The heavens died with him.
> The man is dead.
> The woman is empty
> And so am I.
> The man who was father –
> A father was.

Transcription from the Recording:*

Among other aspects of art therapy we find a means of organizing fantasy which allows the channelling of emotions, sublimation and control. At this stage Rita was still incapable of expressing her feelings and thoughts in words. Sketching or drawing, which was her most natural attribute, emerged only after a prolonged process of reducing her anxieties. Writing poems and improvising tunes revealed to her an

---

*R.P. Recording Archive 1: "Composing Songs in Music Therapy"

Plate 1. "Dead City"

aspect of her personality of which she had so far been unaware, but which she had now integrated in a positive manner into her visual creative abilities.

These variegated artistic expressions served as a new basis for conversation with her psychiatrist, once Rita had agreed to show him her works. This facilitated a greater profundity of artistic expression during music therapy, an elaboration within, by means of the artistic agent, in this case leaving verbal working through to psychotherapy. During the process that Rita underwent, art served as a window through which emotional content could be glimpsed, both in form and in color, as well as in sounds and in words.

The use of linguistic metaphor is something which intensifies during latency and adolescence, since it aids the youngster to veil his or her language. Ambiguous metaphors assisted Rita in giving veiled expression to what she was experiencing: the "Empty Church," the "Mother-Woman empty," and so is she. The "Dead City," "Dead Heavens," and a dead father; the crosses which link the empty church to her father's death, and the whole town seeming to serve as the father's grave. Such metaphors, derived from her Catholic upbringing, held great significance for Rita and her attempts at self-expression. Not only did they bring her pain out into the open, thus moderating it and lessening its intensity, they also constituted aesthetic creations which could be considered, perused and listened to.

Regarding the tune she improvised, it contains sudden jumps which in her performance resembled screams.* The finale also somehow peters out, the tune changes meter, is not anchored in any central sound and lacks a clear sense of direction. This could be interpreted as total lack of balance, but also as a courageous attempt at free-style creation with no instrumental support and in a style totally at variance with the relaxation music she had been hearing in the first stages of therapy.

It seemed to me that the latter interpretation was the more appropriate, and that after five months of limited verbal interaction, with an emphasis on a lessening of anxieties, Rita was now beginning to display certain mental powers and confidence which gave hope for a positive prognosis.

In the drawing of the "Dead City," there are opposing motifs whose combination gives a sense of the dramatic: the drooping crosses, as opposed to firm, straight lines; the use of three bold primary colors (red, blue and yellow) firmly enclosed within clear boundaries, giving a sense of imprisoned strength; even when a soft, curving line is introduced, it is trapped within a strict rectangle. These features can be distinguished in the bold colors and firm linear formations which cover the entire page, despite the images of death and desolation, the cross, as well as being a symbol of death and mourning, can also hint at hope. About a month after the Dead City, there began to emerge a whole series of sketches of infants. Immediately after completing the first (see Plate 2) she composed words and music for it, while studying the picture:

---

*Cassette 1: ibid.

Like a bad baby
Reaching out for the world's web, to tear it apart
Screaming with its eyes
At its good mother –

Transcription from the Recording:*

In her later drawing of the "Traffic Light" (see Plate 3) Rita endows the infant with talons or knives at its fingertips, but at the same time these might be wings. The talons rip at the web of the world that maltreats her, while simultaneously helping her to escape. The web is depicted as a spiral within which she finds herself trapped, but despite the fear there is an attempt to break out. As with the Traffic Light drawing, the eyes are expressionless black orbs, such is the infant which, in her phrase "screams with its eyes."

Rita depicts herself as bad and her mother as good. On the one hand she has internalized the badness she experienced in childhood and identifies herself as being bad, but on the other hand she uses the defence mechanism of Undoing and describes her mother as Good. My assumption here was that she was referring to her biological mother who was anything but good to her. Probably the very concept of mother-hate arouses within her deep-rooted anxieties which she is still unable to confront.

During this amazing outburst of sudden activity, Rita began to express those fantasy-fears which troubled her, and to master them by transferring them to, and developing them within, various artistic modalities. Furthermore, at this stage (as opposed to previously), she was losing her inhibitions about displaying open aggression. In her day-to-day behavior, however, she remained quiet and withdrawn. It would take another six months before she would dare express aggression outside the music therapy room.

As far as her music was concerned, this was characterized by a descending chromatic movement through the first six bars, something which gave it a dirge-like character.

The verb "to tear" appears, in her mother tongue, at the end of the sentence, the upward jump of a full octave on the ninth bar gives this word a sudden, dramatic

---

*R.P. Recording Archive 2: "Composing Songs in Music Therapy"

Plate 2. "Web"

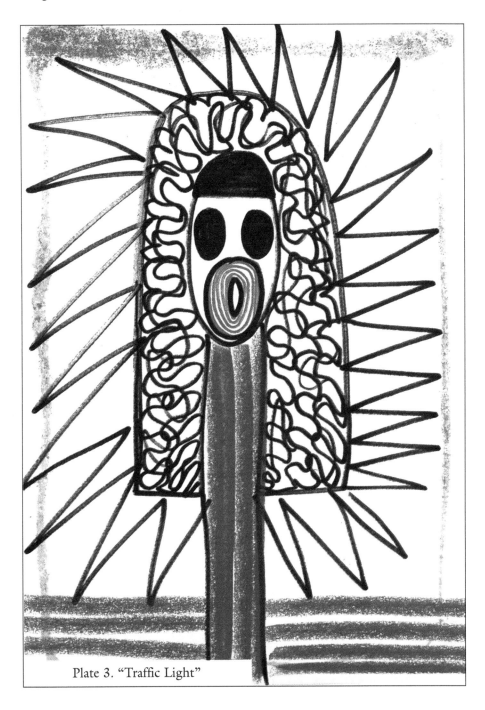

Plate 3. "Traffic Light"

stress. In the four ensuing bars Rita repeats the words "screaming with its eyes," thus giving added emphasis. The closure is on the opening note which is maintained under the words "at its good mother." Emphasis is originated by monotonous repetition. It is possible that Rita felt the need to express this phrase as some kind of a relic of magical thinking, as if unvarying repetition would transform the words into a magic truth. Whatever the case, even without her being consciously aware of what she was doing in music, it was music which reinforced her verbal content.

About two months after the first Infant sketch, Rita produced a drawing of a black-and-red "Traffic Light" (see Plate 3) based this time on a poem she had already composed:

> Screaming like a traffic light
> With deadened eyes
> No world
> Not for me.
> That sound
> That good sound
> Not for me.
> Everything I touch,
> Destroyed, dead and gone.
> All that could be
> Gone.
> Not for me.
> And the nightmare
> Those eyes
> Always
> Gazing down at me –
> The cross
> Oh, merciful Jesus
> Always they crucify
> Strike the same place.
> I am the evil,
> It is I who weep
> I who wound.*

As in the previous picture, the eyes and the harsh light are familiar motifs; so are the cross and the self-blame for evil. But now there is a certain subject development: she sees herself as undeserving of the good things such as "That good sound" (presumably a reference to relaxation music heard in the initial stages of therapy). Since she is bad, and everything she touches is destroyed and dies, goodness "is not for me." It is possible that here we encounter guilt feelings regarding the death of her adoptive father, as if within her magical thought framework he died, as it were, through her own touch.

---

*R.P. Recording Archive 2: As above

Here too we can perceive the internalization of the character of the biological mother, in which Rita pictures herself not only as the evil and the wounder, but also as the weeper.

Verbally, she showed no interest in, or need for, explanation of those "crucifying eyes," although it was clear that she had vivid and harsh memories of her mother's threatening face looking down at her. This was something which justified the extreme caution regarding use of the supine position during relaxation exercises.

In the Traffic Light picture, Rita portrays herself as a rigid object disseminating a razor-sharp radiation. The eyes are opaque, as if blind to the world, as if to say: "being blind means being invisible, and hence invulnerable." The mouth is the red light (in previous drawings the mouth does not appear) sounding a warning, perhaps screaming it. The mouth is the center, perhaps a representation of the infant still screaming within her. In this instance, as already mentioned, the picture came after the poem, something which perhaps suits a mouth which already exists and is possibly learning to speak.

On the other hand Rita felt no need to improvise any music for this poem. During the following few months we devoted the major part of therapy sessions to open expressions of anger and aggression. This was done by playing large percussion instruments, and music popular with adolescents at that time. I also encouraged Rita to compose songs for various performances within the confines of the hospital.[10]

Rita emerged as a ready and willing composer and songwriter and seemed to enjoy appearing at occasional performances in which I would support her on the piano, and recruit a percussion group from among the other patients. Such music, which answered the physical and emotional needs of adolescents and was characterized by repetitive drum beats, extreme dynamics, simple melodies, and lyrics which appealed to teenagers, served to enhance Rita's standing in the eyes of her peers, and certainly reinforced her own self-confidence. As a result of these activities, toward the end of this first year, when a group of five adolescents (including Rita) were released from hospitalization they continued to attend weekly music therapy as outpatients.

Once released from hospital, Rita shared an apartment with two others of her own age group and found a job at the sales counter in a music shop.

During this period the "Infant Drawings" continued for a time. Two additional examples: In the first (see Plate 4) Rita refers to herself in the first person:

> I am the baby
> With the red feet
> With the red hands
> Ripping and tearing*
> Yelling and sprouting
> In a scream.**

---

*Words unclear in original recording; this is a possible translation.
**R.P. Recording Archive 4: "Composing Songs in Music Therapy"

Plate 4. "Red-Handed Baby"

Rita continues to scream, to rip and to tear, and to bleed from the hands and feet with which she arrived more than once at the hospital—she describes them as "red," the eyes remain blank, the mouth again disappears, but in the poem it does in fact play a role. Despite the fact that the infant stumbles, the lines and colors continue to display a certain decisiveness and strength. Even the lyric includes such a word as "sprouting":

> Yelling and sprouting
> In a scream –

About a week after the sketch and the poem, the tune emerged.
Transcription from the Recording:

Again we encounter the chromatic phenomenon which adds dramatic tension to verbal content. However, in this instance there is a chromatic rise, as opposed to the descent we witnessed previously. This rising scale is impressive within itself: Rita holds a pause between bars, and where the infant is "ripping and tearing" she jumps a seventh, and retains this sound for the words "Yelling and Sprouting," then continues a semitone in order to stress the final words: "In a Scream."

There can be no doubt that here we see a clear correlation between words and music, additional proof that the music therapy patient does not need a priori familiarity with the medium. All that is needed is that she be exposed to sufficient stimuli and the opportunity for spontaneous reaction in order to create her own form of personal expression and the chance of revealing within herself her own "music child."

There ensued a further year of group music therapy in which emphasis was laid on socialization, group creative activity, group discussion of individual and mutual creativity, and physical-musical experiences suited to the needs and urges of the adolescent, etc.

The following year saw an additional improvement in Rita's condition which found expression in greater self-confidence, relationships with her own age group, and a stability in her relationship with her adoptive mother. At this point I would like to introduce another of her creations (see Plate 5) in which she refers to herself in the first person. In this case music and words were created together, while the picture came later.

I am the baby
That stretched out its hands
And managed from the void to emerge

Transcription from the Recording:*

Rita has already recognized the infant's ability to emerge "from the void" and to reach out.

Similar to her previous sketch (see Plate 2) the "Web of the World" is again represented as an entrapping spiral, but its colors are now soft and varied. Color emerges from color and they intermingle. The infant remains featureless, but its arms are longer, reaching out to the world. Technically, Rita began with the inner yellow circle, and then expanded it with both colors and space, only as a last stage did she add the infant. It would seem that she had no need any more for aggressive expression and could now afford to reveal a certain tenderness, perhaps the "good woman" within her.

This time the tune was tonal (d minor), but at its conclusion with the words "from the void" she reverted to that same chromatic mannerism we have already mentioned. On the final word "to emerge," she returned to the central note, closing it off by a descending octave. The song emerges as stable, and its tonal framework certainly serves as a true reflection of Rita's mental condition. As we have already seen, many patients who undergo music therapy with no previous musical experience, reveal a parallel between verbal and musical development, and integration of personality.

The last example presented here (see Plate 6) was not accompanied by music. Rita made this sketch and composed this poem during a group session devoted to guided imagery through music. In place of verbal discussion, each patient was invited to express his experiences by means of the art medium most suited to him at that moment.

Like a bird which can fly
Like a bird to the clouds
Like a bird
Which grew wings.
Its feather's no longer clipped
They are fine, and well-shaped
To a body, complete, which is mine.
Like a new bird blazing with color
like a bird first spreading its wings
This is me.**

---

*R.P. Recording Archive 15: As above
**R.P. Recording Archive 17: As above

Plate 5. "Reach Out"

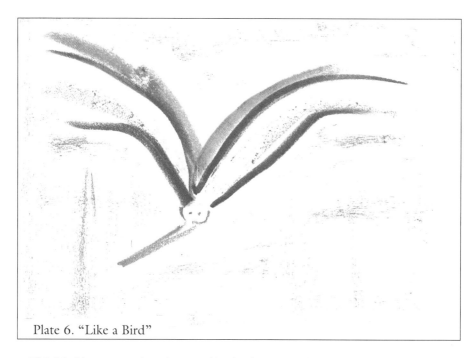

Plate 6. "Like a Bird"

This bird has grown its wings and its body is complete, it senses its own beauty and its ability to fly into the clouds. Rita claims center place in her own picture—the surrounding space is now open before her.

Three months later Rita concluded her treatment and left the music therapy group.

CONCLUSION

In this chapter I have presented examples of the use of appropriate relaxing music as a prelude to treatment of continuing anxiety. As an example I chose an adolescent girl who suffered severe and continuous traumas during her first three years. Despite the fact that she was later adopted by a warm and loving family and enjoyed the best of family life and a good education, she remained emotionally scarred, and this served to sabotage her personal and societal development. During mid-adolescence, a period of significant psychological and physiological change, she underwent an additional trauma with the death of her adoptive father. As a result, her situation deteriorated, she attempted suicide and was committed to a psychiatric hospital. During a five-month period of individual music therapy she underwent a process of relaxation and guided imagery, and thus learned to decrease her psychophysiological symptoms of anxiety and to cooperate in psychotherapy.

In the next stage, described here as the "Creative," music therapy concentrated on the traumatic elements which emerged in various forms of artistic expression: drawing, poetry, improvising music, and later on composing pop songs and group work on material suited to a teenage mentality.

By means of the examples already presented, it was possible to follow the process of ego formation from childhood trauma and a self-image of an "Evildoer with a Cross to bear," to the release of the tortured infant within her and its transformation into a free-flying bird.

By expressing emotional content through a variety of artistic media, she was able to achieve more confidence and greater insight. In this respect one can see in the patient's expressions an example of what Freud called an artistic reorganization of neurotic symptoms and urges. Organization which serves both as sublimation and communication (Freud 1909).

At the same time this can also be seen as a model which supports the Kleinian school of thought regarding the nature of art as correcting and rehabilitating the infant's anxieties and destructive impulses towards the object (Klein 1929). According to Melanie Klein, the subconscious strives to rehabilitate those objects which the imagination has destroyed (and which in Rita's case were destroyed in reality).

Both in her poems and in her drawings of infants Rita displayed a developmental line. At the outset the infant was depicted as "Bad," a year later—after her release from hospital (as an outpatient)—she openly identified with the infant as herself, as a creature which despite its sufferings grows and develops. After a further year we encounter an infant which reaches out and "Emerges from the Void." Through these three examples one can perceive a rehabilitation of the "inner-infant" image by means of artistic expression, and through this process an improvement in object relation, something which also found expression in verbal psychotherapy.

This same phenomenon can be perceived concerning her self-image as an adolescent, or maturing person, according to the following examples:

1. Dead City. She is dead and empty like all the people and objects which surround her.

2. Traffic Light. She is still unworthy: "No world, not for me. Everything I touch, destroyed, dead and gone." Nevertheless, there is already a reference to accusing eyes gazing down at her (presumably an oblique reference to her biological mother).

3. Like a Bird. In this example from the final stages of therapy she can already view herself in a positive light, like someone whose wounds have been treated and is now undergoing a process of renewal. Still delicate—but complete.

Instead of submitting to deep-rooted fearful imaginings, Rita found a way to master them through artistic expression. This was a tripartite role: visual, verbal, and musical.

In conclusion I would point out an additional developmental line which emerged during Rita's treatment. At the outset we encountered an anxiety-ridden young girl, lacking any initiative, who underwent receptive music therapy. As a result she gradually began to cooperate and turn the passive process into the active, during which she learned to overcome anxiety states. Once she had gained sufficient self-confidence she was then able to translate painful content into powerful artistic expression. Such strength and self-control led to growing self-confidence and faith in her own self and in others: in other words—growth and independence.

VII

ALON

FROM THE JUNGLE
TO THE KING'S PALACE

D.I.M.T. with a child suffering from MBD and elective mutism

INTRODUCTION

This concluding case history presents the problems facing the music therapist when confronted with a combination of both psychological and physiological handicaps. For these reasons I have chosen to relate the case of
Alon, who was born at term, probably with a minimal neurological defect which
was only detected when he first entered primary school. In his early years Alon
suffered from various physical complaints and also developed elective mutism.

At the outset of music therapy the strategy was that of "holding" with an emphasis on stability and calm. Despite the importance of this for Alon's emotional
condition, it should be stressed that as long as his psychological problems were
dealt with in the above mentioned atmosphere no positive changes were accom-
plished. On the other hand, once the therapeutic approach was modified and the
neurophysiological ailments were treated by stimulative music, there began a dramatic change in his psychological state. This example indicates the need, from time
to time, for a balance between the use of relaxing and stimulating music during
therapy, and demonstrates music's potential for awakening emotional processes
through the physical being, and thus creating a breakthrough to verbal expression
and to hitherto repressed content.

ALON: PATIENT PROFILE

Alon, the youngest of six children, had a normal birth. His mother was an art
teacher and his father was an office worker. Alon was bottle fed for his first four
months and then preferred semiliquid foods up to the age of six. His parents were
extremely concerned by his recurrent upper respiratory infections, which ham-
pered his ability to perform essential functions such as breathing, sucking and
eating. Perhaps due to this, they paid less attention to the delay in Alon's motor
skills, and to his limited ability for verbal communication which emerged during
pre-kindergarten child care. In fact Alon would speak only at home.

When he was three and a half years old Alon underwent tonsillectomy and
adenoidectomy. While these operations succeeded from a physical point of view,
the psychological symptoms of disturbed communication became more severe. As
a result Alon was referred to a psychological clinic and was diagnosed as suffering
from elective mutism.[1] E.E.G. examination revealed no pathology, and due to
Alon's noncooperation it was impossible at this stage to carry out an accurate
neurodevelopmental examination.

The difficulties encountered in psychotherapy raised the question of alternative
approaches, and so his family, together with the consultant psychologist, referred
Alon to music therapy, with the indication that music could serve as a preverbal
medium capable of circumventing speech.[2]

Since Alon never spoke outside of the family circle, I decided to conduct the first
intake and observation in his own home before starting in the music therapy clinic.
In this way I was able to observe his behavior and how he would make contact
within an environment in which he would make use of speech, as opposed to the
outside world.

Before going into details about the psychological aspects of the case and the elective mutism syndrome, I would like to present a brief outline of the dominant features observed during the intake process which describe Alon's sensory, motor and vocal development.

VOCAL DEVELOPMENT

1. Able to pronounce all syllables and to speak within the family circle, and to a limited extent during music therapy.
2. While speaking, emphasizes the musical characteristics of speech, rather than its verbal meaning.
3. No emotional correspondence between speech content and its musical components.
4. Strong tendency to alliteration.
5. Stops speaking when sensing even a minor threat.
6. Vocal intensity in the music room limited, from *pp* to *p*.
7. Tendency to swallow syllables and accelerate toward the end of sentences.
8. Is, however, able to pronounce all syllables.

SENSORY-MOTOR DEVELOPMENT

1. General hypotonia.
2. Inadequate ability to hop or jump according to chronological age.
3. Cannot skip.
4. Crawling normal, but slow for his age.
5. Left-right drum beating unskilled, often drops the drumsticks.
6. Does not maintain consistent beat-unit; has difficulty in repeating a rhythm pattern.
7. Plays xylophone at random, and has difficulty maintaining visual-motor contact.
8. Inability to cross midline in play.
9. Inadequate pincher grasp and finger separation.
10. Poor graphic skills.
11. General dependence on Activities of Daily Living (A.D.L.).
12. Avoids physical contact.
13. Needs and enjoys vestibular stimulation.
14. Other sensory channels appear normal.

According to this data Alon would seem to be a hypotonic child with immature motor development, as well as apraxia of both gross and fine motor skills.

Speech was orderly, but its musical aspects, which in my view are linked with emotion, were impaired. It is quite possible that it was his hypotonia which caused poor dynamics, babbling and acceleration.

So far so good regarding Alon's vocal and sensory-movemental development. In order to fill in the picture we must now consider his psychological development.

Elective mutism has been defined as "persistent refusal to talk in one or more major social situations, including school, despite ability to comprehend spoken language and to speak" (DSM-III-R 1987, 88).

Differential diagnosis includes speech defects emanating from mental retardation, autism, hearing problems, depression, etc. Elective mutist children, however, can talk and understand even though there can occasionally occur a delay in the development of speech and difficulties of articulation, particularly after emigration and a conflict of languages.

The mutism is accompanied by additional symptoms: social isolation, physical repulsion, negativism, compulsive traits, passive aggression, fear of change and dependence on key figures, shyness, temper tantrums, school refusal, etc. (ibid.). This begins after the acquisition of speech, but is often only fully revealed within an educational framework. It can last for a few weeks, occasionally even for a few years. The average is about one percent of those referred to psychological treatment, slightly more girls than boys. Families are often typified by overprotectiveness and by a prolongation of the child's infancy.

Psychiatric literature describes the causes of elective mutism as being liable to emerge from early oral trauma, early hospitalization, as well as already mentioned, bilingual conflicts resulting from emigration (Harold et al. 1981, 904).

The negative trends and the mutism are generally directed at the parents, even though the silence is expressed away from home. More than once this dynamic of nonspeech has been observed between parents themselves (Browne et al. 1963).

Regarding Alon, his own mutism, as observed in educational and therapeutic setting, was expressed in a total lack of verbal communication outside the family circle, as well as in a syndrome of isolation, physical repulsion and shyness, in compulsive behavior and in passive aggression.

THERAPEUTIC ANALYSIS AND CONSIDERATION

Alon suffered from a wide variety of developmental problems:

1. Neurological defects which included hypotonia and apraxia whose treatment had been postponed due to the greater urgency of other medical disorders. Rejection of touch could have been either the result of neurological immaturity, or an emotional side effect of surgery. The desire for vestibular stimulation might indicate movemental deprivation, but perhaps also a lack of initial experience at an early age. In other words Alon showed an attempt to improve his low muscle tone, which had been hampering development.

As already mentioned, motor deprivation may harm body scheme development and thus undermine the child's overall sense of confidence. Functions such as following the mother while crawling on the floor and comprehending "object permanency" may be impaired. This is also the case at a later stage, when connecting with and playing with other children. And indeed during Alon's treatment the assumptions based on observation were in fact verified: it emerged that his neurological damage, worsened by his physical condition, had served as a significant factor in his emotional development.

2. Medical problems at an early age, such as the upper respiratory infections, in an area considered to be from a developmental point of view essential to the infant's oral gratification.

Melany Klein (1955 in Mitchell 1986) stresses that oral frustration may well increase sadistic oral impulses aimed at the mother. In other words, along with the internalization of pleasurable substances, the infant also internalizes pain and dissatisfaction and so links these with the source of nourishment. At an early stage breast or bottle, which serve as part-objects, are conceived by the infant as total and a total part of itself. This connection is reinforced by the mother who regards food as representing herself. Normal feeding symbolizes acceptance of motherhood, but food refusal signifies rejection. The more the infant develops negative experiences the greater its sadistic fantasies, and hence guilt feelings and anxieties. One of the most primitive infantile defense mechanisms is "splitting," the ego divides between "good" and "bad," thus enabling it to destroy the "bad" object. "Splitting, provided it is not excessive and does not lead to rigidity, is an extremely important mechanism of defense which not only lays the foundation for later and less primitive mechanisms, like repression, but continues to function in a modified form throughout life" (Klein in Segal 1974, 36).

Indeed during Alon's treatment "splitting" emerged as a central theme. Anna Freud emphasizes the links between normal functioning of the oral area and normal psychological development. According to her, while eating in itself is a biological function (a response to the visceroceptive stimulus of hunger and of salivating), eating problems, even though organic in origin, can serve as the basis for development of neurotic anxieties. When the mother has to feed her infant against his will he is liable to develop feelings of hostility and frustration toward her; similarly the gradual variations of diet define his future preferences and rejections.

"Organic feeding disorders become the basis for the nonorganic types. Neurotic disturbances arise more easily where loss of pleasure in the function of eating has prepared the ground for them" (A. Freud 1946, 131). As we shall see, this was proven during therapy when there began to emerge elements of oral-sadism.

Indeed, it seemed to me that the combination of basic neurological immaturity, and frequent illnesses in U.R.T. during infancy had affected Alon's oral area which serves as the focus of contact and pleasure in the first stages of life. This problem became more crucial as the result of surgery on already sensitive and painful organs. According to Erikson (1950), normal development of the oral area is central to the creation of basic trust and primary object-relation.[3]

Roberston and Bowlby (1952) and Bowlby (1960), researched the effects of hospitalization on children under the age of four. Observation revealed that even those who were hospitalized for short periods underwent the following stages: protest (due to anxiety at being separated from the parent), despair, and then denial (these latter two serving as defense mechanisms). It appears that even after the 1950s, when parents were permitted to remain in hospital at the child's bedside, the same stages could be observed. The very experience of being cut off from home, and the traumas of hospitalization, surgery and treatment, sufficed to create such reactions. Jessner and Kaplan (1949) stress that mouth and throat operations, despite the fact that these generally demand only brief hospitalization, are liable to be very psychologically injurious.

It can be assumed that Alon, who in any case underwent a difficult period of oral development, became fixated at the protest stage and expressed this by elective mutism and isolation.

Roth et al. (1967), suggests that the more complex the child's progress from one developmental stage to the next, the greater the imprints of the preceding stage.

On the assumption that his mutism was a symptom of deep anxiety and that stressing it might be of no help, I told Alon that "in the music room it's forbidden to talk, here we just play, and converse, through music." In this paradoxical approach I saw a chance of diminishing his mutism by means of extremely exaggerating it. It seemed that at this stage Alon should be accepted as is, and that the role of the therapist was to create a supportive atmosphere for expression. Similarly he should be given, in a symbolic manner, the chance to experience a sense of holding, with the therapist assuming the role of "the good enough mother," a term coined by Winnicott (1971).[4]

My assumption was that it would be best to deal first and foremost with Alon's passive aggression and to let it find expression in an atmosphere of trust, both through diverting aggressive emotions to the primary agent (music) and then by transmitting those same emotions to the secondary agent (therapist). Similarly, due to both physical and psychological considerations, it would be preferable to deal with oral and respiratory problems by means of wind instruments, flutes, trumpets, whistles, etc., thus circumventing the need for speech.[5]

His posture problem seemed to be less urgent, his psychological condition seemed to demand more immediate attention. In retrospect this might have been an error of judgement since effective therapy should include body-mind integration from the outset. Nevertheless, during the first fourteen months of therapy Alon made slow but steady progress; he was gaining confidence and basic trust. At home he would talk as usual, but in the music room extremely briefly (something he started doing the moment that "paradoxical rule" was proposed). He still had no verbal contact with children or adults within any other framework. During music therapy sessions his voice remained introverted and subdued; despite any encouragement he remained incapable of shouting, or of expressing anger. It was as if he had a hidden lump in his throat.

All this time he was being treated by modal and tonal music with a permanent continuity, rhythmic repetition, mid-range pitch, simple melodies and traditional harmony. Most themes were adopted from his own fragmentary efforts, and were repeated as they were, or when necessary arranged by the therapist: sometimes by playing, as an unaccompanied song, or in a combination of both.

This kind of music, which developed during observation, gave him room for creativity without being pressured, and freedom to game-play without educational and other demands. In other words, the musical organization described below actually served as a clearly supportive framework within which he was able to act freely.

This supportive framework was created within the therapeutic space: vacant in its centre, but with instruments readily available next to, and hanging on, the walls.

In this way Alon could choose movement, instrumental playing, or listening, according to his needs. The role of the therapist was to reassure the self-confidence derived from the music and the space in which it took place, and at the same time to encourage significant expression with no anxieties. This was done both by music and words.

Despite the fact that Alon's self-confidence increased, it should be emphasized that his posture remained slack and defeatist and he had difficulties in expressing his emotions.

Since music therapy cannot be defined as one of the exact sciences, it was hard to predict whether another form of music, ecstatic for example, would automatically provoke a different response. It is possible that these fourteen months were essential for the establishment of basic trust. Whatever the case, at the end of this period there occurred a number of changes both at home and within the educational framework which led to a severe regression in Alon's condition.

There were a change in kindergarten teachers and the loss of a father figure for a number of months. It appeared that anxiety in the face of loss influenced him to such an extent that his mutism became total even at home, his movements came to resemble the stereotype of an autistic child, and he would mouth into the microphone sighs, gurgles and the sound of vomiting. I interpreted these as a sign of despair and almost passive protest, which demanded a reassessment of the therapeutic approach.*

THE JUNGLE

The sudden worsening of Alon's condition seemed to indicate that supportiveness, constancy, musical and verbal mirroring, even relaxing conditions, were still not enough to enable him to stand against the anxiety-ridden changes with which he was confronted at this stage.

In kindergarten he began to undergo developmental-occupational therapy, but the results were not evident, either at home or in the music room. Quite the opposite, it seemed as if muscular hypotonia and "mental hypotonia" were being more and more closely linked. Despite grave doubts about a drastic change in the manner of therapy, I nevertheless decided on such a step, knowing that certain boundaries would still be retained: the therapeutic space, the therapist, the content, and the familiar musical instruments.

This new approach was aimed at creating something similar to the dynamics of ecstatic healing rituals in which movemental, some times vocal, and other expressive elements are taken to the extreme (see Chapter 1). In these the shaman drums and dances, serves as a model for the patient and thus legitimizes freedom of movement, and dramatic role playing.

As a consequence, at our next session Alon was confronted with some ten minutes of music: drums recorded at a voodoo ceremony in Haiti. I had also set up in the music room something resembling a tent and explained to Alon that this was the "lair of the beast."

---

*A.H. Recording Archive, Cassette 10: "Music Therapy as a Bypass to Speech"

There were several considerations involved:

1. There was a chance that such music might stimulate the child into spontaneous movement leading to increased muscle tone, swifter movement and hence to an outlet for aggressive energy.

2. Within Alon's magical thinking, animals might be employed as metaphorical sources for strength and brutality.

3. The tent might represent a limited intermediate area[6] as a place of refuge. On the other hand, the more expansive intermediate area (the room itself) could be the space into which he would emerge, expand, and try out new experiences.

At this stage of assessment and interpretation there was no guarantee that Alon would in fact react to such musical stimulation, to the offer of the "lair," or indeed to the vocal-movemental example he was due to get from the therapist.

In retrospect it can be said that the new (ecstatic) music and the borrowed metaphor of the beast's lair had a dramatic impact on Alon from the very first moment. He began to run around the room as if in a trance, leaping, somersaulting, roaring, hurling cushions, beating on drums and cymbals—all this, it should be noted, according to the tempo and intensity dictated by the recording with no need for intervention or modeling on the part of the therapist.

Once this was all over, he crept into the lair and started speaking through the tent wall, acting out the role of a vicious man-eating tiger. At this stage I supported his aggressiveness with drum beats and verbal mirroring.*

By role playing within the beast's lair, Alon split the world into "goodies" and "baddies." He placed himself among the "baddies" while counting me (and the piano) among the "goodies." His role was to devour; my role was that of the victim. In a similar manner he divided up the musical instruments: drums, cymbals and the flute were bad, while guitar, piano and fiddle were good. This revealed the stage of fixation in which he was at present situated and the need to deal with splitting.

An example of the content he expressed verbally from within the tent:

The snake will bite you, strike you—like all the other beasts you'll be caught. Your face will be devoured, your tent collapse—the stinking drum be banished. They'll hate it, be angry and tear the jungle apart. You'll be dead, they'll give you a dangerous drink— poison. Retarded beasts will beat the mother of this sweet child—will strike the sweet sun and the blue heavens....

The above is only a small example of what Alon came out with during that same session, but it serves to show just how much built-up fury he had inside, and how much energy had been required to repress it.

It was the stimulus of ecstatic music and its consequent physical freedom which led to his ability to express his aggressions through music-play, and hence communicate them to his therapist. My task at this stage was to contain, support through music and words, and give the child the feeling that his aggression was not necessarily destructive of the object.[7]

---

*A.H. Recording Archive 12: "Reinforcing Emotional Content with Music"

About halfway through this therapy session Alon emerged from his lair and continued to speak in a kind of incantation,[8] accompanying himself on a drum with an accurate rhythm composed of repetitive structures:

It should be noted that after such intense movemental activity Alon's muscle tone undoubtedly increased, something which found expression in his stable rhythm on the drums. Whereas previously he would often lose hold of the drum sticks he now played with great strength and confidence. There was a certain paradox between his drumming and his incantation. I saw his drumming as the expression of his aggression, and his quiet intoning as that of his introversion and anxiety. Gradually the drumming, which by its nature is a physical activity, led to an increase of vocal dynamic and a closing of the gap between physical and verbal expression.

In his book *Human Aggression*, Anthony Storr (1968) emphasizes that aggression is not a reflex which vanishes when the stimulation which triggers it ceases, but rather a complex of physiological reactions which remain long after the original stimulus has been removed. Storr stresses the importance of finding a physical outlet for aggression which can enable the physiological symptoms to be gradually moderated.

During aggressive reaction, the adrenaline secretion into the bloodstream increases, thus creating a condition similar to the activity of the sympathetic system.[9] This can explain why Alon's frenzied musical activity (drums, movement and voice) was effective on two levels: the organization of movement and posture, and the release and hence moderation of aggressive energies.

In his case the kind of calm, melodic music employed during the first months of therapy would have been of no avail. Nevertheless it should be noted that D.I.M.T. does not limit treatment to the cathartic level of ecstatic healing ritual, but goes on to verbal elaboration and development by various techniques used in psychotherapy.

It appeared that the tempestuous music employed touched upon a sensitive spot in Alon's inner life which needed to be exposed and had not been reached by the verbal mirroring and nonmusical games activities usually practiced in child therapy. The music served to unlock a gate behind which lay a dense jungle.

Following the dramatic outburst of speech described above, the therapeutic space became Alon's jungle (as he saw it) in which he was free to act out the wild beast and transmit to the therapist his aggressive feelings to his full satisfaction. Only later was it possible to develop them verbally. Clear awareness of a make believe situation enabled him to be aggressive with no risk of guilt feelings.

At this stage, whenever I tried to start a session without an ecstatic musical opening, Alon would have difficulty entering into the role and would revert to his previous introverted dynamic. The music served not only as an opening, but also as a support for aggressive content when expressed in words, and as a summation and closing of the session.

Gradually, over a period of about sixteen months, the gap began to close between the introverted, mute and hypotonic child, and the impulsive, screeching wild animal.*

During the jungle stage the therapy session took on a kind of loosely built sonata format whose parts varied in duration and content according to the patient's needs and the therapeutic aims. As his skills increased, less time could be devoted to the technical stages of the opening and closing, and more to tackling psychological problems.**

Structure of the Therapeutic Session

A. OPENING	Ecstatic music, spontaneous movement.	10–15 min.
B. EXPOSITION	Speech: Alon defines roles and subjects	
C. DEVELOPMENT	Song, instrumental playing, movement, role playing, speech (realization and elaboration of exposition).	B + C = 30–40 min.
D. SUMMARY	Recapitulation: singing or conversing between patient and therapist	
E. CLOSING (Coda)	Soothing singing and/or playing: Relaxation: return from fantasy to reality:	D + E = 10–15 min.

During the jungle period it was impossible to ignore obvious oral elements, in particular fantasies of oral sadism: "I am an animal which eats you up; I bite, I poison, I swallow; I'll eat you, and Mom, and Dad." There was also a clear splitting between good and bad figures; and at the same time between music and between instruments. Such observation on the part of the therapist, relying on the psychodynamic definitions of psychosexual development as well as on the Kleinian concept of splitting were of great help in clarifying therapeutic goals and their realization.

In addition to the use of musical means and equipment, the lair, puppets and other properties to be found in the therapy room, Alon would also ask to hear recorded music, in particular such as would express evil. Out of a wide selection of works which were at his disposal and which he could try out on the tape recorder, at this stage he showed an overwhelming preference for two in particular: John Cage's *Solo No. 1*, and parts of Luciano Berio's *Sinfonia*, both of which employ unconventional vocality. Alon's choice, it seemed, was directly connected with his own psychological syndrome, and the free style of these works gave him the legitimacy he sought in order to make use of his own voice in a variety of ways within a wide dynamic.

---

*A.H. Recording Archive, Cassette 20: "Reinforcement of Emotional Content Through Music"
**A.H. Recording Archive, Cassette 26: "Aggressive Emotions in Music Therapy"

The end of this stage of therapy was reached when he began to express his aggressions not as a tiger or other wild animal but as Alon himself. Likewise he began to realize that good and bad can coexist, and that it was permissible to speak about fearful fantasies and even direct them toward his parents or other family members without being hurt and without destroying or losing them.

THE RECORDING STUDIO

After some sixteen months during which the therapeutic space was the jungle, Alon now transformed it into "the recording studio." This was made possible by his emerging strengths which enabled him to more closely approach the realities of the music room, and with the lessening of his need for aggressive expression. Alon now turned himself into a singer/musician and cast me in the role of recording engineer and/or musician when necessary. The structure of the therapy session remained similar but the opening and closing were reduced to a few minutes. The jungle had clearly turned into the studio when Alon started a session by chanting the following composition:

> This studio is new and strong—a very beautiful studio—the other studio was a little bit very old. We'd come into the studio, and what a stink it had! Until we started the music, skunks kept coming in through the door. Then we strengthened that studio. We lit lights when it was dark. We had to light two spotlights on the drums. Leaving is forbidden—we even locked the door. Leaving is forbidden: out there are the skunks who fart everything up—and after the skunks will come a bear and a monkey.
> Q: Do you feel safe in this studio?
> A: It's all O.K. We have to be in a studio. This is our home.*

This was his way of metaphorically describing the process he had undergone in building up a sense of trust in the therapy room (it used to be old and stank, now it is new, strong and handsome) and in music (the brightly lit drums which later banished the skunks with their music).

By speaking in the first person plural ("We'd come in—we started to play—we lit lights," etc.) he was acknowledging a joint effort and his faith in the therapist. On the other hand he still demonstrated anxiety about the outside world (skunks, bears, monkeys, figures from the previous jungle period), hence the locking of the door and "leaving forbidden."

The studio was "our home," a haven in which he could act out his fantasies without any risk. There was no doubt that the jungle images were a projection, or aggressive and dangerous representation, of inner content. I was still uncertain about Alon's ability at this stage to organize himself within the confines of the studio, and to gather enough strength to be able to function in a wider perspective than that of the existing therapeutic space.

This studio period lasted for some three months, during which Alon played the singer, accompanied himself on a variety of instruments of his own choosing, and emphasized the pure musical result no less than the emotional content.[10] Whereas

---

*A.H. Recording Archive, Cassette 30: "Organization Through Music"

during the previous stage he had preferred works by Cage and Berio, he now chose, from time to time, a wide range of pieces including Paul Winter's *Callings*, short excerpts from Mozart, classical jazz, songs by Israeli folk composer Sascha Argov, local children's songs, Jewish liturgy (mainly in the Sephardic style), and more. It seemed as if this expansion of choice served as the symbol for a similar expansion of his own potential for emotions and experiences. This was most evident in the variations within the dynamic and content of his verbal expression.

During this period Alon would speak quite freely within the music room, but not at the kindergarten. Nevertheless it was decided, on the basis of music therapy recordings which revealed his verbal and mental abilities, as well as on the opinion of a psychologist, to transfer him to a special class in a regular school.[11] At the outset of the school term he still did not employ speech as a means of communication, but this situation gradually improved, as did his overall organizational abilities.

As already noted, in music therapy Alon had begun to lay stress more and more on aesthetics, on rhythmic and melodic organization, and had begun to be extremely free in expressing his emotions both in music and in words.

The stimulative stage was now a mere two to three minutes of jumping on a trampoline with break dance music. Music drama was often within a framework of his own devising which recalled the Balinese gamelan ensemble. Alon would seat himself in the middle, surrounded by various percussion instruments, and would sing and accompany himself on whatever he fancied. Shifting from instrument to instrument and the need for coordination developed his movement skills and enabled him to achieve rich and variegated expression. Indeed the balance between tension and relaxation, retention and release, planning and improvisation (typical elements of musical creativity) were at their most evident during this studio period. In general, this was a period typified by organization and control, by the ability to repel or delay sudden impulse, by greater freedom of expression of sensations and emotions, by an accumulation of knowledge and experience, by the ability to express dissatisfaction, and by the forming of self-will. All these are characteristics of normal development during the psychosexual anal stage, and indeed this was a consideration which helped in determining therapeutic strategy.

Despite a certain similarity between the tent or lair and the gamelan circle, moving in and out of the circle displayed flexibility and ease. The lair was for hiding, whereas the circle was a symbol of the entire therapeutic space. Both Alon's movements and posture revealed a greater openness to his surroundings, as opposed to the curling-up introversion or the extravagant reactions to ecstatic music which typified the jungle period. Such openness could be discerned by a balance between contraction and extension: in other words stability opposing the force of gravity, and by inference, confidence in confronting the outside world. After about three months there were new subjects for discussion. Alon would raise them partially in his role as singer/musician, partially in verbal conversation:

Disasters: "The old lady upstairs died and they took her away to hospital in an ambulance."

Existential threats: "The skunks came back and got into the studio and the animals won't let the singer appear," etc.

Despite the fact that such content tended to renew his anxieties, Alon was by now able to face them without resource to his previous aggression and also without regression. He now had new and more varied strategies: relaxing by means of calming music, or performing a kind of musical dialogue in which he would play a variety of roles.

Skunks: "Mister singer, we've come to spoil your song."

Singer: "You're nothing more than a load of stinking skunks and I can scare you off. Scram! I've got drums and xylophones which can finish you off just like that!"

During one session he was seeking ways to resuscitate a woman who had died. He chose a doll which symbolized her and tried to revive her by breathing through a flute resting on her bosom. Convinced that this would not work he said, "Impossible. The dead are dead and it's all nonsense. She's got to be buried." And he did so—he discovered a "grave" beneath the mattress, laid the doll to rest and covered her with a blanket and then said, "That's it. We're finished for today. We've got to tidy up the room."* Here we can see how Alon employed rational thought when magical thoughts and deeds could not help him solve problems. I assumed that such subjects were linked with past disasters and could now be ventilated and elaborated. This marked the end of the studio stage. Alon was now ready for further development.

THE ROYAL PALACE

Gradually the recording studio became transformed into the "royal palace," a "wizard's tower" or a "knight's fortress." The fantasies were concentrated around a royal family generally composed of king, queen and prince.

At the outset of this stage Alon would arrange festivities, pageants and concerts within the palace. He would alternate as master of ceremonies, musician, actor, king and prince. I was cast as either queen or musician.

After about three months there began to emerge themes of sexual fantasy, envy and aggression. On one occasion the fantasy of the prince's marriage seemed to arouse great anxiety in Alon and he began to curse himself harshly with a soft percussion accompaniment. Since this episode seemed to signify some kind of exorcism, I should like to describe it in detail.

Alon arrived for therapy, and after a brief opening initiated a royal wedding for the prince which soon turned into the wedding of "The evil king and queen. He doesn't care if the Jews will die, won't be able to move, will be weak, will be sick, drink poison, won't go to the doctor, will die and won't be able to move."

At this point, having linked his fantasies of the royal family to his own, Alon paused for a moment and continued to direct his curses at himself, employing a soft drumming accompaniment with a constant relaxing rhythm:

"You're a dumbo, you're a son-of-a-bitch. You're stupid. You're an 'Ostimuck.' You're nothing. You should be hit. Weak, don't exercise. Don't go to the doctor. Drop dead! You'll never move."

*A.H. Recording Archive, Cassette 35: "Words and Music in Therapy"

Then he suddenly stopped, looked at me and yelled, "And don't you dare sing that stupid song. You hear? I can't stand this song. It's stuck to me. Yeah! Get rid of this song!"

I tried, by mirroring, to demonstrate that by singing it he had brought this song out, but he insisted that only music could banish it. And so I sang him a "Song of Exorcism" in which the piano accompaniment used chromatics to stress dramatic elements with a low range and a tense harmony. At the same time voice and words were repetitive with a calm and objective dynamic. Alon eventually relaxed, and requested a short repeat just in case some of the curses had remained within him. I added a few incantatory phrases using a few of his own words here and there as if it were a magic formula:

> The song has gone, has gone from you
> The song has gone – and vanished
> The song was gone when you sang it
> And now it pesters you less.

Alon seemed to be satisfied, and said, "Enough, enough. Let's do one more song and then finish."*

THE SONG OF EXORCISM

It would seem that during his entire therapy Alon had placed his trust in music as a means of relaxation, or self-defense, or a means of clarifying difficult situations. Even when he would shut himself off in the beast's lair he would sing and play, and even permit me to invade his privacy by means of singing or playing. Similarly, on occasions he would block the entrance to his lair with musical instruments but would still make use of singing and playing to transmit emotional messages. Some of these came across loud and clear even without the use of words. However, when he felt sufficiently confident he would add meaningful words to his instrumental playing. It should be mentioned here that above and beyond the significance that the music therapist attaches to the choice of instrument, most patients regard the instrument as capable of sounding threats while not being threatening in themselves, as opposed to verbal-vocality whose content is considered to be comparatively unequivocal.

During the first stage of therapy (before his regression) Alon had become acquainted with various musical instruments and had experienced the modeling of various ways of self expression through music and song, with the aid of careful and limited interpretation on the part of the therapist.

With his jungle outburst of speech he had begun to bestow emotional qualities on certain instruments, to express this verbally and to utilize his playing as a metaphor and an externalization of his emotions. During the organizational studio

---

*A.H. Recording Archive 45: "Magic Thinking and Its Expression in Music Therapy"

stage he played for its own sake, emphasizing control, aesthetics and harmony, and paying attention to the end product.

During the king's palace stage, whose content was without doubt of an oedipal character, his use of instruments became more sophisticated. For example while accusing himself he accompanied his harsh words with a gentle rhythm on drums and rattles, thus creating an ambivalence which enabled him to express his feelings without risk.

However, once the curses became too strong for him, he applied to me for musical support. In that instance I supported him by singing a soft repetitive incantation of key words while at the same time describing on the piano the tensions and anxieties they portrayed.

This is significant because in fact this was the first time that Alon had directly appealed to me for assistance: not for the tiger, not for the singer but for him, himself. He was not satisfied with the words offered in response: the devil within which expressed itself in song had to be exorcised by the same means, by song. Only after administering such first-aid could Alon be prepared to verbally describe what had happened.

This was a process in which music's preverbal role was dominant, and in which one could convey without words the musical message: "It seems that you fear the feelings which the curses arouse," as well as by incantation and repetition to ease the anxiety. The cursing occurred only twice, one week after another, and then Alon seemed to regain a certain emotional stability, and some five months before the conclusion of music therapy he began to talk at school and to become involved in social activity to a remarkable degree.

During his last five months of music therapy he continued to raise oedipal themes, particularly in variations on the tale he had created.

There was a king, a queen and a prince. They lived in a palace. At night cruel knights kidnapped the prince and turned him into a weak dumbo-boy. Then they regretted it and brought him back to his bed. Instead they killed the king, his father. The queen and the prince disappeared to another place, to another country.

All of these variations were based on the same motif which he had improvised (possibly from part of a well-known Israeli song he had once heard):

In the development of this story there was a systematic plot line which symbolically described Alon's growth and development. At the outset he improvised a song with no instrumental accompaniment. Next he chose certain instruments and accompanied his own singing with a dynamic identity between voice and instrument. Later he requested piano accompaniment which he received in carefully moderated doses.

At the sixth session Alon sang his story with a slight alteration of content:

When the king, queen and prince heard the knights storming the palace, they fought them. The prince was his father's staunchest supporter and the king said to him, "You are brave and strong." And in the end everyone celebrated, and the prince married Snow White, and the king married the queen, and this, this was the end.

Musically, Alon's singing here is clear and rich in dynamic expression. The piano accompaniment is mainly contrapuntal, both musically and emotionally. Voice and instrument interact smoothly. The keen listener will be able to distinguish that here the music therapist is not simply following the patient, but that there exists a blend between two partners.*

From a psychological point of view Alon had found a reasonable solution by identifying with a father figure, reconciliation with reality, and a building of self-confidence.

The following table can serve to analyze and compare the various stages of the therapeutic process:

Content Raised by Patient	Patient's own Description of Therapeutic Space	Means Used to Realize Fantasies
ORAL FEATURES (15–16 Months)		(Actual age of patient: 6–7½ yrs)
1. Oral-sadistic fantasies: I am a predator, venomous, devouring, You, Mom and Dad, and other animals	Jungle, Beast's Lair	Recorded ecstatic music heavy percussion piano tent puppets and dolls recordings chosen by patient: Cage, Berio.
2. Splitting of Good and Bad: I am bad, Mom and Dad are good. Some instruments are good, some bad.		
ANAL FEATURES (3 Months)		(Actual age of patient: 7½–7¾ yrs)
1. I am a singer and musician, in control of the outside world	Studio	Metallophones xylophones, autoharp Japanese bells, small gong click sticks, flute, guitar, piano, microphone, glove puppets.
2. Disaster and death, realistic solutions		
OEDIPAL FEATURES (10 Months)		(Actual age of patient: 8–8½ years)
Marriage, birth, death, jealousy, identification with father figure, reconciliation	Palace	Drums, xylophones, zanza, autoharp, fiddle, dulcimer piano, guitar, hand puppets

*A.H. Recording Archive, Cassette 50: "Comparison of Oedipal Subjects"

CONCLUSION

I deliberately selected Alon's case as a suitable summary of this presentation of the Developmental-Integrative Model in Music Therapy. His case demanded a holistic approach which could perceive both neurological and psychological problems at one and the same time.

As in the other case histories previously described, music played a variable role according to the demands and stages of therapy in progress, on the assumption that both physical and psychological needs can respond to music's intrinsic qualities and its stimulating and relaxing features:

Ron needed a way to relax in order to sense his body in a positive manner and to rid himself of the tensions expressed by overanxiety.

Anat needed physical awakening in order to combat the force of gravity, to straighten up and to face the world as best she could.

Jacob needed to re-internalize keystones of music in order to rehabilitate his own cantorial ability.

Rita needed relaxation in order to overcome deep-rooted anxieties and to achieve creative self-expression without losing control.

Alon was initially treated with protective, relaxing music without taking into account his need for excitation and stimulation. (Maybe this is why the first stage of his therapy took so long). The change of therapeutic strategy led to significant, even dramatic changes in all behavioral levels, and to a balance between tension and relaxation, stimulation and soothing.

Flow and control, movement and arrest, these are the basics both of the art of music and the development of the human infant.

Deliberate use of basic musical elements and of music as a part of more complex artistic forms allows us to channel that same flow and control in order to re-create preliminary states of relaxation, excitation and alertness. Furthermore, as a result of clinical practice we know that sounds which serve to moderate physical and mental blocking are also capable of penetrating intellectual control, thus enabling the patient's threatening contents and fantasies to be brought to the surface (Sekeles 1989).

Music which is capable of arousing such content assists in the process of working through and dealing with these, sometimes on its own, but generally—according to the principles of D.I.M.T.—through a combination of both music and the word.

CONCLUSION

I n this work I have attempted to shed some light on a number of basic questions which concern all who work in the field of music therapy and which still remain unsolved:

One of the central dilemmas remains the difficulty of defining just to what degree Art Music of a complex texture can affect the listener. True, research has proven the psychophysiological effects of basic musical elements (repetitive beat-units, acceleration, deceleration, vocal and dynamic range), however it remains an unsolved riddle how to determine the exact effect a complex musical composition can have on the listener in general, and the patient in particular. Indeed, without a close familiarity with the patient's associative world and emotional linkages with any definite musical style, or any specific composition, the therapist will find it extremely difficult to encourage the patient and help him through a positive change. The choice of music to be used during therapy, or an understanding of the patient's choice of any given piece, serve only as a prelude to their mutual journey, during which both therapist and patient will encounter many questions to be solved together.

In addition, research which has attempted to catalogue music by way of analyzing emotional criteria has not produced any unequivocal results; often they even contradict one another. It could well be that this is one of the reasons why the majority of music therapy models refrain from overusing readily available compositions, and prefer to make use of vocal and/or instrumental improvisations. The improvised themes and motifs are created by the patient or suggested by the therapist, as a basic element in music therapy. In other words, creative activity is to be preferred over the use of ready-made recordings, despite the obvious fact that the artistic level of the improvisation will never, or seldom, match that of a well executed piece.

This leads us to an additional aspect of music therapy: the attitude of the therapist to the music produced during the therapeutic session. The therapist must be able to accept and contain any and all of the patient's attempts at musical expression exactly as they come, and in particular to avoid any "artistic" criticism. In fact we strongly believe that any music therapist whose musical training and skills impinge upon his ability to listen and convey a sense of acceptance and empathy is not suited to this profession. Since the music therapist must first and foremost be a trained musician with professional skills, he/she must now undergo a thorough change of attitude: criticism and professional judgement must be replaced by acceptance and receptivity. It is our view that the patient must feel free in the music room to give musical expression to his feelings in any way he chooses, while at the same time being aware of the fact that any or every musical variation has its own meaning, and might open the way to greater self-awareness.

Musical expressions, be they accidental or fragmental, can nevertheless serve as a means of bringing to the surface repressed emotions, can help the patient link and identify with them, and reveal blockages (both physical and mental) which hamper normal function and/or free use of mental and physical resources. It emerges therefore, that the applicant for music therapy need not necessarily possess musical skills or even be acquainted with the medium, just as the applicant for movement therapy need not be a dancer, nor the applicant for drama therapy an actor. Nevertheless, how can anyone express themselves in music or movement if they have no knowledge of the medium?

The solution presented here is based on the assumptions of D.I.M.T. with reference to relevant research material. These assumptions maintain that the basic foundations of the art of music emerge from a spontaneous reaction within various parts of the human organism: internal organs activated and rhythmically set by the biological clock, external limbs which by their own specific characteristics permit the creation of rhythmic structures, the vocal system, etc. The ability to "be" with music, either receptively or actively, gradually develops according to the degree by which these keystones are given external stimulation. Whatever the case, musical development begins in the womb: it is influenced by primary sounds heard in utero, encouraged after birth by feedback (movemental, vocal, tactile) on the part of the parent, and then gradually developed toward the outside world. The more the creative urges develop, along with absorptive skills and overall expressive ability, so does musical creativity improve. Indeed we occasionally encounter children and adult patients who, as a result of musical stimulation during therapy sessions, are awakened to channels of expression and creativity which they never knew before. Now and then such creative potential becomes the means for complex artistic expression, even the basis for the patient's professional rehabilitation, but in general the patient's musical expressivity is quite simple. Its importance is not based on its artistic value but rather on its ability to convey emotional content, ventilate and moderate anxieties, and enable their elaboration in music and in words.

At the same time one must recall that a patient who is a trained musician must undergo a process of moderating his artistic criticism and in particular his accepted conventions and aesthetic considerations, otherwise he is liable to employ structured music (with which he is most familiar) as a defense mechanism rather than as an agent for change and mental growth.

Another major question in art therapies in general, and music therapy in particular, is the degree to which the therapist can intervene verbally. This is a matter which concerns many therapists, and also arouses controversy. The more the model is based on a psychological concept (such as Analytical Music Therapy, developed by Mary Priestley, 1975, 1978), the greater the tendency to utilize the verbal techniques employed in psychotherapy. On the other hand a model based first and foremost on music (such as Creative Music Therapy, developed by Paul Nordoff & Clive Robbins, 1971, 1977, 1983), makes very little use of verbal psychotherapy, preferring action and "doing" to psychological insight as it is generally understood.

The Developmental Integrative Model prefers a balance between both words and music and encourages the natural links between the two. Sometimes patient and therapist will conduct a dialogue in the form of an accompanied recitative in order to free the words from intellectual inhibitions, or from physical disabilities, and give them a free flow. Now and then words and music are employed in a structured or improvised song framework, on other occasions the words can serve to describe physical and emotional experiences which occur during the musical process, to elaborate the major events, work them through and develop better insight (Sekeles 1995, 6–16).

All this is done through a variety of approaches and techniques which are dependent on the degree of the patient's awareness, insight and ability to verbally communicate. Whatever the case, from the examples displayed here in various case histories we can learn that patients defined as mildly or even severely retarded, might develop verbal skills during music therapy and actually compose verses with a sense of beauty and aesthetics.

Finally there arises the question as to whether music therapy is a scientific field. This is something which preoccupies both practicing music therapists and those working in related research. Most music therapists are in the main concerned with the day-to-day practical problems of their patient's special needs and hence have little time to spare for theoretical research. As presented here there are indeed aspects of music therapy which can be measured scientifically, whereas at the same time there are many others which prove themselves in practice but as yet have no scientific proof.

The difficulty in finding a scientific basis for such phenomena is in general rooted in the fact that these are complex processes which demand interdisciplinary research. It should be stressed that at present there exists a certain lack of contact between the clinical practice of music therapy and scientific research. The main reason for this is that scientific research generally limits itself to spheres which neither directly nor indirectly are of any great help toward an understanding of the therapeutic process.

To my mind, research projects which should be encouraged and developed are those emerging from the observation and study done by the people on the job. For example, research into the effectiveness of repetitive drumming on the physical organism and the emotional state. Clinical observations were handed over for laboratory examination, and as a result additional work systems were developed which now employ rhythmic structures for therapeutic purposes.

Whatever the case, it is my contention that at this stage of development in the field of music therapy, it would seem that the only way open to us by which we may assess the therapeutic process is to make use of the potential knowledge at our disposal, in music, psychology, medicine and any other related field, which teaches us to observe normal development and thus deal with aberrations.

A combination of all these, at the right time and in correct proportions, can enable the therapist and the patient to sail the right course, with music helping to point the way.

APPENDICES

APPENDIX 1

Analysis of Instrument Playing
Therapeutic Viewpoint
A Few Examples of 25 Instruments Examined (Sekeles 1981)

Instrument	Point of Sensory Contact	Limbs Used	Movement	Required Range of Movement in the Joint	Reaction to Force of Gravity	Hand-Hand Coordination
				(On a Scale of One to Ten)		
Bells idiophones	Arms, hands, hips, ankles etc.	Wherever attached	Flexion, extension rotation	1–10	Depends on posture 1–2	1–2
Stand-Drum 40 cm. circ.	Fingers, palms	Hand(s)	Flexion, extension (wrists), fisting, movement or arrest in shoulder and elbow	1–10	1, 2–4	1–10
Autoharp	Finger-tips	Both hands	Pinching, flexion, opposition, movement and arrest	3–10	Instrument rests on surface 1, 2	3–6
Metallophone chimes	Fingers, palms	Hand(s)	Pinching, flexion, opposition	2–10	1, 2	3–10
Kazoo	Fingers, lips	Fingers, lips and vocal chords	Pinching lip-pursing, breath, song	5–10	2–3	0
Standing electronic organ	Finger-tips,	Fingers, hand(s), foot	Flexion, opposition, planti- and dorsi-flexion	2–10	1–2	2–10

Instrument	Posture	Strength Required (On a Scale of One to Ten)	Difficulty Assessment	Instrument Change Due to Disability
Bells idiophones	Varied, depends on activating limb	1–2	1–2	Can be attached to any limb, thus suited even to severe disabilities
Stand-Drum	Body and hand stability, seated and standing	1–10	1–10	a) Attaching drumsticks to hands b) Change of drumming angle
Autoharp	Body and hand stability	3–10	3–7	a) Attaching plectrum to finger or to wrist b) Alteration of instrument position, as needed c) Color coding of keys
Metallophone chimes	Body and hand stability	2–10	2–10	a) Reducing extent of keyboard b) Realignment of instrument c) Single-handed playing d) Playing with Interval Stick (3rd, 5th, chords)
Kazoo	Stability of holding hand	2–10	2–10	
Standing electronic organ	Body and hand stability	1–2	1–10	Stabilizing the wrist-joint

In matching these instruments to the developmental stage and the needs of the patient or a healthy person, we find the following:

Bells and idiophones (Age—from birth and onward): attachment of the instrument to any limb leads to any movement (even inadvertent) activating a sound. The Developmental Possibilities are:
1. Auditory feedback to movement and the motivation to repeat it
2. Practice and improvement of integration between hearing, sight, and movement
3. Means of developing movemental planning
4. Simple activity which can be linked to listening, movement, etc.
5. Playing while lying in bed.

Drum stand (Age 2 years and onward): when the torso is stable. The possibilities:
1. Improvement of hand-hand coordination
2. Improvement of hand-eye coordination
3. Improvement of rhythmic perception and performance
4. Release of aggression
5. Control (mastery)
6. Motor-activity on different developmental levels.

Autoharp: suits the developmental stage in which there is a separation of the two vertical halves of the body: pinching and plucking with one hand, and pressing with the other (which might also be interchangeable). The possibilities:
1. Developing coordination between hands
2. A swift musical result with an uncomplicated harmonic accompaniment
3. Descriptions of emotions ranging from gentle to aggressive
4. Playing in bed.

Metallophone, chimes: stage where grasping the drumstick and movement-direction are fairly competent, separation of the two vertical halves of the body. The possibilities:
1. Swift musical result, (e.g., using the Orff technique)
2. Hand-hand coordination
3. Eye-hand coordination
4. Work on continuity (sequences)
5. Planning of accurate movement
6. Visual, emotional, and other descriptions
7. Taking part in group activity and creating interpersonal dialogue
8. Work on fine movement and expression
9. Playing in bed.

Kazoo: demands understanding of breathing and vocality (approx. 4 years and onward). The possibilities:
1. Development of vocality when there is no speech, or speech impediment due to either physical or psychological causes
2. Enables a dialogue without words
3. Work on the oral area (motor or oral deficiencies)
4. It is entertaining
5. Playing in bed.

Electronic organ: demands finger separation and hand-foot coordination, as well as separation of the two vertical halves of the body. The possibilities:
1. Minimal movement producing maximum sound.
2. Swift musical result
3. Variety of description and expression
4. Work on finger separation
5. Hand-hand coordination
6. Eye-hand coordination
7. Eye-hand-foot coordination.
8. Work on continuity (sequences)
9. Enrichment of playing by electronic means.

APPENDIX 2

Musical Elements: Their Origins and Roles

Element	Origin	Audibility	Control	Musical Function
Rhythm, (beat-unit)	Inherent rhythms: brain, heart, lungs, diaphragm, sex.	Inaudible, unless by means of special equipment	Brain stem, autonomic nervous system	Organization, sensed or heard
Tempo	As above	As Above	As Above	Velocity, acceleration, deceleration
Rhythmic structures: (motifs, phrases)	Motor-system: development of voluntary muscle system from in utero to optimal ability. (inherent and developed)	Can be visually observed as movement: audible only if movement provokes sound	Central nervous system: cortex	Organization of an internal time division, enabling change and development
Divisions, parts	Rhythmic cycling of the human organism (inherent and developed)	Can be visually observed or sensed: not always audible	Multi-systemed	Overall organization: the contours of creation
Pitch	Vocal and respiratory systems (inherent and developed)	Audible	Central nervous system	Source of motifs, phrases, melody, and harmonic organization
Timbre	Vocal and respiratory systems, as well as body-sound (inherent and developed)	Audible	Central nervous system	Color and atmosphere
Intensity, volume, (dynamics)	As above	Heard and sensed	Central nervous system	Dynamic organization of musical piece. Atmosphere

Psychophysiological influences of such elements

RHYTHM

Repetitive and with no acceleration: a reduction of muscle tone, stabilized breathing, confidence, and psychophysiological relaxation leading to sleep.

With acceleration: increased muscle tone, accelerated breathing, blood flow, pulse rate, etc. Psychophysiological awakening to a degree of ecstasy.

RHYTHMIC STRUCTURES

Repetitive structures with no change in tempo: similar to repetitive beat-units, could signify fear of change, perseverance, compulsion, etc.

Changes of rhythmic structure: maintain the attention both of listener and performer, enable a change of muscle tone according to therapeutic necessities, as well as creative variations within a repetitive framework.

DIVISIONS, PARTS

Demand a basic sense of beat-unit, rhythmic structure, on occasions tonality and melodic structure of phrase. This is a more advanced psychological and physiological developmental stage, enabling the organization and control of microcosmic elements within a macrocosmic framework.

PITCH

This is directly translated into feeling: a wide range has the effect of dramatization and emotionalism, whereas a limited range leads to relaxation. Sudden high notes stimulate a state of alertness; in cases of anxiety or oversensitivity, high-pitched sounds can emphasize pathology.

TIMBRE

Can cause a sense of pleasure or displeasure, acceptance or rejection, can elicit free associations in Guided Imagery in Music (GIM) and in other therapeutic dynamics.

INTENSITY, VOLUME (Dynamics)

A central factor for emotional expression matching or not matching a given situation. Influenced by educational background, degree of daring, and internal resources. The gap between the patient's basic emotional resources and their expression in terms of musical dynamics can often indicate a pathological condition.

APPENDIX 3

Music Therapy Observation Report
(Music Therapy: David Yellin College)
1981–1983 (Sekeles, ed.)

Observation location	Duration	Date	Hour	Reported to: (specify function)	Received by:
Name of referee	Age	Address		Educational framework	Family framework
Reason for referral to music therapy		Previous and present therapeutic frameworks			Diagnosis
External impression:		Dress	Overall appearance		Manner of entry
Equipment employed		Dominant characteristics		.	

MOTOR SYSTEM (Movement)

Gross motor activity of trunk and limbs: posture of body and limbs, muscle tone, movemental range, energy investment, movement continuity, dominant half of body, symmetry between both halves of body, all possibilities of movement axes, (both active and passive), coordination (various aspects including sensory-movemental coordination), sense of balance, spatial organization, movement planning (praxis).

Fine motor activity: finger independence, pinching, opposition (thumb against palm), range, strength, continuity, planning, hand dominance.

SENSES

Sensory deficiencies and/or sensory immaturity: oversensitivity, undersensitivity, white noise, sensory integration, sensory-motor integration, the stage of sensory-motor development.

VOCALITY (both Musical and Verbal)

Normal functioning of vocal and respiratory systems, volume, clarity of diction, tempo, acceleration/deceleration, rhythmic and melodic continuity, range, pitch, imitative ability, normal and abnormal melo-rhythmic expression (e.g., ecolalia, stammering), hoarseness, vocal expression, vocal stress, intonation, verbal and musical integration, vocal creativity, vocal and verbal communication, linkage between linguistic and verbal ability, linguistic alternatives, ability to express emotion and imagination.

RHYTHMICALITY

Natural tempo, preservation of tempo, continuity and maintenance of beat-unit, spontaneous rhythmic reaction, imitative ability, ability to improvise on a repetitive beat, capacity for a rhythmic dialogue, maintenance of meter, counting. Pathological expressions (perseverance, compulsiveness, etc.).

INSTRUMENTAL PLAYING

Planned movement (range, energy investment, efficiency, muscle tone), hand-hand coordination, between other limbs involved in music playing, dominance, symmetry, crossing midline, playing as opposed to the force of gravity, creativity and improvisational ability, imitation, specific expressions and characteristics, imagination and ability to express emotions.

HEARING

Deficiencies, range, over or under sensitivity, white noise. Linkage between hearing system and other sensory systems (intersensory integration), linkage between hearing and movement (sensory-motor integration), auditory distinction (pitch, timbre, volume, direction, singular or multiple sounds), complex distinction (intervals, tune, scale, combinations), identification, memory, ability to describe what is heard, interpretation of what is heard into feelings, or extra-musical experiences. Time needed for memorizing and identifying.

LISTENING

Readiness, directed or free listening, continuity, memory, the need for extra-musical support, emotional effect, metaphorical transference, tendencies and rejections, relaxing or exciting influences (both emotional and physical), the preferred repertoire of musical selections and their characteristics.

EMOTIONAL ASPECTS

Making contact, awareness, adaptability and readiness for cooperation; the effect and its application to a given situation. The degree of flexibility, motivation, devotion, confronting frustration, emotional calm or chaos, initiative, concentration, the will to face up to challenges old and new, self-control, confidence, discipline, aggression, passive aggression, sensitivity or insensitivity, criticism, exactitude, organization, planning, systemization, reactions to positive or negative comment, reality judgement, imagination, flexibility, stability, leadership or following, spontaneity, inquisitiveness and curiosity, a sense of humor, ways of getting out of uneasy situations, compulsory and ritualistic habits, idiosyncrasies.

COGNITIVE ASPECTS

Understanding instructions, verbal organization, a vocabulary and its utilization, distinguishing between essential and subsidiary, long-term and short-term memory. Preferred memory: auditory, visual, tactile, kinesthetic, etc. Analysis, simplification, symbolization, abstraction, the ability for complex thought, the ability to confront new situations, problem solving, specific learning abilities, stage of cognitive development.

SOCIAL ASPECTS

Introversion, extroversion, manner of communication, role-playing within a group, ability to share and create feedback, tactics of sociability, etc.

SUMMARY AND RECOMMENDATIONS

1. Summary of diagnostic findings through music
2. Recent situation of referee patient
3. Recent developmental stage (physical, emotional, cognitive, social)
4. Developmental gaps
5. Approach and techniques used during observation/therapy
6. Recommendations for continued music or other therapy
7. Prognosis as observed in music therapy
8. Preservation of material (recordings, reports, video)
9. Name, role and signature of reporter/therapist.

NOTE: The purpose of these report-sheets is the provision of guidelines for assessment: naturally they can be utilized in various ways. They are designed for both individual and group therapy observation.

NOTES

CHAPTER I

1. In ethnomusicological literature, as well as in recent writings concerning music therapy, shamanism is employed as a general term for almost all forms of ethnic healing. In this work I chose to include those healing rituals which match Eliade's definitions (1972) and which distinguish between healer, witch doctor, herbalist, etc. and shamanism as it is known in Siberia and Central Asia. Eliade acknowledges that such phenomena occur in other regions of the world, provided they conform to the following principles:

a) The use of techniques by which the shaman falls into a trance (an altered state of consciousness).

b) That when in this state of trance the shaman's spirit is capable of leaving his body and making magic journeys, ascending to the heavens or descending to the depths of the sea and the bowels of the earth.

c) That the shaman's studies include a knowledge of dreams, trance, ecstatic flights, gods and spirits, the myths and genealogies of the ancestors, secret languages, and the drumming, songs and dances of ritual.

The word shaman apparently comes from the dialect of the Manchurian Tungus tribe, and "sha" (meaning "He who knoweth") is to be found in other languages and dialects throughout North and Central Asia. The shaman is never subject to the spirits, rather it is he who rules over them, as well as over fire. In those tribes in which shamanism is prominent (Eliade mentions in the main the Turko-Tatars, the Samoyed, the Tungus and the Chuckchee), there is a common belief in a Heavenly God, with between seven and nine offspring who inhabit the lower levels of the heavens. With these demigods the shaman has a special relationship and it is they who assist him in his healings: in this case spiritual healing in its broadest connotation, and not necessarily concerned with the imbalance of the body's biology. The shaman's functions, in accordance with his training, are not limited to healing alone, he is also a religious and political leader, a musician and a dancer. He has inherited his role from the gods, or they have elected to bestow it upon him. A self-proclaimed shaman is unacceptable, and no shaman may perform his duties without the approval of the tribe and its ancestors.

Eliade stresses that on occasions the selection of the shaman may be preceded by an overemotional or ecstatic event, and there are those who see a continuous process of self-therapy in the role of the shaman. Indeed Eliade mentions the case of a shaman from the Yakut tribe who began to sing at the age of twenty and when he had gained sufficient confidence began to study shamanic ritual. At the age of sixty he was described as possessing unlimited energy and to be capable of drumming and dancing all night long. Were he not to perform ceremonies for any length of time he would begin to feel unwell (Eliade 1972, 28).

On the other hand Eliade stresses that there are no grounds for the belief that the shaman is prone to psychotic attacks: he is always in full control of his actions and is capable of manipulating the participants in a masterly fashion. One example is a shaman from the Tungus tribe who conducts his rituals in a circular tent of limited capacity, densely packed with people. He performs in heavy garments with his eyes closed, making broad movements, but nevertheless never bumps into anyone and finds whatever or whomever he needs at any given moment with remarkable accuracy—evidence of strict rehearsal and an acute sense of direction.

Even at the height of an ecstatic trance, Eliade notes, the shaman remains in command of a number of his faculties: visual observation and clarity of thought, accompanied by an intelligence higher than the tribal average, adaptability and a great deal of knowledge (ibid., 29–30).

2. For examples of such integration between music and movement see the case histories of Ron and Anat. An example of the integration of music, singing and drawing is the case history of Rita, and of music combined with song and dramatic play acting, Alon. In each case these were compilations of materials which emerged during therapy according to the personal needs of the patient.

3. In music therapy today, this is one of the most accepted forms of conversing through music, the therapist creates a fixed rhythmic and harmonic framework which repeats itself, while therapist and patient converse in song on this given basis. This technique is especially effective in cases of anxiety or of speech problems. See case history of Alon.

4. In a previous unpublished work (1981), I compared the music of 46 ecstatic and 52 hypnotic rituals.

5. Traditional societies believe in the despatching of extrahuman or superhuman forces or agents as the harbingers of disease. Such belief is based on the religious tenets regarding the unity of the world and the duality of the forces active within it. Traditional healing therefore, holds that balance and harmony are expressed by the fact that Man and Nature represent absolute goodness. Any imbalance which occurs between the two can lead to a total disruption of this harmony which is typified by order, health and perfection. Such imbalance can be caused by actions which go against those taboos which clearly define the differences between good and evil (Yoder 1972).

6. Frances Desmond is considered to be one of the most important pioneers in the research of Indian music. Between the years 1907–1957 she recorded some 2,000 examples from a vast number of North American tribes. Her collection is housed in the Folklore Archives of the Library of Congress in Washington D.C. and includes examples of healing rituals from fourteen tribes, some of which have been issued by the Ethnic Folkways Library.

7. Ida Halpern, a musicologist from British Columbia, compiled this anthology in 1966 for the National Museum of Canada. It includes songs from seven tribes. Dr. Halpern concentrated on the Kwakiutl (from the northern extremity of Vancouver Island) and the Nootka (to the south).

8. According to Harner (1973, 155–175), this drug takes effect within minutes as an overall stimulant to the senses which leads to haziness and a sense of levitation. Visions are at first pleasing and aesthetic but soon develop into the horrific. Since

the shaman describes in detail his own sense of levitation and what he sees, it would seem that certain visions such as snakes, jaguars, and other beasts of prey tend to repeat themselves. An experiment conducted by Naranjo (1973, 176–190) on 35 volunteers in Santiago, Chile, revealed that the symptoms the drug produces are not necessarily culture dependent: 33 experienced the separation of the soul from the body, of these 10 experienced levitation and rotating movement, 7 saw beasts of prey and reptiles, 8 experienced their own death, 5 saw demons, and only 3 saw angels, Jesus or the Virgin Mary (visions which are alien to the culture of the Napo). The remaining 2 reported a feeling of well-being with no visions at all. Naranjo claims that the hallucinatory motifs induced by the drug must be seen as universal, and that some of them exist in cultures and parts of the world which neither the Chilean shaman nor some of the participants in the experiment have ever seen. It should further be mentioned that the visions also included music (in the main drums, whistles and flutes), as well as images of gods and demons, singing and drinking the drug in the company of human beings. It should be noted that these are the typical elements of the ecstatic healing ritual, while the one under discussion is hypnotic or soothing.

9. This is a typical phenomenon of many healing rituals. The Hamadsha make use of melodic structures (the Ariah), each of which is aimed at exorcising specific spirits (Sekeles 1979). The same is true of the tunes played at the Zar ceremonies (ibid.). Indian tribes employ rhythmic motifs in order to target specific ailments (Densmore 1927). The Sioux healer has special songs for each and every sickness. There are also secret songs for particular afflictions which must never be applied to another. There can be no doubt that within the framework of healing ritual, the attitude to song or music as an influence on spirit or demon, is similar to that of a specific cure.

10. For a description of such acceleration see Siberian Tungus (Shirokogoroff 1935, 326, 329), Haitian Rituals (Courlander 1944, 45) and the Moroccan Hamadsha (Crapanzano 1973, Chapter 12)

11. This transformation from patient to healer is a well-known phenomenon in many brotherhoods, such as the Zar in Ethiopia, the Indian Salish and others. In the San tribe who dwell in the northwestern regions of the Kalahari Desert, no less than ten percent of both men and women become healers. This is a tribe which holds a weekly healing ritual in which all the villagers take part. Song and ecstatic dance take on a major role as an energy outlet (Katz 1982, 344–369). This phenomenon is also perceptible in Western civilizations where people encountering and trying to tackle certain problems come up with innovative therapy (Alexander, Feldenkrais), hence the need for the therapist to undergo therapy in order to better comprehend the therapeutic process, and to gain a personal insight.

12. A further example can be found in the Ethiopian Zar ceremonies (Messing 1956; Kahana 1983). Both researchers stress that the Sudanese (a minority in Ethiopia and an enslaved people in the past), participate in the rites as equals. This is also the case for women, whose social status in Ethiopia was always discriminatory.

13. This seeking of a healing melody which can reach out and touch the patient, characterizes modern music therapy and the models it employs by making use of improvisation as a central tool, for example in "The Creative Model of Music Therapy" developed by Nordoff and Robbins (Bruscia 1987, 21–73). The essential difference is that the Moroccan ghiyya player has an already prepared repertoire, whereas the music therapist must make his choices according to the therapy in progress. The common denominator is the never ending need to follow the reactions of the patient as music is performed, in order to know whether or not the musical material employed touches on the genuine needs of the patient.

14. Unusually rapid breathing which leads to a lack of oxygen and a consequent dizziness, muscular spasms and so forth. This is an accepted technique in certain ecstatic rituals (Malagash *Exorcising Evil Spirits*, see charts).

15. See Vogel *Technique* (1984) and Case History: Ron).

16. Rutherford (1986) stresses that Eskimo Rituals do not employ the drum. I, however, witnessed such a ritual in June 1980 performed by Eskimos from the village of Sivuqaq in Alaska in which they made use of huge frame drums, ranging from a hand spread in width to the height of a ten-year-old child. Such frame drums are held by bone handles and accompany the Eskimo incantations.

17. During my work in a psychiatric hospital I instructed the patients how to build their own drums (as well as other musical instruments), and to decorate them according to their own imagination. These decorations consisted of objects attached to the drum (as in Siberia) as well as drawings on the drumskin itself (as with the Indian tribes). There could be no doubt that the emotional attachment of the patient to his own handmade drum was much deeper and more significant than his attitude to any acquired or purchased instrument; and this despite the fact that any belief in the drum as a symbol was alien to his inherited culture, unlike that of traditional societies.

18. The frequencies of brain waves can be defined as follows:
Alpha: 8–13 Hertz (relaxation and inner concentration).
Beta: 14–30 Hertz (alertness).
Delta: 4–5 Hertz (deep sleep)
Theta: 4–7 Hertz (light sleep for adults, possibly awakedness for children). Children's brain waves usually stabilize around the age of eight (Greenfield & Sternbach 1972).

19. See *Ethos* (1982, 10:4) for researches into shamanism and endorphins (Montreal 1980). In 1974 John Hughes succeeded in isolating in the brains of large domestic animals a material which resembled morphine blocked by nalaxon. In 1976 a group of researchers discovered Beta endorphin and Simon coined the definition Endogenous morphine-like product.

20. It is possible that pain relief by means of blocking stimuli could explain the playing of the Aulos (known for its strong vibrations) on the bodies of patients in

Ancient Greece who suffered from lower-back pains (Chomet 1875). Teirich (1958) also writes of the use of music in autogenic exercises with the vibrations directed at the solar plexus, in order to achieve deep relaxation. Similarly, at the First Scientific Seminar for Music Therapy conducted by the International Society for Music Education at Bad Honnef, Germany (1986), a treatment was displayed which could transmit music not only through the regular auditory channels but could also direct the vibrations to specific areas of pain in the body.

CHAPTER II

1. See Jean Piaget (1952), where he focuses on the developmental sequence of thought and intelligence, Freud's views regarding the psychosexual stages, and the theory of learning which claims that behavior, or the potential for behavior is acquired through experience and can therefore be conditioned (Bachrach 1981, 378).

2. Sense: in which the receptors are located in specific organs (ear, eye, nose and the vestibular canals). Sensation: in which the receptors are dispersed, such as tactile sensation or proprioception.

3. See also Case History Ron: The importance of repetitive beat-units in achieving relaxation, and Case History Jacob: the rehabilitation of input and output of beat-units in advanced age.

4. Alfred Thomatis: Otolaringolist, who established the Institute of Cannes-Sur-Mere on the French Riviera, and lectures on psycholinguistics. Dr. Thomatis concludes that there exist links between hearing/speech, and psychological problems, and between traumatic pregnancy and childbirth. In his form of therapy the patient undergoes a repeated simulation of the birth process through the use of recordings of sounds similar to those heard in the uterus whose volume is gradually increased. After birth, treatment proceeds through play and art therapies in order to enhance the infant's growth.

5. An example of integration while playing may be found in the case of an Israeli guitarist who was injured in the spine (D-1) and became paraplegic below the level of the injury. Although the head and arms remained functional, he had difficulty playing the guitar due to imbalance and instability of the torso. In the absence of the senses, sensations and locomotion needed for optimal performance, alternatives had to be sought, in this case external support and a suitable seating accommodation succeeded in solving the problem.

6. On the subject of Sensory-Motor Integration see the works of Ayres (1970b, 1972b, 1970).

7. See Appendix 1: Analysis of Instrumental Performance from a Therapeutic Viewpoint.

8. For example, constant repetition of a single motif, the use of nonsense syllables, drastic expansion or limitation of the vocal range, sudden dynamic changes

and accentuations, and so on. All of these permit the transmission of emotional messages by vocal means, and open up therapeutic possibilities.

9. Increase of tempo holds good not only for amateur musicians, or in our case patients, but also for professional musicians who perform the same work at different hours and on different occasions in a different tempo, sometimes for objective, but generally for subjective reasons.

10. Auditory communication is based on teleception, which also characterizes other sense organs located in the head (nose, eyes), as opposed to tactile communication between mother and infant, which demands physical contact.

11. Eric, a paranoid schizophrenic, was treated with receptive music therapy for a full year due to his inability to communicate verbally or by any other means, including active music. After about a year of total mutism (during which he nevertheless regularly and punctually attended individual sessions) he began to cooperate verbally, and on his own initiative to compose his own music. His compositions sprang from within his private world, as did certain special annotations he would employ in addition to the standard principles of scoring (Sekeles 1978)

12. In his book *Creativity and Disease* (1985) Philip Sandblom quotes numerous examples of artists who suffered from various maladies. These quotations suit Freud's viewpoint of the artist as a personality which invests its neurotic symptoms in its creative work (Freud 1908, 1909). For example Beethoven, who wrote that only his art prevented him from fulfilling his suicidal tendencies, or Paul Klee who wrote that he "created in order not to weep," or Grahame Greene who defined writing as a form of self-therapy, and expressed amazement that anyone who does not write, paint or compose music can escape the madness, melancholy, panic and fear which are part of the human condition.

13. The number of clinical and supervised hours is officially anchored in the constitution of the Israel Association of Creative and Expressive Therapies (1985), something which guarantees professional advancement. On the other hand no one can be forced into undergoing therapy so this is no more than a recommendation. Alongside the familiar reasons why the therapist himself should undergo therapy, lies the fact that the transformation from being a musician to becoming a music therapist is something that requires a considerable psychological investment which can be greatly helped by verbal and/or artistic psychotherapy.

14. I have frequently encountered patients for whom the exact reproduction of any motif they produced was of the utmost importance. This demands either absolute hearing or a relatively sensitive ear. One example is that of Naomi who was hypersensitive to sound and music, and extremely sensitive to pitch. The establishment of mutual trust between us involved first and foremost a completely faithful response to her music. Since this is not a phenomenon involving a high degree of intelligence, I have also observed it in the retarded, the autistic, and on occasions among cases of neurological damage and immature sensory development.

15. One example is Dan (aged 12), an autistic child who makes partial use of body language as alternative communication. He is unable to speak and is severely retarded, but is nevertheless capable of comprehension when addressed in simple phrases. In order to forge a link between sessions, at the Opening, he will listen intently to a recording of the previous Closing (always jointly performed in song accompanied by the piano and additional instruments of his own choosing). On arrival Dan, who can be restless and aggressive, is always impatient for this Opening to which he listens in absolute silence, utilizing it to enter into a state of concentration and creativity. Another example is that of Naomi (aged 8) who suffers from extreme emotional disturbances. On arriving for a session she will await the therapist's playing and has invented the saying "I've entered the magic room." This is a slogan which helps her to enter and cooperate in the elaboration of subjects which are not necessarily always enjoyable.

16. Both speech and song contain prosodic sound qualities considered critical to the voicing and understanding of language. The sounds produced by the larynx are characterized by volume, basic frequencies and by their quality. They are capable of altering the significance of a single word or an entire sentence, and it is they who are responsible for the transmission of vocal-emotional messages. D.I.M.T. works on the prosodic elements of language, similar to the vocal play of the infant, as a prelude to verbal-vocality. We have already noted that in the syllabic singing of the Navajo Indians (see Chapter 1), use is made of prosodic elements for a soothing and relaxing effect.

17. Leitmotif: a term coined by Wagner's friend Von Wolzogen in 1878 to define a phenomenon he perceived in the composer's later operas by which characters, concepts and typical situations are represented by musical motifs, which can nevertheless be adapted according to any given dramatic situation (Apel 1969, 466–467).

18. Such models, or basic structures, which are an analogy of the collective archetypes of the unconscious, could be perceived as originating from inherent musical codes, similar to the linguistic codes referred to in the theories of Chomsky. Sadai views such codes as part of a natural system which permits an intuitive perception of music. The more the child is exposed to musical stimulation, the greater the development of his intuition and musical perception. Sadai bases his theories on extensive research of such musical phenomena as tonality, modality, etc. (Sadai 1988, No. 4). Sadai's theory might well serve to explain why patients who have no experience whatsoever of musical creativity can, in their own time and after sufficient stimulation, express themselves in a variety of ways, mainly vocally but also by the use of instruments, as if they had been formally trained. It could be said that such progress is the result of inherent musical structures.

19. The linkage between words and music differs between the various therapeutic models. In D.I.M.T. the linkage is wide and variegated, for example:
a) Music as a substitute for words (such as in cases of severe or profound retardation).
b) Music as a breakthrough to speech (Case History: Rita).

c) Music as an arouser of emotion and speech, and as a link between emotion and awareness (see all case histories).

d) Music as a major medium (as in the case of the terminally ill, when the need for a sense of optimal well-being takes precedence over the need for verbalization and awareness).

e) The balance between words and music, when words might prove to be threatening or the music might tend to overwhelm.

f) Mirroring, expansion, interpretation, etc., by either musical and/or verbal means.

CHAPTER III – RON

1. Cerebral palsy is defined as "a persisting qualitative motor disorder appearing before the age of three, due to nonprogressive damage to the brain" (Dorland 1982, 956)

2. "Spastic" is the most common category (30%) among the varieties of C.P. Ron suffered from spastic hemiplegia (on his right side). An infant affected by this syndrome is liable to grow up with an unbalanced development on either side of the body, however such asymmetry will become apparent only at the age of 5 to 9 months. Spastic hemiplegic children miss important stages in their motor development such as being able to sit up from a prone position, being able to crawl on hands and knees, etc. They suffer from a constant sense of imbalance and symmetry and gradually begin to neglect, or even deny, the affected side of the body. This was indeed the case with Ron. He had completely rejected his affected area; his elbow suffered from contracture (an irreversible flexion of the joint), and he would complain of pain in the spastic half of his body.

3. Suffering from such a complex combination of handicaps could, of course, lead to a chain reaction of difficulties, not only in the child's physical development, but also emotionally, societally and intellectually. Concerning the anal stage, Erikson comments, "development of the muscle system gives the child a much greater power over the environment in the ability to reach out and hold on, to throw and push away…as he gets ready to stand more firmly on his feet the infant delineates his world as 'I' and 'You,' 'Me' and 'Mine' " (Erikson 1950, 77). Since body awareness and body image are a direct outcome of sensory, motor, cognitive and emotional development, severe physical handicap from birth may well sabotage the dynamic of natural growth.

4. The processes of intake and observation were undertaken with purely musical resources in order to decide whether individual music therapy was the most appropriate treatment. Here it should be stressed that even though the patient may arrive with his own detailed case history, it is up to the music therapist to conduct his own process of observation, since music can often offer its own unique means of diagnosis.

5. As opposed to Vogel (1984), and my own clinical experience, Schneider describes the use of relaxing music with athetoid patients, however for spastic C.P.

patients he employs stimulating music. This is worthy of further examination; it may well be that the defined aim of such therapy is different (Schneider in Gaston 1968, 140).

CHAPTER IV – ANAT

1. Hypotonia is a "decreased muscle tone due to the loss of the cerebellum's influence on the stretch reflex" (Trombly 1983, 55); it is "treated by overall general stimulation, especially swinging, rolling, spinning in all planes for labyrinth stimulation" (ibid., 82).

2. See Chapter 1: "Stimulative Elements in Ecstatic Healing Rituals."

3. The aim being to create posture and movement which will be more effective in the improvement of body alertness in order to establish a readiness to indulge in movement, learning, singing, conversation, etc. According to research and observation conducted by Ayres (1972) and others, such a state can be achieved through the Postural Responses Mechanism. These responses are dependent on sensory input structures aroused during antigravitational activity.

4. e.g., Tactile, vestibular and proprioceptive functions which are essential to the building of self-confidence and emotional stability. Children suffering defects in such functions are in danger of either developing mental and physical inhibitions, or a restless psychomotor reaction to any stimulus. In both cases, particularly the second, there exists a basically disorganized body scheme. In other words the awareness which permits us to sense the body and its actions without the need of actually watching it, is missing. This sabotages the sense of the body's limitations, the planning of movement, the sense of balance, and so on. This can lead to defects of both physical and mental self-confidence.

5. Neuropathological findings in the brains of Down's Syndrome children are a reduction of the dendritic spines of the visual cortical neurons in infants and children, but not in the embryo (Takashima et al. 1981); a decrease in presynaptic and postsynaptic length and width, but no change in cleft width for fetal Down's nervous tissue (Petit et al. 1982); abnormal electric membrane properties in infants, children, and even in six-week embryos (Scott et al. 1982).

6. Acetylcholine is a neurotransmitter secreted in the neuromuscular synapse of the skeletal muscles. Acetylcholinesterase is the enzyme which breaks it down.

7. "Activity of Daily Living" is a term used in rehabilitation medicine.

8. Plastic surgery, as practiced on many Down's Syndrome children in Israel, certainly improves external appearance and facial expression, however, the shortening of the hypotonic tongue does not help in any significant way to an improvement of speech and diction. Likewise, there is no connection between such surgery and hypotonia.

9. Between 1979–1989 I observed more than twenty Down's Syndrome children whose ages ranged from infancy to adolescence. Apart from three cases, all

were characterized by hypotonic body-posture, hypermotility in situations which demanded concentration and alertness, and an improvement of receptivity as a result of music and movement stimulation of an excitative nature which increased muscle tone.

10. "Complex movement" refers in this case to skipping, cross steps, balancing on one leg, walking on the toes, walking on the heels, separate finger movement for playing instruments and in general, a conscious organization of movement and posture.

11. Transfer from location to location must be done together with a clarification of the extent of stimulation and careful study of the patient. Should the stimulation be over prolonged and too powerful, it might well lead to disorientation and thus lose its effectiveness. The aim is to achieve alertness, as opposed to fatigue, exactly the opposite of the ecstatic traditional ritual which is extremely prolonged and terminates in deep sleep.

12. During such observations I discovered a number of additional aspects:

a) Arrhythmic musical stimuli led to confused reactions and a decrease of muscle tone.

b) Children under the age of three had a global-movemental reaction.

c) There was a clear connection between musical and movemental tempo, between musical intensity and the range and strength of movement, as well as between harmonic tension and postural arrest.

CHAPTER V – JACOB

1. C.V.A.: a cerebrovascular accident (stroke) is commonly caused by thrombosis or total occlusion of a blood vessel due to arteriosclerosis. Another cause is hemorrhage (usually secondary to hypertension). Symptoms vary according to the affected blood vessel. Stroke causes anoxic damage to the nervous tissue. The patient might suffer from hemiplegia or hemiparesis of the side of the body opposite to the site of the stroke. At the same time there might emerge various neurological defects. Psychological problems are also common among post-CVA patients. (Lishman 1987, Chapter 9).

2. The cerebral cortex is divided into two hemispheres. Each hemisphere is composed of four lobes: frontal, parietal, occipital and temporal.

3. Aphasia is a term used to define a wide range of speech and language problems caused by neurological damage. The specific type of aphasia is determined by the location and extent of brain damage. The two major categories are motor aphasia (expressive), and sensory aphasia (receptive). Expressive (Broca's aphasia) primarily causes speech difficulties; receptive (Wernicke's aphasia) causes disturbances in comprehending speech.

4. The Wada test temporarily anesthetizes one hemisphere at a time on separate days preceding surgery, so that the neurosurgeon can perceive which side of the

brain normally controls the power of speech. (Springer & Deutch, 1985, 20). The test is named after its inventor, Juhn Wada.

5. See also Chapter Two: "Rhythmic Cycles."

6. Recordings made before the injury enabled us to assess progress according to the following parameters: exactitude of rhythm, melody and vocal qualities. (Recording archive: 120, 129, 131. I.R. – Vocal comparisons before injury and during therapy).

CHAPTER VI – RITA

1. Maria Montessori (1870–1952) encountered a class of disturbed children while working as a physician in the psychiatric clinic of the University of Rome. As a result of her interest in this matter, as well as her concern for underprivileged pupils, she developed a system of individual teaching which was considered revolutionary at the beginning of this century. Her classrooms were furnished according to the needs and potential of the child. Montessori based her theories on current knowledge of child development, scientific research, as well as experimental pedagogical and anthropological studies. She regarded the child as possessing a far greater personal potential than that recognized in her day and age (Standing 1962).

2. Clive Robbins & Paul Nordoff (1977, 1), use this expression to describe a latent entity within every human being consisting of an inherent musical potential which can find its expression in a certain sensitivity to sound, in a response to rhythmic and tonal organization, and in an ability for expression through music. It is the therapist's role to awaken this "music child" so that it may assist the patient in self-organization and communication both with himself and with the outside world.

3. In their book *Dangerous Families* (1986), Peter Dale et al. discuss the importance of family therapy in the case of an abused child and propose one of the well-established approaches. As far as we know, Rita's adoptive family did not undergo family therapy. They confronted the problems on a purely material level, and attempted to compensate for emotional deprivation within an every day life-style.

4. It should be stressed that during the first stage of hospitalization no diagnosis was determined. According to the policy of the therapeutic team, lengthy observation and treatment should precede diagnostic conclusions. This was especially relevant in the case of adolescents and is now accepted practice in a number of Israeli hospitals.

5. Rolf Muuss divides adolescence into parallel periods of the educational process: ages 9–11—prepuberty and end of primary school; 12–14—intermediate period and middle school; 15–18—midpuberty and completion of high school; 19–21—belated maturity. (Muuss 1988, 14–15).

6. See Poem example #3: "And the nightmare, those eyes, always gazing down at me, the cross, Oh, merciful Jesus, always they crucify, strike the same place...."

7. Joseph Wolpe conducted research into relaxing situations aimed at the study of counter-reactions to fear and anxiety situations. As opposed to the approach of Edmund Jacobson (1938), which required fifty-six consecutive relaxation sessions, Wolpe arrived at a program of six twenty-minute sessions with instructions for continuous self-exercise. Both systems are based on the principle of the contraction and relaxation of muscle groups. Instruction is verbal and the stress is on the causes of anxiety, not on anxiety reaction. This system, publicized in 1958 as "Systematic Desensitization" resembles other behavioral techniques.

8. Suggestive sounds, as previously described, include music based on steady and repetitive beat-units, a moderate tempo ranging from andante to allegro, voice range which does not exceed a ninth, moderate dynamics, and the use of such instruments as the lute, guitar, harp, and lyre. In my experience these characteristics are much more significant than the musical style itself.

9. As already mentioned, therapy sessions were recorded in their entirety. The music was transcribed from these recordings, and the poems translated into English. The illustrations are taken from color slides.

10. A unique feature of music therapy within the hospital was a regular monthly concert to which the patients would contribute their own creative efforts, and perform them themselves. This was something which contributed to the patient's self-esteem, and also to a certain respect from his peers. It created an atmosphere of artistic encouragement, and emphasized the latent creative talents of human beings, even in illness and distress.

CHAPTER VII – ALON

1. This is a syndrome first described in German literature by Kussmaul (1877) as voluntary aphasia. Tramer used the term to describe the behavior of children who refuse to speak within any framework other than that of their immediate family (Harold et al. 1981, 904).

2. Such primary communication consists of direct messages by way of any given medium, from the infant's crying and body language, to those transmitted by the arts. In this case the communicative medium will be in the main sound and music and all that these arouse. Secondary communication will consist of indirect transmission by way of codes, primarily verbal. The aim being to transmit knowledge in as wide a range as possible. Usually both these communicative systems work in unison on parallel levels. For this reason the messages can be unanimous, ambiguous or even contradictory. Pinhas Noy claims that the language art is derived from the primary levels of one or several of the media used in human communication. For example, music is based on the preverbal levels of the auditory media, painting on the primary experience evoked by visual stimuli, and dancing on the medium of expressive posture and movement (Noy 1972, 245).

3. Despite certain differences of phraseology and concept between various theoreticians such as Anna Freud, Melanie Klein, D.W. Winnicott, Margaret Mahler, and others, there is a consensus regarding the central sphere of each developmental stage and its psychosexual significance. It is possible to accept even post-Freudian classifications, as additions built layer upon layer over the basic developmental theories.

4. Winnicott's term "good enough mother" means a mother figure who is actively aware of the infant's needs and adapts herself to the various stages of its development. Such adaptability allows the infant to gain its gradual independence stage by stage and at the same time gather the strength to face and overcome frustrations. As has been mentioned, this is a role which the therapist can symbolically adopt and thus assist the patient to undergo corrective experiences.

5. In music therapy great attention is paid to the choice of the instruments used for expression. Wind instruments serve as a direct extension of vocal expression and make it easier for a patient who has difficulty with direct vocality. The same is true of instruments which serve as an extension of the hand and arm and thus aid physical expression in patients who fear movemental activity.

6. Winnicott (1971, 3) describes the "intermediate area of experience" as a resting place to serve as a bridge between internal and external realities, an intermediate area in which one can relax and draw forth the strengths needed to confront either internal or external demands. Such relaxation can be acquired through game playing, artistic creativity, and so on (see also Chapter Two, "The Therapeutic Space").

7. See "Transference and Countertransference as Reflected in Music Therapy" (Sekeles 1990—unpublished article).

8. Incantation: a spell which is sung in a magic ritual, also found in art music (e.g., Massenet's opera *Roy de la Hore,* 1877)

9. The autonomic nervous system (ANS) stimulates and controls structures not under conscious control. It is divided into two parts, the sympathetic nervous system and the parasympathetic. The two systems are antagonistic to one another and work in balance, unless the amount of stimulus in one part is increased or decreased. The sympathetic system dominates when a person is in a stress situation, and the parasympathetic is most active in relaxing situations (Liebman 1991).

10. During the previous developmental stage Alon had attributed either "good" or "bad" qualities to the instruments, The big drums and the cymbal played the role of the tiger and other wild beasts, the flute was the poisonous snake, the metallophone and the piano were the good animals and the good people, and hence he hardly used them himself. It should be noted that alongside the sounds these instruments produced, Alon was also influenced by their external appearance. In contrast to this, during the studio period his musical choices became wider and the distinction between good or bad was abandoned.

11. The majority of those responsible were originally in favor of finding him a classroom in a psychiatric institution, due to his continuous passivity and

nonverbality in kindergarten and the impossibility of examining his IQ or his degree of maturity regarding regular primary school. The dramatic changes in music therapy found their expression only gradually, and very slowly, in an educational environment.

BIBLIOGRAPHY

Achterberg, J.; Kenner, C.; and Lawlis, G.F. "Biofeedback, Imagery and Relaxation: Pain and Stress Intervention for Severely Burned Patients," Presented at The Bio-Feedback Society of America, Chicago, March 1982.

Achterberg, J. *Imagery in Healing: Shamanism and Modern Medicine.* Boston: New Science Library, 1985.

Alajouanine, T. "Aphasia and Artistic Realisation," *Brain,* 71 (1948): 229–241.

Alvin, J. *Music Therapy.* London: Hutchinson, 1975.

American Psychatric Association, ed. *DSM-III-R: Diagnostic and Statistical Manual of Mental Disorders.* Washington, DC: American Psychiatric Association, 1987.

Amihai, Y. *Hour of Mercy* (in Hebrew). Jerusalem/Tel Aviv: Schocken, 1983.

Amihai, Y. *From Man Thou Art and to Man Shalt Thou Return* (in Hebrew). Jerusalem/Tel Aviv: Schocken, 1985.

Anderson, M.S.; and Savary, L.M. *Passages: A Guide for Pilgrims of the Mind.* New York: Harper & Row, 1972.

Apel, W. *Harvard Dictionary of Music.* Cambridge, MA: The Belknap Press of Harvard University, 1969.

Appenzeller, O.; Standefer, J.; Appenzeller, J.; and Atkinson, R.R. "Neurology and Endurance Training: vs. Endorphines." *Neurology* 30 (1980): 418–419.

Ayres, A.J.; and Heskett, Wm. M. *Clinical Observations of Disorders in Postural and Bilateral Integration,* Film. Los Angeles: University of Southern California, 1970b.

Ayres, A.J. *Sensory Integration and Learning Disorders.* Los Angeles: Western Psychological Services, 1972.

Ayres, A.J. Southern California Integration Test. Los Angeles: Western Psychological Services, 1972b.

Bachrach, A.J. "Learning Theory," In *Modern Synopsis of Psychiatry III,* edited by H.I. Kaplan and B.J. Sadok. Baltimore: Williams & Wilkins, 1981.

Berger, J.; and Cunningham, C.C. "The Development of Eye-Contact Between Mothers and Normal vs. Down's Syndrome Infants," *Developmental Psychology,* 17, no. 5 (1981): 678–689.

Bettelheim, B. *The Empty Fortress.* Glencoe: Free Press, 1967.

Bever, T.; and Chiarello, R. "Cerebral Dominance in Musicians and Nonmusicians." *Science* 185 (1974): 137–139.

Blos, P. *On Adolescence, A Psychoanalytical Interpretation.* New York: Free Press, Macmillan Publishing Co., 1962.

Bobath, B.; and Bobath, K. *Motor Development in the Different Types of Cerebral Palsy.* London: William Heinemann Medical Books, 1975.

Bogen, E.; and Gordon, H.W. "Musical Tests of Functional Lateralization with Intracarotid Amobarbital," *Nature* 230 (1971): 524–525.

Bonny, H.L. Preferred Records for Use in LSD Therapy. Baltimore: Maryland Psychiatric Research Center, 1969.

Bonny, H.L.; and Fahnke, W.N. "The Use of Music in Psychedelic (LSD) Therapy." *Journal of Music Therapy* 9, no. 2 (1972): 64–87.

Bonny, H.L. *GIM Therapy No. III: Past, Present and Future Implications.* Baltimore: ICM Books, 1980.

Bonny, H.L.; and Savary, L.M. *Music and Your Mind: Listening with a New Consciousness.* Rev. ed. New York: Station Hill Press, 1990.

Boring, E.G. *Sensation and Perception in the History of Perception-Experimental Psychology.* New York: D. Appleton-Century Company, 1942.

Borling, J.E. "The Effects of Sedative Music on Alpha Rhythms and Focussed Attention in High-Creative and Low-Creative Subjects." *Journal of Music Therapy* 18, no. 2 (1981): 101–108.

Bowlby, J. *Maternal Care and Mental Health.* Geneva: World Health Organization, 1952.

Bowlby, J. "Separation Anxiety." *The International Journal of Psychoanalysis* 41 (1960): 89–113.

Bowlby, J. *Attachment and Loss.* London: Hogarth Press, 1969.

Brain, L. *Brain's Clinical Neurology.* 5th ed. rev. R. Banister. Oxford University Press, 1981.

Brinkworth, R. "The Unfinished Child: Early Treatment and Training for the Infant with Down's Syndrome." *Royal Society of Health* 2 (1975): 73.

Brodal, A. "Anatomical Organization and Fiber Connections of the Vestibular Nuclei." In *Neurological Aspects of Auditory and Vestibular Disorders.* Springfield, IL: Charles C. Thomas, 1964.

Browne, E.; Wilson, V.; and Laybourne, P.C. "Diagnosis and Treatment of Elective Mutism in Children." *Journal of American Academy of Child Psychiatry* 2 (1963): 605.

Bruscia, K.E. *Improvisational Models of Music Therapy.* Springfield, IL: Charles C. Thomas, 1987

Buckley, S.; Emslie, M.; Haslegrave, G.; and LePrevost, P. *The Development of Language and Reading Skills in Children with Down's Syndrome.* Book and Video. Portsmouth: Down's Syndrome Project, 1968.

Cannon, W.B. "Voodoo Death," *Psychosomatic Medicine* 19 (1957): 182–190.

Chomet, D.H. *The Influence of Music on Health and Life.* New York: Putnam, 1875.

Clynes, M., ed. *Music, Mind and Brain: The Neuropsychology of Music.* New York: Plenum Press, 1983.

Courlander, H. "Dance and Dance-Drama in Haiti." *The Function of Dance in Human Society.* New York: Boas School, 1944.

Crawford, N. *Soul Vine Shaman.* New York: Sacha Runa Research Foundation, Paper No. 5, 1979.

Crapanzano, V. *The Hamadsha; A Study in Moroccan Ethnopsychiatry.* Berkeley: University of California Press. 1973.

Crapanzano, V.; and Garrison, L. *Case-Studies in Spirit Posession.* New York: John Wiley & Sons, 1977.

Crete, G. "Chamanisme et Musicotherapie Recherche Sonore et Hallucinations Auditives." 5th World Congress of Music Therapy, Paris, July, 1983.

Critchley, M.; and Henson, R.A., eds. *Music and Brain Studies in the Neurology of Music.* London: William Heinemann Medical Books, 1977.

Dale, P.; Davies, M.; Morrison, T.; and Waters, J. *Dangerous Families: Assessment and Treatment of Child Abuse.* London: Tavistock Publishing, 1986.

Deloria, V. "From Wounded Knee to Wounded Knee." In *The World of the American Indian*, edited by J. Billard. Washington, DC: National Geographic Society, 1974.

Densmore, F. "The Use of Music in the Treatment of the Sick by American Indians." *Music Quarterly* 13 (1927): 555–565.

Densmore, F. "Importance of Rhythm in Songs for the Treatment of the Sick by American Indians." *Scientific Monthly* 79 (1954): 109–112.

Deutsch, D., ed. *The Psychology of Music.* New York: Academic Press, 1982.

Dorland, W.A. Illustrated Medical Dictionary. 26th ed. Philadelphia: Igako-Shoin/Saunders, International Edition, 1982.

Drury, N. *The Shaman and the Magician.* London: Henley, Routledge & Kegan Paul, 1982.

Eagle, C.T.; and Gaston, E.T. "The Function of Music in LSD Therapy for Alcoholic Patients." *Journal of Music Therapy* 13, no. 1 (1972).

Eliade, M. *Shamanism, Archaic Techniques of Ecstasy.* Bollington Series. Princeton University Press, 1972.

Erikson, E.H. "Identity and the Life-Cycle: Selected Papers." *Psychological Issues*, Monographic Series 1, no. 1. New York: International University Press, 1959.

Erikson, E.H. *Childhood and Society.* New York: W.W. Norton & Co., 1950.

Evan S-Wentz, W.Y. *Tibetan Yoga and Secret Doctrines.* London: Oxford University Press, 1967.

Feldenkrais, M. *Body and Mature Behaviour.* Tel Aviv: Aleph, Ltd., 1949.

Fishler; Share; and Koch. "Adaptation of Gesell Development Scale for Evaluation of Development in Children with Down's Syndrome." *American Journal of Mental Deficiency* 68 (1964): 542–646.

Foster, G.M. "Disease Etiologies in Non-Western Medical Systems." *American Anthropologist* 78 (1976): 773–781.

Foster, G.M.; and Anderson, B.G. *Medical Anthropology.* New York: John Wiley & Sons, 1978.

Freud, A. "The Psychoanalytical Study of Infantile Feeding Disturbances" In *Psychoanalytical Study of the Child II.* New York: International University Press, 1946.

Freud, A. *The Ego and the Mechanisms of Defense* (in Hebrew). Tel Aviv: Dvir, 1977.

Freud, S. "The Relation of the Poet to Day-Dreaming," 1908. In *Collected Papers* Vol. 4, no. 9. New York: Basic Books, 1959.

Freud, S. "Five Lectures on Psychoanalysis," 1909. London: Standard Edition XI, 1953–1973.

Freud, S. "Recollection, Repetition and Working Through," 1914. *Collected Papers* Vol.2, no. 32. New York: Basic Books, 1959.

Freud, S. *Inhibitions, Symptoms and Anxieties*, 1926. London: Hogarth Press, 1936.

Gaston, E.T., ed. *Music in Therapy.* New York: Macmillan, 1968.

Garbourg, P. *The Secret of the Sphincters* (in Hebrew). Tel Aviv: Pelleg, Sifriat Ma'ariv, 1982.

Ghez, C.; and Fahn, S. *The Cerebullum: Principles of Neurological Science.* Amsterdam: Elsevier, 1981.

Gesell, A. *Developmental Diagnosis.* New York: Paul B. Hoeber, 1947.

Green, E.; and Green, A. *Beyond Biofeedback.* New York: Delta, 1977.

Greenfield, N.S.; and Sternback, R.A., eds. *Handbook of Psychophysiology.* New York: Holt, Rinehart & Winston, 1972.

Halpern, J. *Indian Music of the Pacific North-West Coast.* New York: Folkways Records, 1967. Recorded collection.

Harner, M.J., ed. *Hallucinogens and Shamanism.* New York: Oxford University Press, 1973.

Herzog, G. "Music in the Thinking of American Indians." *Peabody Bulletin* (May 1933).

Hooker, D. "Evidence of Pre-Natal Function of the Central Nervous System in Man," *Neurophysiological Approaches to Therapeutic Exercise*, edited by O.D. Payton, S. Hirt, and R.A. Newton. Philadelphia: F.A. Davis Company, 1977.

Howery, B.I. "Music Therapy for Mentally Retarded Children." *Music in Therapy*, edited by E.T. Gaston, Chapter 3. New York: Macmillan, 1968.

Ilan, E. *Psychotherapy with Children and Youth* (in Hebrew). Tel Aviv: Sifriat HaPoalim, 1979.

Jacobson, E. *Progressive Relaxation.* University of Chicago Press, 1938.

Jacobson, E. *Anxiety and Tension Control.* Philadelphia: Lippincott, 1969.

Jessner, L.; and Kaplan, S. "Observations on the Emotional Reactions of Children to Tonsillectomy and Adenoidectamy," *Transaction of the 3rd Conference on Problems of Infancy and Childhood*, edited by G.E. Senn. New York: Josiah Macy Foundation, 1949.

Jilek, W.G. *Salish Indian Mental Health and Culture Change: Psycho-Hygienic and Therapeutic Aspects of the Guardian-Spirit Ceremonies.* New York: Holt, Reinhart & Winston, 1982.

Jung, C.G. "The Archetype of the Collective Unconscious." *Two Essays on Analytical Psychology.* 2d ed., 90–114. London: Routledge & Kegan Paul, 1966.

Kahana, Y. "The Zar Spirits, A Category of Magic in the System of Mental Health Care in Ethiopia." *International Journal of Social Psychiatry* 31, no. 2 (Summer 1985): 125–144.

Kampinsky, W.H.; and Ward, A.A. "Effect of Section of Vestibular Nerve upon Cortically Induced Movement in a Cat." *Journal of Neurophysiology* 13 (1950): 295–304.

Kaplan, H.I.; and Sadock, B.J., eds. Modern Synopsis of Psychiatry III, Baltimore: Williams and Wilkins, 1981.

Katz, R. "Accepting Boiling Energy," *Ethos* 10 (1982): 344–369.

Kephart, N.C. *The Slow Learner in the Classroom.* Columbus, Ohio: Charles E. Merill Publishing, 1960.

Kimura, D. "Right Temporal Lobe Damage." *Archives of Neurology* 8 (1963): 24.

Kimura, D.; and Archibald, J. "Motor Functions of the Left Hemisphere." *Brain* 97 (1974): 337–350.

Klein, M. "Infantile Anxiety Situation Reflected in a Work of Art and in the Creative Impulse." *International Journal of Psychoanalysis* 10 (1929).

Klein, M. *The Psychoanalysis of Children*. London: Hogarth Press and The Institute of Psychoanalysis, 1932.

Klein, M. "Notes on Some Schizoid Mechanisms," 1946. *The Selected Melanie Klein*, edited by Mitchell. J. Penguin Books, 1986.

Klein, M. "The Psychoanalytical Play-Technique: Its History and Significance," 1955. *The Selected Melanie Klein*, edited by Mitchell. J. Penguin Books, 1986.

Kleinhaus, M.; and Sela, P. *Hypnosis* (in Hebrew). Internal Publication, Ramat Gan, 1986.

Kohen-Raz, R. "Developmental Patterns of Static Balance Ability and Relation to Cognitive School Readiness." *Pediatrics* 46 (1970): 276–281.

Kreitler, S. *The Psychology of Symbols* (in Hebrew). Tel Aviv: Papyrus, Tel Aviv University, 1985.

La Barre, W. *The Ghost Dance: The Origin of Religion*. New York: Delta, 1970.

Langer, S.K. *Philosophy in a New Key*. 3d ed. Cambridge, MA: Harvard University Press, 1982.

Laplanch, J.; and Pantalis, J.B. *The Language of Psychoanalysis*. London: Hogarth Press and The Institute of Psychoanalysis, 1985.

Leboyer, F. Shantala. *Un Art Traditionel Pour le Massage des Enfants*. Paris: Seuil, 1976.

Liebman, M. *Neuroatonomy*. 4th ed. Baltimore: University Park Press, 1991.

Leibowitz, Y. *Body and Soul: The Psychophysical Dilemma* (in Hebrew). Tel Aviv: Defense Ministry Publication, 1982.

Lishman, W.A. *Organic Psychiatry*. Oxford, London: Blackwell Scientific Publishing Co., 1987.

Lloyd, R.; Solomon, G.F.; Dorf, M.; and Greenblat, M. *Explorations in Psycho-Neuroimmunology*. New York: Grune and Stratten Inc., 1987.

Ludwig, A.M. "Altered States of Consciousness." In *Trance and Possession States*, edited by R. Prince, 69–95. Montreal: Buck Memorial Society, 1968.

Maxwell, J.A., ed. *America's Fascinating Indian Heritage*. New York: Reader's Digest Association, 1978.

Melzak, R.; and Wall, P.D. "Pain Mechanism. A New Theory." *Science* 150 (1965): 971–979.

Merriam, A.P. "The Importance of Song in the Flathead Indian Vision Quest." *Ethnomusicology* 9 (1965): 91–99.

Messing, S.I. "Group Therapy and Social Status in the Zar Cult in Ethiopia." *American Anthropologist* 60 (1956): 1120–1126.

Mossman, P.L. *A Problem-Oriented Approach to Stroke Rehabilitation*. Springfield, IL: Charles C. Thomas, 1976.

Murooka, H. "Analysis of Intra-Uterine Sounds on the Newborn Infant." *Journal de Gynecologic Obstetrique et Biologie de la Reproduction* 5 (1976): 367–376.

Muuss, R.A. *Theories of Adolescence* (in Hebrew). Tel Aviv: Sifriat HaPoalim, 1988.

Naranjo, C. "Psychological Aspects of the Yage: Experience in an Experimental Setting." In *Hallucinogens and Shamanism*, edited by M. Harner. New York: Oxford University Press, 1973.

Neher, A. "Auditory Driving Observed with Scalp Electrodes in Normal Subjects." *EEG and Clinical Neurophysiology* 131 (1961): 449–451.

Neher, A. "A Physiological Explanation of Unusual Behaviour in Ceremonies Involving Drums." *Human Biology* 34 (1962): 151–160.

Nordoff, P.; and Robbins, C. *Therapy in Music for Handicapped Children.* London: Victor Gollancz Ltd., 1971.

Nordoff, P.; and Robbins, C. *Creative Music Therapy: Individual Treatment for the Handicapped Child.* New York: John Day Company, 1977.

Nordoff, P.; and Robbins, C. *Music Therapy in Special Education.* 2d ed. Saint Louis, MO: MMB Music, 1983

Noy, P. "About Art and Artistic Talent." *International Journal of Psychoanalysis* 53 (1972): 243–249.

Noy, P. "Insight and Creativity." *Psychological Approaches.* Department of Behavioural Studies, Beer Sheba Univ., 1983. Presented before the New York Association of Psychoanalysis, 1976.

Noy, P. "The Problems of Art in Psychoanalytical Thinking" (in Hebrew). *Psychological Approaches*, 347–358. Department of Behavioural Studies, Beer Sheba Univ., 1983.

Olds, C. *Fetal Response to Music.* Wickford, Essex: Runwell Hospital, 1984.

Panneton, R.K. "Prenatal Auditory Experience with Melodies: Effects on Postnatal Auditory Preferences in Human Newborns." PhD dissertation, University of North Carolina, 1985.

Paul, G.; and Trimble, R.W. "Recorded vs. 'Live' Relaxation Training and Hypnotic Suggestion: Comparative Effectiveness for Reducing Physiological Arousal and Inhibiting Stress Response." *Behaviour Therapy* 1 (1970): 285–302.

Pelletier, K.R.; and Herzing, D.L. "Psychoneuroimmunology: Towards a Mind-Body Model." *Advances* 5, no.1 (1988), 27–65.

Petit, T.L.; LeBoutillier, J.C.; Alfano, D.P.; and Becker, L.E. "Synaptic Developments in the Human Fetus: A Morphometric Analysis of Normal and Down's Syndrome Neocortex." *Experimental Neurology*, 1983.

Peushell, S.M. *The Young Child with Down's Syndrome.* New York: Human Science Press, 1984.

Peushell, S.M., ed. Down's Syndrome: Development and Learning (in Hebrew). Jerusalem: Yated, 1987.

Piaget, J. *The Origins of Intelligence in Children.* London: International University Press, 1952.

Piaget, J. Child Psychology (in Hebrew). Tel Aviv: Sifriat HaPoalim, 1974.

Prechtl, H.F. "Minimal Brain Disfunction Syndrome and the Plasticity of the Nervous System." *Advances in Biological Psychiatry* 1 (1978).

Priestley, M. "Countertransference in Analytical Music Therapy." *British Journal of Music Therapy* 9, no. 3 (1978): 2–5.

Priestley, M. *Music Therapy in Action*. 2d ed. Saint Louis, MO: MMB Music, 1985.

Prince, R. "Shamans and Endorphines: Hypothesis for a Synthesis." *Ethos* 10, no. 4 (1982).

Rahmani, L. *Brain and Learning, Processes and Defficiencies* (in Hebrew). Papyrus, Tel Aviv University, 1981.

Rahmani, L. *An Approach to Clinical Psycho-Neurology* (in Hebrew). Tel Aviv: Diyunon, 1984.

Resnick, P.J. "Child Murder by Parents: A Psychiatric Review of Filicide." *American Journal of Psychiatry* 126 (1969): 325–333.

Robertson, J. *Young Children in Hospital*. London: Tavistock Publishing, 1957.

Robertson, J.; and Bowlby, J. "Responses of Young Children to Separation from their Mothers." *Courrier de la Centre Internationale de L'Enfance* 2 (1952): 134–142.

Rosenheim, A. *Man Encounters Himself, Psychotherapy: The Experience and the Process* (in Hebrew). Tel Aviv: Schocken, 1990.

Rosenzweig, M.R.; Bennet, E.L.; and Diamond, M.C. "Brain Changes in Response to Experience." *Scientific American* 226 (1972): 22–29.

Roth, R.M.; Hershenson, D.; and Berenbaum, A. *The Developmental Theory of Psychotherapy: A Systematic Electisism*. Chicago: Illinois Institute of Technology, 1967.

Rutherford, W. *Shamanism: The Foundations of Magic*. Wellingborough: Aquarian Press, 1986.

Rutter, M. *Maternal Deprivation Reassessed*. Harmondsworth: Penguin Books, 1972.

Sadai, Y. "Cognitive Musical Structures"; "Symbol, Archetype and Myth in Music"; "Is Music a Language?"; "The Epistemology of Music" (all in Hebrew). Unpublished Lectures, 1988.

Salk, L. "The role of the Hearbeat in the Relation Between Mother and Infant." *Scientific American* (May 1973).

Sandblom, P. *Creativity and Disease: How Illness Affects Literature Art and Music*. Philadelphia: George F. Stickley Co., 1985.

Scartelli, J.P. "The Effect of Sedative Music on Electromyographic Biofeedback Assisted Relaxation Training of Spastic Cerebral Palsied Adults." *Journal of Music Therapy* 19, no. 4 (1982): 210–219.

Schneider, E.H., ed. *Music Therapy 1962*. Lawrence, KS: Allen Press, 1963.

Schneider, E.H. "Music Therapy for the Cerebral Palsied." In *Music in Therapy*, edited by E.T. Gaston, Chapter 10. New York: Macmillan, 1968.

Scott, B.S.; Petit, T.L.; Becker, L.E.; and Edwards, B.A.V. "Abnormal Electric Membrane Properties of Down's Syndrome DRG Neurons in Cell Culture." *Developmental Brain Research* 2 (1982): 257–270.

Scott, P.D. "Parents Who Kill Their Children." *Medicine, Science and Law* 13, no. 2 (1973): 120–126.

Seashore, C. *Psychology of Music*. 1938. Reprint. New York: Dover Publications, 1967.

Segal, H. *Introduction to the work of Melanie Klein.* New York: Basic Books, 1974.

Sekeles, C. "The Use of Music with Psychiatric Patients to Elicit Speech and Language." 7th International Congress of World Federation of Occupational Therapy, Jerusalem, March 1978.

Sekeles, C. *Music in the Healing Rituals of Non-Literate Societies* (in Hebrew). Hebrew University, Jerusalem, 1979.

Sekeles, C. "The Effect of Specific Musical Components in Healing Rituals of Non-Literate Societies." AAMT Music Therapy Conference, Imaculata, PA, March 1981.

Sekeles, C. "Cultural Aspects of Vocal Expression in Therapy." 5th World Congress of Music Therapy, Paris, July 1983.

Sekeles, C. "Sound and Music in the Treatment of Hypotonic Down's Syndrome Children." First Research Seminar of ISME, 1986, 22–39. Saint Louis, MO: MMB Music 1989.

Sekeles, C.; and Cohen, E. "Integrated Treatment of Down's Syndrome Children Through Music and Movement." 4th International Conference of Young People Dancing, Vol. 2, 19–28. London, July 1988.

Sekeles, C. "Music as a Balancing Agent Between Fantasy and Reality in the Treatment of Emotionally Disturbed Children." 5th International Congress of Music Therapy and Music Education for the Handicapped, Congres Centrum Leeuwenhorst, Noordwijkerhout, August 1989.

Sekeles, C. *Observation and Diagnostic Charts in Music Therapy* (in Hebrew), David Yellin College, Jerusalem, 1990.

Sekeles, C. "Music as a Therapeutic Agent: The Developmental-Integrative Model in Music Therapy" (in Hebrew). PhD thesis, Hebrew University, Jerusalem, 1990.

Sekeles, C. "The Many Faces of the Drum" (in Hebrew). *Therapy Through the Arts* 1, no. 3 (1994): 7–19.

Sekeles, C. "The Voice of the Body: Reflection of the Soul" (in Hebrew). *Therapy Through the Arts* 2, no. 1 (1995): 6–16.

Shahar-Levi, Y. "Revealing and Concealing in Body-Language: A Glance Into the World of Movement-Therapy" (in Hebrew). *Sihot, D* 1 (1989): 31–25.

Shetler, D. "Prenatal Music Experiences: Prelude to Musical Life." *Music Educators Journal* 71, no. 7 (1985): 26–27.

Shiloah, A. *The Epistle on Music of the Ikhwān Al Sāfā.* Tel Aviv: Tel Aviv University: School of Fine Arts, 1978.

Shirokogoroff, S.M. *Psychomental Complex of the Tungus.* London: Kegan Paul, French, Trubner, 1935.

Somerville, M. "Learning to Talk Through Singing." *Exceptional Child* 24 (1958): 286.

Springer, S.; and Deutch, G. *Left Brain, Right Brain.* New York: Freeman & Co., 1985.

Standing, M.E. *Maria Montessori, Her Life and Work.* New York: Mentor-Omega, 1962.

Storr, A. *Human Aggression.* New York: Penguin Books, 1968.

Takashima, S.; Becker, L.E.; Armstrong, D.L.; and Chan, F. "Abnormal Neuronal Development in the Visual Cortex of the Human Fetus with Down's Syndrome: A Quantitative Golgi Study." *Brain Research* 225 (1981): 1–21.

Tart, C.T., ed. "Introduction." *Altered States of Consciousness.* New York: John Wiley & Sons, 1969.

Teirich, H.R. *Musik in der Medizin.* Stuttgart: Gustav Fischer Verlag, 1958.

Trombly, C.A., ed. *Occupational Therapy for Physical Disfunction.* Baltimore: Williams & Wilkins, 1983.

Vaugham, G.F. "Children in Hospital." *Lancet,* June 1 (1957): 1117–1120.

Verney, T.; and Kelly, G. *The Secret Life of the Unborn Child.* London: Sphere Books, 1981.

Vogel, B. "Prenatal Stimuli Through Music-Therapy." *British Journal of Music Therapy* 15, no. 3 (1984).

Weistuch, L.; and Lewis, M. "The Language Interaction Intervention Project." *Analysis and Intervention in Development Disabilities* 5 (1985): 97–106.

Winnicott, D.W. "Ego Distortion in Terms of True and False Self." *The Maturation Process and the Facilitating Environment.* London: Hogarth Press and The Institute of Psychoanalysis, 1965.

Winnicott, D.W. *Playing and Reality.* Harmondsworth: Penguin Books, 1971.

Wolpe J. *Psychotherapy by Reciprocal Inhibition.* Stanford, CA: Stanford University Press, 1958.

Yoder, I. "Folk Medicine." *Folklore and Folklife,* edited by R.M. Dorson. University of Chicago Press, 1972.

Zausmer, E, Peuschell, S.M.; and Shea. "A Sensory-Motor Stimulation for the Young Child with Down's Syndrome." *MCH Exchange* 2 (1972): 1.

Zimrim, H. *Abused Children: A Multifaceted Problem* (in Hebrew). Tel Aviv: Papyrus, Tel Aviv University, 1985 (Hebrew).